# DIVERGENT PATHS

# DIVERGENT PATHS
## ECONOMIC MOBILITY IN THE
## NEW AMERICAN LABOR MARKET

ANNETTE BERNHARDT, MARTINA MORRIS,
MARK S. HANDCOCK, AND MARC A. SCOTT

Russell Sage Foundation • New York

## The Russell Sage Foundation

The Russell Sage Foundation, one of the oldest of America's general purpose foundations, was established in 1907 by Mrs. Margaret Olivia Sage for "the improvement of social and living conditions in the United States." The Foundation seeks to fulfill this mandate by fostering the development and dissemination of knowledge about the country's political, social, and economic problems. While the Foundation endeavors to assure the accuracy and objectivity of each book it publishes, the conclusions and interpretations in Russell Sage Foundation publications are those of the authors and not of the Foundation, its Trustees, or its staff. Publication by Russell Sage, therefore, does not imply Foundation endorsement.

**Library of Congress Cataloging-in-Publication Data**

Divergent paths : economic mobility in the new American labor market / Annette Bernhardt . . . [et al.].
p. cm.
Includes bibliographical references and index.
ISBN 0-87154-150-5
1. Occupational mobility—United States.  2. Labor mobility—United States.  I. Bernhardt, Annette D., 1964–

HD5717.5.U6 D58 2001
331.12'7973—dc21                                                2001019329

The paper used in this publication meets the minimum requirements of American National Standard for Information Sciences—Permanence of Paper for Printed Library Materials. ANSI Z39.48–1992.

Text design by Suzanne Nichols

RUSSELL SAGE FOUNDATION
112 East 64th Street, New York, New York 10021
10 9 8 7 6 5 4 3 2 1

# Contents

# About the Authors

**Annette Bernhardt** is senior research associate at the Center on Wisconsin Strategy, University of Wisconsin, Madison.

**Martina Morris** is the Blumstein-Jordan Professor of Sociology and Statistics at the University of Washington, Seattle.

**Mark S. Handcock** is professor of statistics and sociology in the Center for Statistics and the Social Sciences at the University of Washington, Seattle.

**Marc A. Scott** is assistant professor of educational statistics at the School of Education, New York University.

# ═ Acknowledgments ═

This book has been some time in the making. What began as a two-year project—"We will analyze the data in the first year and write it up in the second"—ended up taking five years to complete. The country has gone through two presidential elections, each of the authors has changed jobs at least once, the NLSY collected two more rounds of data, and the pace of events posed the constant question of whether we were writing about contemporary or historical events. None of us will ever underestimate the complexity of such a project again. It would not have been finished but for the support of many different people and institutions. Columbia University provided the seed grant for the project and the encouragement to undertake the first steps. The Russell Sage and Rockefeller Foundations then provided solid and sustained support for the work, from its conceptual development, through the years of wrestling with the data, to the final synthesis of the findings. Support like this is rare, and we are all deeply grateful to the Foundations. Several analyses in the book were also conducted as part of overlapping projects, funded by the William T. Grant Foundation and the National Center for Research on Vocational Education.

The Institute on Education and the Economy (IEE) at Teachers College, Columbia University, and the Population Research Institute at Pennyslvania State University provided the infrastructure needed to conduct the research. We are especially grateful to Lisa Rothman, associate director of IEE, for her patience, support, and expertise at all stages of the grant process. The Population Studies Center at the University of Pennsylvania provided a rich intellectual environment during a leave of absence for Martina Morris midway through the process. The Center on Wisconsin Strategy, University of Wisconsin–Madison, generously supported Annette Bernhardt during the final stages of writing.

Special mention must be made of the pivotal role that IEE played in the development of this book. Tom Bailey, its director, provided

x    Acknowledgments

incisive intellectual feedback, helped to secure foundational support, and enabled Annette Bernhardt and Marc Scott to make this book a top priority during their tenures at IEE. Much of the thinking behind the policy discussions in this book began in collaborations between Tom Bailey and Annette Bernhardt. A majority of Marc Scott's efforts were conducted while in residence at IEE; the Institute also funded his work on the final stage of the book after he had taken a position at New York University.

We would like to thank Stefan Jonsson, Jane Zavisca, Barbara Gelhard, and Jay Cross for superb research help over the years. Steve McClaskie at the Center for Human Resource Research at Ohio State University provided invaluable assistance on data questions. We would also like to thank the editorial and production staff at the Russell Sage Foundation, who worked quickly and professionally; our manuscript is much the better for their efforts. Finally, we owe many intellectual debts to Eileen Appelbaum, Tom Bailey, Rose Batt, Jared Bernstein, Samuel Bowles, Laura Dresser, Peter Gottschalk, Robert Hauser, Chip Hunter, Dave Marcotte, Doug Massey, David Neumark, Paul Osterman, Joel Rogers, Judith Singer, Bruce Western, and Erik Olin Wright.

# = Chapter 1 =

## The New Labor Market

A LMOST three decades ago, Daniel Bell's *The Coming of Post-Industrial Society* foretold the shift from an economy based on the production of goods to one based on knowledge and technology. Bell and others saw great potential in this shift: It would change the nature of work, with professional, technical, and service occupations gaining dominance and education becoming the sole determinant of success. It would fundamentally alter the nature of capitalism, by moving power out of the market and transferring it to those engaged in the production of knowledge. It would result in social planning that was rational and analytical. New tensions and conflicts might emerge, but in the end, the vision was of a social system based on "theoretical knowledge as the axis around which new technology, economic growth and the stratification of society will be organized" (Bell 1973, 112).

It is ironic that immediately following the publication of Bell's book, a period of economic decline set in. First came the Organization of the Petroleum Exporting Countries (OPEC) crisis, stagflation, and the onset of manufacturing layoffs. The twin recessions in the early 1980s only served to reinforce the sense that America was losing its competitive standing in the work economy. Robert Hayes and William Abernathy (1980), in a landmark article entitled "Managing Our Way to Economic Decline," squarely placed the blame on complacent business strategies, citing U.S. productivity figures and rates of investment in research and development that lagged behind those of the other industrialized countries. A glut of popular books soon followed, diagnosing the country's ills and calling for Japanese-style management and production systems (Dertouzos, Lester, and Solow 1989). Some employers, such as Xerox and General Motors' Saturn plant, did respond with innovative reform, but on balance we did not see a wholesale adoption of the high-performance workplace, despite evidence of its productivity benefits. The Japanese model was instead

1

supplanted by another approach that seemed to emphasize just the opposite: the lean and flexible staffing that has become something of a fixture in the postindustrial landscape. By 1996, a full 78 percent of establishments reported using at least one type of flexible staffing arrangement (Houseman 1997).[1]

Regardless of how circuitous the path has been, however, thirty years later it does appear that Bell's predictions are starting to come true—on some dimensions at least. Fully 80 percent of Americans worked in the service sector in 1999, productivity growth is finally ticking upward, and technology- and knowledge-based industries are the fastest-growing sectors in the economy.

Change has come at a steep cost, however. Starting in the mid-1970s, real wages stopped growing and even declined for certain groups in the labor force, a marked reversal from the postwar economic boom. To make matters worse, the degree of inequality in wages grew by roughly 30 percent. Either one of these trends alone is cause for concern, but in combination, they indicate a truly worrisome deterioration in workers' economic welfare. By the mid-1980s, articles on the declining middle class began to appear in both the popular and academic press. For a time there was even serious debate as to whether America might not be better off trying to resuscitate and rebuild its manufacturing base (Magaziner and Reich 1983; Cohen and Zysman 1987). Soon thereafter, the changing face of poverty generated a heated controversy on the growth of the "urban underclass." Early on, these trends were framed in the context of job flight overseas and especially the decline of inner-city manufacturing jobs (see Kuttner 1983; Auletta 1982; Wilson 1987).

By the beginning of the 1990s, however, the dominant explanation had shifted to the growing wage gap between "skilled" and "unskilled" workers. Two reports, *A Nation at Risk* (U.S. Department of Labor, U.S. National Commission on Excellence in Education 1983) and *America's Choice: High Skills or Low Wages!* (Commission on the Skills of the American Workforce 1990), pointed to the poor performance of American students on international achievement tests and argued forcefully that the problem lay in our education system and its failure to adequately prepare young workers. Although these reports were highly influential and yielded broad policy initiatives such as the School-to-Work Opportunities Act of 1994, it is surprising how quickly they, too, have become anachronistic in light of the resurgence of American competitiveness.

Viewed in retrospect, then, the past three decades have witnessed considerable turbulence both in the economy and in our attempts to understand what has been happening to it. The latter is not surprising, in that the focus of researchers and policy analysts is necessarily constrained by time and place. Nevertheless, perhaps we are now at a point where we can step back and begin to form a more sober assessment of the transition to postindustrialism. This is not to imply that the transition is complete—of course it is not—but rather to recognize that we now have much more information than Daniel Bell and his contemporaries had thirty years ago.

What stands out above all is the rise in economic inequality. It has not yet been reversed, despite the longest period of economic expansion in the postwar era and one of the tightest labor markets on record; and despite our best efforts we can only partially explain it. This may change, however, as researchers begin to take a long-term perspective and take stock of how economic restructuring has affected the nature of work and opportunity in America. This question is no longer simply a matter of growing wage differentials; it is increasingly about what it means to have a job and to build a career. The nature of competition and product markets, the structure of workplaces, and wages, compensation, and attachments to employers all look very different now than they did at the height of industrial capitalism. Compared with the postwar period, the American employment relationship appears to be changing—in how the workplace is organized, how workers are matched with jobs, and how wages and the terms of employment are set. In addition, as workplaces are restructured, potentially strong effects on economic mobility arise, effects that researchers are only beginning to address: "Perhaps the most important implications of the new employment relationship concern increased inequality in the workplace and, ultimately, in society as a whole" (Cappelli et al. 1997, 11).

The goal of this book is to push researchers and policy makers toward a sustained focus on how the life chances of American workers have changed. A true evaluation of postindustrialism cannot rest solely on employers' competitiveness in the global economy; it requires a more balanced assessment of who benefits and who loses. Greater inequality has become firmly rooted in the new labor market, and we can no longer afford to write it off as a short-term structural adjustment. The effect on workers is likely to be permanent, manifesting itself throughout the course of the career and in the eventual attainment of a family-supporting income. Upward mobility—the hallmark of this country—hangs in the balance.

Ultimately, the question is whether we are seeing the emergence of a more fluid and open labor market, in which workers freely move to take advantage of rapidly changing opportunities, or a more rigid and segmented labor market, in which mobility from entry-level to good career jobs is declining and some groups of workers are increasingly cut off from the chance ever to attain a stable well-paying job. The latter possibility has prompted Richard Freeman to warn of an emerging apartheid economy: "Left unattended, the new inequality threatens us with a two-tiered society . . . in which the successful upper and upper-middle classes live fundamentally different from the working classes and the poor. Such an economy will function well for substantial numbers, but will not meet our nation's democratic idea of advancing the well-being of the average citizen. For many it promises the loss of the 'American dream'" (Freeman 1997, 3).

The research reported in this book consists of an empirical inquiry into the nature of upward mobility and career development in this new postindustrial economy. Our strategy is to compare the experiences of two groups of young adults during the critical stages of their careers, when the majority of wage growth occurs and when long-term attachments to employers are formed. The first group entered the labor market in the late 1960s at the tail of the economic boom. The other began working in the early 1980s, after the onset of economic restructuring. This latter group is the first generation to experience the emerging labor market in full strength, and we use them to better understand how the rules governing success have changed, especially for the majority of workers, who do not attain a four-year college degree. By tracking their movements between firms and the consequent path of their wage growth, we can observe how economic restructuring has affected the opportunities to achieve a stable job and upward mobility. In this way, we hope to introduce a balancing perspective into current policy discussions, which have tended to be swamped by the economic boom and by the needs of the stock market—for example, lack of wage growth is now applauded as an economic indicator. It is time to put long-term trends in worker welfare back on the table.

## The Rise in Inequality

There is by now a substantial history to research on cross-sectional trends in earnings and wages. The basic facts are as follows. Starting in the early 1970s and continuing to various degrees through the 1990s, earnings for male workers stagnated and even declined—this after several decades of strong and consistent growth (see figure 1.1). At the same time, inequality increased dramatically, again a departure from the past. Men in the lowest decile of the wage distribution saw their real hourly wages decline by 11.4 percent between 1973 and 1999, while those in the top decile held stable until the mid-1990s,

**Figure 1.1    Median Annual Earnings for Full-Time, Year-Round Workers, 1960 to 1998 (1998 Dollars)**

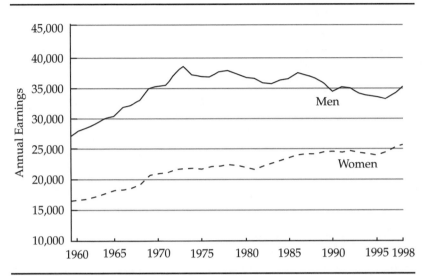

*Source:* Data from U.S. Bureau of the Census 1999.

when their wages grew by 9.2 percent; even the tight labor market and strong economic growth of recent years has not been able to erase this polarization (top panel of figure 1.2). Women, on the other hand, experienced real wage growth during this period, which contributed to a shrinking of the gender gap, although they did share in the trend toward greater wage inequality starting in the early 1980s (bottom panel of figure 1.2). Other measures show similarly disturbing trends. The poverty rate reversed its long-standing decline and started growing again, and the convergence of black and white wages has come to a near standstill.[2]

One of the engines driving these trends is changing the relative rise in the returns to education. Workers with college degrees did not see significant growth in their wages during the 1980s and 1990s but were generally able to hold their own ground. Workers with less education, however, saw large declines in real wages. The increase in the high school wage penalty between 1979 and 1995 varies from one labor force group to another (from around 30 percent to 60 percent); nevertheless, it is a broad-based trend and one of the central facts of the changing structure of earnings inequality (Mishel, Bernstein, and Schmitt 1997b; Autor, Katz, and Krueger 1998). Thus the prevailing dictum in both public and academic spheres is that "skill" has become increasingly important in the American labor market.

**Figure 1.2   Change in Hourly Wages by Wage Percentile, from 1973 to 1999**

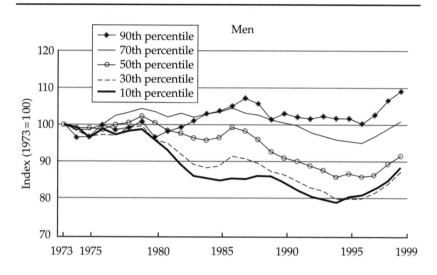

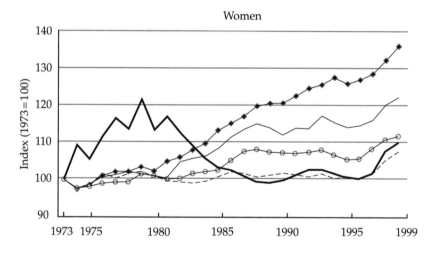

*Source:* Data from Mishel, Bernstein and Schmitt 2001.

The education story is a descriptive one. It does not answer the critical question of just why education has become more valuable. Much of labor economics research in this area has therefore been devoted to identifying what has caused the shift in demand.[3] The two main candidates within this framework are technology and the globalization of trade. The trade story, however, has been surprisingly difficult to document, notwithstanding the much-cited relocation of manufacturing jobs out of the United States.[4] Almost by default, then, technological change has become the leading explanation. From this perspective, substantial numbers of American workers are not meeting the demand for technological acumen and thus find their wages declining, while at the same time, skilled workers are reaping the benefits of their qualifications.

This is an intuitively appealing and parsimonious account of the rise in earnings inequality, but as a comprehensive account it is not entirely satisfactory. Until recently, the skill-biased technological change argument was made by fiat, inferred from the structure of the growing wage differentials themselves (for example, Bound and Johnson 1992). We have begun to see studies that attempt to empirically demonstrate the effect of technological change in the aggregate (for example, Krueger 1993; Berman, Bound, and Griliches 1994), but these efforts compete with detailed case study research offering a more complex picture, one in which technology has served to both upskill and de-skill jobs, and close analysis of changes in skill requirements of jobs over time yields a mixed picture (see the reviews by Philip Moss [2000] and Peter Cappelli [1996]). Another key wrinkle is that the timing and rate of technological innovation do not easily match the timing of the rise in wage inequality (see Autor, Katz, and Krueger 1998; Howell and Wolff 1991; Mishel, Bernstein, and Schmitt 1997a). Perhaps most important, the changing returns to education explain only about a third of the total increase in inequality. More than half has occurred within groups of workers of the same age, education, and experience, and this residual has so far not been explained, except to assume that it simply reflects other "unobservable skills" that have also come into greater demand because of new technologies.

The utility of such a sweeping assumption is doubtful, especially given that other candidates have not yet been fully explored. To wit, it has become clear that firms are responding to increased competition and are restructuring work in ways that are not easily captured by the argument for technology-driven change. The business press abounds with examples of innovative companies that have created high-quality and high-paying jobs; yet just as prevalent are accounts of low-wage strategies, de-skilled jobs, the imposition of two-tiered wage systems, and substitution of contingent for full-time workers. Although there is no doubt that profound technological change has occurred, the story that unfolds across a number of industries is that firms often use the same technology (computers, for example) to reorganize jobs differentially, upskilling in some parts of the organization, automating and routinizing in others; thus, restructuring and technology interact to produce different outcomes for workers, within the same industry and even the same firm. Frank Levy and Richard Murnane, in their classic literature review of the wage inequality field, end with a recognition of this diversity: "Some firms may choose to compete for larger shares of standardized products produced by low wage workers carrying out relatively simple tasks. Other firms may choose to tailor production to a high value-added, high quality product at the upper end of the same market. Both strategies may prove successful in generating profits, but with quite different consequences for workers' wages" (Levy and Murnane 1992, 1374).

In explaining the variability in firm strategies, observers have pointed to changes in corporate governance, deregulation across a host of industries, the decline of unionization and bargaining power, and the stagnant minimum wage.[5] This is simply to reiterate a longstanding argument of institutional economists: firms' choices about the setting of wages and the allocation of labor are made within a network of constraints, which derive not just from product markets but also from institutions and regulations, as well as past choices and strategies made by the firms. Thus there is a growing sense that the environment in which firms make choices and pursue competitive strategies has shifted and that trends in the labor market and wage inequality are part of an unfolding system of industrial relations. If so, what does this new system look like?

## A New Employment Relationship

For close to half a century, American industry profitably worked within the paradigm of mass production, the features of which are well known (Kochan, Katz, and McKersie 1986; Jacoby 1985). By World War II, the craft production system of the nineteenth century had given way to monopoly capitalism, driven by the centralization of capital and the consequent dominance of large firms. Under Fordism, products became standardized, growth was contingent on market stability and expansion, and Keynesian macroeconomics came to play an important role in balancing supply and demand.

Of interest to us here is what happened to the social organization of production. The old foreman system of shop-floor control was replaced by a combination of technical and bureaucratic control of the workplace (Edwards 1979). Unions played a critical role in this reformulation of industrial organization. The union was given a voice in setting wages, working conditions, and grievance procedures; in return, management had control over planning and company decision making.[6] For jobs lower in the skill hierarchy, work was broken down into simple, discrete tasks according to the principles of Taylorism. For jobs higher up the skill hierarchy, employers enjoyed a customized training system: because workers learned on the job, they brought firm-specific knowledge, tested skills, and commitment to each new position to which they were promoted. The result was a diverse system of job categories, each component of which was rigidly defined. Wages were attached to particular jobs, and on-the-job training and seniority activated the promotion process. Coupled with limited ports of entry, the result was strong job security and middle-class wages for a sizable core of workers.[7]

Thus the allocation of labor, worker mobility, and wage determination came to be largely governed by the internal labor market. It is important to understand that the benefits of this system also incurred a set of costs. Because employers made at least an implied and often a formal commitment to workers, their flexibility on a number of fronts was constrained (restrictive labor legislation also played a role in this). They could not easily hire from the outside nor change the number of workers being used, the tasks and functions they performed, or the wages and benefits they were paid.

Starting in the mid-1970s, the terms of this trade-off apparently deteriorated for American employers. The mass production system had reached the limits to its expansion, primarily because it could not maintain high levels of productivity gains in markets that were increasingly contested, saturated, and deregulated. Business leaders, policy analysts, and academics argued that the United States was facing another critical transformation of economic organization and that companies must therefore fundamentally alter the way they organize the process of work and production. New managerial models were developed, with the goal of restoring productivity growth and American competitiveness.

In practice, however, the way this goal is achieved varies enormously. Cost reduction has become an overriding basis of competition, and the problem, of course, is that internal labor markets are costly to maintain. Full-time, permanent workers with long tenures need to be paid high wages and benefits that can add as much as 30 percent to the wage bill. Some will sit idle during slack demand, and others will decline in productivity as their skills become obsolete—rigid job classifications do not easily accommodate products and technology that are in constant flux. At the same time, competitiveness has become a matter of flexibility in who is hired, for how long, for how much, and for which tasks (Hyman 1988).

Thus we are currently seeing a wide spectrum of firm-level restructuring and innovation in the search for flexibility.[8] A stylized shorthand for this spectrum is the distinction between "high road" and "low road" strategies. At one end lies the high-performance firm, characterized by just-in-time production, flat job hierarchies, and the use of total quality management (Dertouzos, Lester, and Solow 1989; Lawler 1986; Kochan and Osterman 1994; Womack, Jones, and Roos 1990). The success of these reforms is intimately tied to innovative human resource policies, such as self-directed teams, job rotation, and more-sophisticated employee incentives (Walton 1985). In addition, because a firm's success depends on the skill and creativity of its workforce, it provides high wages, job security and mobility, and frontline decision making. At the other end of the spectrum lies the "lean and mean" firm, which emphasizes the bottom line. The production process is characteristically bare-bones, with labor costs and quantities used to make constant adjustments to market changes in product mix and demand (Harrison 1994; Cohen and Zysman 1987; Colclough and Tolbert 1992; Wood 1992). Frequently involved are union avoidance, the use of two-tiered wage structures, subcontracting as a means of reducing the size and cost of labor, and the surprising retention of some tenets of scientific management such as job fragmentation and de-skilling for part of the workforce. Rather than grooming workers for future advancement, these firms are more likely to minimize the number of full-time jobs, adjust to fluctuations in demand with contingent workers, and rely on the external labor market to provide skilled and up-to-date workers.

In truth, the dichotomy of high road versus low road is artificial and too rigid. Often, a mix of strategies is adopted within the same organization. For example, subcontracting and reliance on contingent workers may well be concomitant with high-performance strategies that protect the firm's "core competencies" and therefore an inner group of stable, participative employees (Pfeffer and Baron 1988; Appelbaum and Batt 1994). Similarly, firms emphasizing the bottom line often exhibit innovative production practices that conform closely to the calls for flexible specialization and benefit well-placed workers in the organization (Rosenberg 1989; Piore and Sabel 1984). Thus, though we may well be seeing a divergence in firm practices, we are also seeing firms that increasingly contain both primary and secondary practices within them. In addition, relationships between firms have become more complicated, with deeper and wider networks of suppliers and contractors; and the externalization of work may produce more similarity in jobs within a given occupation than within a firm or an industry. As a result, the practices that govern hiring, screening, training, and labor supply—the labor market—also become occupation based.[9] In short, not only are internal labor markets changing differentially, but so, too, are the external markets that link the internal ones, to varying degrees in different sectors. Understanding this matrix of changes and how it has contributed to growing inequality is clearly one of the key challenges for future research.

It is also important to reiterate that the diversity in firm behavior has been driven not only by market forces but also by distinct changes in the institutional environment (Freeman 1996; Blau and Kahn 1999). Prime among these is the well-documented decline in unionization and its spillover into a distinct lessening of worker voice in general (Freeman and Medoff 1984) as well as legal changes in the regulations that govern the employment relationship (Friedman et al. 1994). Also intertwined has been governmental deregulation of a series of traditionally unionized industries, which has had strong effects on the distribution of work practices and wages (Vogel 1996). Researchers are only now beginning to document the profound impact of the shift in corporate governance toward shareholder control and institutional investors and the constant pressure for performance that has resulted (Christopherson 2001; Berg and Appelbaum 1996). Empirically measuring these types of institutional changes and their effects on firms is enormously difficult—never mind the task of untangling how recent institutional and market changes have been related. We do have some evidence of an ultimate impact on workers, however, because both deunionization and the declining minimum wage have contributed to the growth in wage inequality (the exact size of the effects varies by study; see Dinardo, Fortin, and Lemieux 1996, Freeman 1995, Card and Krueger 1995).

Thus the story of firm restructuring is a complex one. It does not lend itself to a simple, straightforward narrative of exactly how and why the American employment relationship has changed—and continues to change. Fully answering these questions will require more research at the firm level and also the passage of more time. There is no doubt, however, that a fundamental reorganization of work and production is under way in the American workplace, reflecting a "breakdown of the industrial relations system that was shaped by New Deal labor policies and the early institutionalization of collective bargaining" (Kochan, Katz, and McKersie 1986, 21).

## The Effects on Upward Mobility

Clearly, more research needs to be done to elucidate the roles of both technology and firm restructuring in explaining the rise in economic inequality. However, our purpose in this book is not to adjudicate between these two explanations; in fact, arriving at a definitive account is not possible. The central dilemma in this field is that there exist no data that allow one to systematically link organizational restructuring and technological innovation to trends in worker outcomes. Such a project would require representative and longitudinal data over time (back to the start of the 1970s), with information at the firm level (changes in organizational ownership, subcontracting, occupational structure, employment, and salary levels across a large sample of firms) and at the worker level (changes in wages, work history, skill levels, family circumstances), providing the ability to match all workers to all firms. For better or worse, we will never have such data; even if we were to start collecting it now, the past thirty years are lost to us.

This means that the inequality debate will be resolved only indirectly, by triangulating between different sources of information. So far, we have cross-sectional data on wages, and we have case studies of firms and industries. The missing piece of the triad is longitudinal data on what has actually happened to workers' careers as they move through the restructured labor market and the mechanisms that have driven those changes. Cross-sectional data on wages can give us a representative snapshot of workers' well-being over time but provide only weak information on the causes that are operating. Firm and industry studies give us a more dynamic picture of actual changes in the workplace but do not reveal net effects on worker outcomes. The third piece of the puzzle, changes in upward mobility for a national sample, can begin to link these two sources of data. Ultimately, the way that global trade, new technology, and firm restructuring make themselves felt in the wage distribution is by changing the actual career paths that workers build and the degree of upward mobility they are able to achieve over the long run.

The point is simple: lying underneath the one-dimensional distribution of wages that researchers usually analyze is a complex and multidimensional set of individual mobility paths. Our goal in this book is to describe how the structure of mobility has changed over the past three decades and to draw out the implications for the rise in inequality.

It may seem like an odd time to take on the question of upward mobility. Productivity growth has improved, unemployment and inflation are low, and corporate profits as a percentage of gross domestic product are climbing. Workplaces have become more efficient, the adoption of new technologies is brisk, and American global competitiveness is on the upswing (Mowery 1999).

From the perspective of workers, however, there is a growing sense among the public that individuals' life chances are becoming more uncertain and more unequal (Frank and Cook 1995; Hacker 1997). This is not just a matter of good jobs versus bad jobs. At root, the public's concern with trends such as downsizing and dependence on contingent workers has to do with the opportunities for workers to attain stable employment and upward mobility over the long run and the question of whether those opportunities have deteriorated. The intuition is that the strategies that firms have adopted in the search for competitiveness are affecting the structures that enable worker mobility. Both internal and external to firms, these structures include how work is organized, how workers are matched with jobs, how wages and the terms of employment are set, and who has voice in that determination (Doeringer and Piore 1971; Granovetter 1981). These processes ultimately give rise to the wage structure, "the complex of rates within firms differentiated by occupation and employee and the complex of inter-firm rate structures" (Dunlop 1957, 128). It is the systematic paths by which workers move through that wage structure over time that form the key feature of the labor market and that can tell us whether the distribution of mobility paths has changed (Spilerman 1977).

More concretely, if employment is being weaned from internal labor markets for significant numbers of workers, then this affects not only their current jobs but also their long-term career prospects. What happens to promotions, raises, and "climbing up the ladder" when employers hire externally for skilled jobs and invest less in entry-level training, especially for new technology? How do workers with only a high school diploma gain access to firms at which job titles have been collapsed and decision making has been pushed down to multiskilled, autonomous employees working in teams? What happens when low-skill jobs are removed from the organization altogether through subcontracting and outsourcing, to specialized "niche" firms that frequently pay less for the same work? How does flexible staffing and reliance on temporary, part-time, and leased workers affect ports of entry into the firm and workers' ability to accumulate a broad set of skills?

The traditional routes to upward mobility break down under these conditions. In shifting some of the risk of doing business onto their workers, employers have also shifted the locus of career development: "Pressures from the product market are brought inside the company to employees by making compensation and job security contingent on organizational performance. Pressures from the labor market manifest themselves through more hiring from outside, career development increasingly across (rather than within) organizations, and greater use of contingent and contract labor" (Cappelli et al. 1997, 209). It is likely that skilled workers in professional occupations can create new career paths that preserve their opportunities; but for occupations further down the ladder—more numerous in absolute terms—the consequence may well be declining opportunities for upward mobility.

For example, table 1.1 shows the occupations with the largest projected job growth from 1996 to 2006. We might imagine that systems

| Occupation | | | |
|---|---|---|---|
| Database administrators, computer support specialists, and all other computer scientists | 249 | 118 | Bachelor's degree |
| Marketing and sales worker supervisors | 246 | 11 | Work experience in a related occupation |
| Maintenance repairers, general utility | 246 | 18 | Long-term on-the-job training |
| Food counter, fountain, and related workers | 243 | 14 | Short-term on-the-job training |
| Teachers, special education | 241 | 59 | Bachelor's degree |
| Computer engineers | 235 | 109 | Bachelor's degree |
| Food preparation workers | 234 | 19 | Short-term on-the-job training |
| Hand packers and packagers | 222 | 23 | Short-term on-the-job training |
| Guards | 221 | 23 | Short-term on-the-job training |
| General office clerks | 215 | 7 | Short-term on-the-job training |
| Waiters and waitresses | 206 | 11 | Short-term on-the-job training |
| Social workers | 188 | 32 | Bachelor's degree |
| Adjustment clerks | 183 | 46 | Short-term on-the-job training |
| Cooks, short order and fast food | 174 | 22 | Short-term on-the-job training |
| Personal and home care aides | 171 | 85 | Short-term on-the-job training |
| Food service and lodging managers | 168 | 28 | Work experience in a related occupation |
| Medical assistants | 166 | 74 | Moderate on-the-job training |

*Source:* U.S. Department of Labor 1998.

analysts and general managers, though not wholly protected from the vicissitudes of a volatile labor market, can still eventually find a protected "core" job or, at the very least, build real wage growth as they move between employers. For cashiers, salespersons, information clerks, and nursing aides, however, the prospects look less promising. The gap between these "starter" occupations and "career" occupations has gotten bigger, and not just because of skill requirements. Especially in the service sector, the consolidation and siphoning off of key operations does not augur well for eventual mobility (for example, national customer-service phone centers in banking and telecommunications, or the temporary health-worker industry).[10] It may be that other actors will emerge to replace some of the functions of the traditional internal labor market, as seems to be occurring in several large temp agencies such as Manpower. Whether such market-driven solutions can by themselves provide opportunity to low-skilled workers remains to be seen.

Much of this is conjecture, and so the larger point is that we simply do not know enough about what has happened to upward mobility. Although the trends in wage inequality have generated a prodigious amount of literature, little of it has examined the issue of mobility. Labor economists have generally restricted their focus to analysis of the determinants of the cross-sectional trends, and sociologists have generally concentrated on the differential impacts observed by race, sex, and region. However, the growth in cross-sectional inequality is equally consistent with a scenario in which young workers start in low-wage jobs and move to high-wage jobs by adulthood, or one in which some workers get stuck in a cycle of low-wage jobs while others experience strong wage growth over the course of their careers. The latter scenario clearly carries much higher stakes, in terms of overall social consequences and the challenge for public policy.

Mobility is therefore the key to a definitive assessment of the emerging postindustrial economy. For mobility is where the link between labor market structure and individual life history is made, where we gain insight into the dynamic processes that actually generate inequality, and where we assess how well America is meeting its meritocratic ideal.

As researchers begin to ask how firm restructuring has affected economic inequality, then, it is natural that we return to individuals' work histories to analyze the dynamics of the new labor market. In fact, this strategy is basically the only one open to us, because firm-level data on mobility structures over time do not exist at a representative level. Current research has therefore begun to focus on analyzing longitudinal data sets, taking up such questions as whether wage growth has deteriorated, whether the rate of job changing has increased, and how each of these processes unfolds over the life course (for example, Gottschalk 1997; Neumark, Polsky, and Hansen 1997; Duncan, Boisjoly, and Smeeding 1996; Gittleman and Joyce 1996). Mobility is again at the center of analysis.

Our study falls squarely into this emerging field of longitudinal research on job stability and wage attainment. We compare the career development and economic mobility of two cohorts of young white men based on data from the National Longitudinal Surveys.[11] The original cohort entered the labor market in the mid-1960s at the tail of the economic boom, and was followed through the end of the 1970s to the early 1980s. The recent cohort entered the labor market in the late 1970s and the early 1980s, after the onset of economic restructuring, and was followed through the mid-1990s. For each of the years that the two cohorts were followed, rich and detailed information was gathered on school enrollment, educational attainment, work history, wages, and job characteristics such as occupation and industry. This type of data is unique because it affords us a window on the complex process by which upward mobility is built over the key stages of the career. In addition, because the two cohorts are tracked across the same age range for the same length of time, comparing their progress enables us to isolate the impact of differences in economic context— the late 1960s and the 1970s versus the 1980s and early 1990s.

Our logic is that if indeed a new labor market structure is emerging in this country, then the recent cohort of young adults has been the first generation to experience it in full strength, and the impact should be observable in their work histories and wage growth trajectories. This is not to minimize the significant and often painful changes that mature workers have undergone over the past three decades. Our focus, however, is on upward mobility and career development, the majority of which occurs within the first decade and a half of work experience.

Moreover, cross-sectional research shows that young adults have been particularly hard hit by changes over the past several decades. Table 1.2 shows median weekly earnings for twenty-five- to thirty-four-year-olds in the major occupation groups for 1979 and 1996. The first panel describes a general decline in real earnings, most pronounced for traditionally unionized occupations such as machine operators but also strong in the low-end service and clerical occupations. These declines do not just reflect the economy-wide trend in earnings—the second panel shows that the earnings of young adults have declined as a percentage of all adults' earnings, as well, with similar patterns by occupation. We also know that the widening gap

**Table 1.2  Earnings of Workers Aged Twenty-Five to Thirty-Four, by Occupation, 1979 and 1996**

| Occupational Category | Median Weekly Earnings | | | Median Weekly Earnings as a Percentage of Earnings of All Adults | | |
|---|---|---|---|---|---|---|
| | 1979 (Dollars) | 1996 (Dollars) | Percentage Change | 1979 | 1996 | Change |
| Executive, administrative, and managerial | 761 | 658 | −13.5 | 87.1 | 75.8 | −11.3 |
| Professional specialty | 720 | 699 | −2.9 | 83.3 | 79.4 | −3.8 |
| Technicians and related support | 655 | 601 | −8.3 | 88.9 | 87.5 | −1.4 |
| Sales occupations | 662 | 541 | −18.2 | 91.6 | 86.7 | −4.9 |
| Administrative support, including clerical | 612 | 438 | −28.4 | 93.4 | 83.7 | −9.7 |
| Service occupations | 474 | 356 | −24.8 | 97.3 | 90.1 | −7.2 |
| Precision production, craft and repair | 675 | 508 | −24.7 | 96.3 | 86.1 | −10.2 |
| Machine operators, assemblers, and inspectors | 569 | 408 | −28.3 | 95.3 | 87.9 | −7.4 |
| Transportation and material-moving occupations | 642 | 446 | −30.5 | 98.0 | 88.5 | −9.5 |
| Handlers, equipment cleaners, helpers, and laborers | 523 | 362 | −30.8 | 96.8 | 92.1 | −4.7 |
| Farming, forestry, and fishing | 391 | 310 | −20.8 | 99.5 | 96.3 | −3.2 |
| Total | 651 | 499 | −23.3 | 94.1 | 83.2 | −10.9 |

*Source:* Schrammel 1998.

between college graduates and those with less education has been most pronounced among young adults (Katz and Murphy 1992). In this context, the findings of a recent study on training are especially worrisome: young adults with high levels of formal education are significantly more likely to participate in employment-related training, including that provided by the employer, than are less-educated youth (Hight 1998).

Trends such as these give us an initial snapshot of what has happened to young adults in the new labor market, and the message is not encouraging. Again, however, they cannot speak to the deeper issues of economic mobility and career formation under postindustrialism. That is the purpose of this study.

## Plan of the Book

A detailed summary of our findings is given at the end of most of the chapters; here, we simply give an outline of content. This first chapter has taken a broad view of current changes in the labor market and the historical context from which they emerged. In the next six chapters, we turn to a detailed analysis of our longitudinal data to reveal how the structure of long-term mobility has changed. In the final chapter, we return to the broad themes laid out here and discuss the implications of our findings, with respect to both trends in the employment relationship and the policies that are needed to address them.

In chapter 2, we provide an overview of the two National Longitudinal Survey cohorts, discussing our research design, samples, and measures and giving an in-depth treatment of the comparability of the two data sets. This material is key to understanding all of the analyses that follow. Chapter 3 also provides important background material by describing basic labor market trends over the past three decades. We document changes in educational attainment, in the mix of industries and occupations, in the amount of work experience gained, and in the transition from school into the labor market.

In chapter 4 we ask, Has job instability changed? One of the most important stages in career development is the process of job search, or "job shopping," wherein young adults experiment with different types of employers and work settings and hopefully are able to find a match that best suits their needs. It is also the case, however, that too much job changing is detrimental over the long run. Moreover, there has been much recent concern among the public that the "lifelong" job is on the wane and that job instability is growing. We therefore take a close look at the rate of job changing, exploring whether it has increased in the 1980s and 1990s for young adults, and how the tenure distribution has changed.

In chapter 5 we ask, have the consequences of job instability changed? Regardless of whether or not there has been a secular rise in job instability, there might still be significant changes in its effects on workers' wages and careers. In fact, we know that the majority of lifetime wage growth occurs early on in adulthood and that much of it is driven by shifts to better-paying jobs. Has this dynamic changed in the new labor market, and are there any differences by education level?

In chapter 6 we ask perhaps the most important question: Has long-term wage growth changed? There are two parts to this analysis. The first examines the extent to which upward mobility has declined and become more unequal for the recent cohort as compared with the original cohort. Note that two aspects of economic well-being are being captured here, one absolute and the other relative. A change in the average amount of mobility means that everyone's boat is either rising or falling. Growing inequality in mobility means that some workers' boats are rising whereas others' are falling. When both absolute and relative mobility deteriorate at the same time, the effects on those with modest opportunity can be devastating. The second part of the chapter then turns to an analysis of the factors associated with the changes in wage attainment. We are particularly interested here in the role that job stability plays in the ability of workers to achieve long-term wage growth and in the extent to which education mediates this process.

Chapter 7 grounds the foregoing analyses with a detailed look at low-wage workers. Little is known about the actual careers of workers stuck in low-wage, high-turnover jobs over the long run. Yet such information has become particularly relevant with the advent of "work first" policies and the subsequent experiences of former welfare recipients. We therefore exploit the longitudinal power of our data and describe the labor market dynamics that underpin the "low-wage trap." We conclude in chapter 8 by stepping back and discussing what our findings imply about the causes that have driven the growth in inequality, as well as the policies that are most likely to reverse it.

# = Chapter 2 =

# An Introduction to the National Longitudinal Survey Cohorts

T HE PROJECT of this book—to describe how career development and upward mobility have changed, a period of fundamental economic transition for the United States—has strong data requirements: we want to track individual workers as they build their careers and to observe this process in different economic periods. Few data sets exist that can fulfill both functions. We make use of two cohorts from the National Longitudinal Surveys (NLS). The first is the National Longitudinal Survey of Young Men (NLSYM): this nationally representative sample of young men was first interviewed in 1966, tracked until 1981, and reinterviewed yearly in that time span (except for four skipped years). The second is the male sample of the National Longitudinal Survey of Youth (NLSY): this nationally representative sample of young men was interviewed in 1979 and has been interviewed yearly through 1994. Throughout, we refer to the former as the original cohort and to the latter as the recent cohort.

It is important to understand that the NLS data are not representative of the entire age range in the working population. Rather, these two cohorts are followed from the ages of fourteen to twenty-one until the ages of thirty to thirty-seven. We are therefore witnessing the maturing of young workers over time, as they move from school into the labor market and build their careers. The power of this research design lies in the fact that we observe both cohorts across a full sixteen years, at exactly the same ages, with comparable information on education, work history, and job characteristics. Thus, the key difference between the cohorts is the economic context in which they begin to build their careers.

The original cohort entered the labor market in the middle to late 1960s at the tail of the economic boom and was followed until 1981.

21

Although some changes, such as the flight of manufacturing overseas, were already starting to occur during this period, the language of "downsizing," "reengineering," and "workforce reduction " had not yet become part of the national vocabulary, and many firms were still following traditional employment and production practices. In contrast, the recent cohort entered the labor market in the early 1980s, after the onset of economic restructuring, and was followed through the mid-1990s. By this point the shift to postindustrialism was in full swing, marked by public concern about growing inequality, job instability, and the rise of contingent work and "flexible" staffing practices.

Comparing the progress of the two cohorts therefore enables us to isolate the impact of differences in economic context on economic mobility. Our logic is that if indeed a new labor market structure is emerging in this country, then the recent cohort of young adults has been the first to experience it in full strength and the impact should be observable in their work histories and wage trajectories. This is not to ignore the important effect that restructuring has had on older workers but simply to recognize that the dynamics are different. In mid- or late-career, how one adjusts to new labor market demands will be determined by a complex set of constraints, including family responsibilities, skills, and occupational history. Some older workers will be protected by residual formal or informal contracts in their firms (though others will not be, as shown by the research on workers displaced during the 1970s and 1980s). By contrast, what we learn by watching young adults as they start their careers in a radically changed environment helps us to map what the future labor market will look like. The advantage of our study, then, is that neither cohort is confounded by the presence of older workers, who still carry the legacy of past employment practices in their career paths.

Moreover, any changes that we identify between the two cohorts will have strong implications for their members' lifetime wage growth and career development. This is a point we emphasize repeatedly throughout the book. The term "young men" may give the mistaken impression that the NLS data only cover a narrow segment of the working population. In fact, the age range covered by the sixteen years of longitudinal data in the NLS captures the most important years of career development. During the first decade and a half of labor market experience, workers finish their schooling, make the transition to the labor force, and lay the groundwork for an eventual long-term relationship with an employer. Roughly two-thirds of lifetime wage growth occurs during this formative period, largely determining the paths of upward mobility (Murphy and Welch 1990). If we want to understand the dynamics of labor market inequality—who ends up where and why—then the early career is the place to look.

Finally, we should highlight how the NLS data complement other data typically used in the inequality field. On the one hand, nationally representative cross-sectional data, such as the Current Population Survey and the census, are good for establishing how the wage structure has shifted; but they quickly lose power when we ask questions about mechanisms and lifetime impacts. Organizational and industry-level case studies, on the other hand, do a much better job of speaking to the actual dynamics in the workplace that have contributed to rising inequality—such as the introduction of new technologies and the shifting of jobs outside of the firm; but their drawback is the limited scope of case study data, which makes it impossible to generalize their findings to the workforce as a whole.

The NLS longitudinal data provide a bridge between these two sources of information. By tracking two nationally representative samples of workers over the course of their careers, we can identify how the structure of upward mobility has changed—a question that cross-sectional data cannot answer. As we watch the unfolding of these workers' careers, we can also identify some of the actual mechanisms that have yielded the polarization in wages—but for a representative sample of workers that case studies cannot provide. The bridge provided by longitudinal data is therefore a crucial step forward. It brings a wealth of new evidence to the table for testing the different explanations for the rise in inequality. Organizational studies are good at generating, but not testing, predictions about the way that restructuring has altered career mobility between and within firms. We can take those predictions and match them up against the patterns actually observed in the NLS data: for example, we can look for flatter wage trajectories marked by frequent job changes, which might be consistent with a weakening of internal labor markets and a rise in labor market segmentation. In the absence of national data tracking both firms and their workers, this type of indirect testing provides the best opportunity we have for resolving the inequality debates.

## Samples

The baseline sample selection for both cohorts is as follows (further selections are done later for different analyses). We choose all respondents who were between the ages of thirteen and twenty-two in the first year of the surveys. We select non-Hispanic whites only: attrition

**Figure 2.1   Years Surveyed and Age Ranges for Two NLS Cohorts**

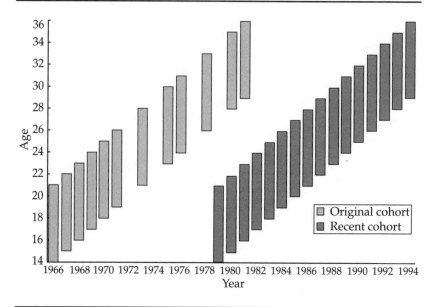

*Source:* Authors' compilation.

among nonwhites was extreme in the original cohort, which seriously compromises any effort to conduct race-based analyses.[1] We also drop the poor white supplemental sample and the military supplemental sample from the recent cohort (NLSY). Because both are purely supplemental samples, they do not affect the representativeness of the main sample (in terms of income, for example).[2]

The resulting sample sizes are 2,743 for the original cohort and 2,434 for the recent cohort. Respondents can be observed for a maximum of 16 years, although many respondents missed at least one survey, and some dropped out of the survey altogether. The mean number of years observed for each respondent is 9.0 years in the original cohort and 13.8 years in the recent cohort. The number is lower for the original cohort because four years were skipped in that survey (specifically, 1972, 1974, 1977, and 1979). The resulting structure of our data is illustrated in figure 2.1, which shows the years surveyed and the age range in each year for the two cohorts. As mentioned, the ages of respondents are fourteen to twenty-one years in the first survey year and thirty to thirty-seven in the final survey year. We focus our analyses on those aged sixteen and older; respondents who en-

Table 2.1    Years Used from the Two NLS Cohorts for Different Analyses

| Panel Number | All-Years Comparison | | Twelve-Year Comparison | Matched Two-Year Comparisons |
|---|---|---|---|---|
| | Original Cohort | Recent Cohort | | |
| Year 1 | 1966 | 1979 | * | |
| Year 2 | 1967 | 1980 | * | Years 2 and 4 |
| Year 3 | 1968 | 1981 | * | |
| Year 4 | 1969 | 1982 | * | Years 4 and 6 |
| Year 5 | 1970 | 1983 | * | |
| Year 6 | 1971 | 1984 | * | Years 6 and 8 |
| Year 7 | | 1985 | | |
| Year 8 | 1973 | 1986 | * | Years 8 and 10 |
| Year 9 | | 1987 | | |
| Year 10 | 1975 | 1988 | * | * |
| Year 11 | 1976 | 1989 | * | Years 11 and 13 |
| Year 12 | | 1990 | | |
| Year 13 | 1978 | 1991 | * | Years 13 and 15 |
| Year 14 | | 1992 | | |
| Year 15 | 1980 | 1993 | * | * |
| Year 16 | 1981 | 1994 | * | |

Source: Authors' compilation.

tered the survey at the age of fourteen or fifteen are "picked up" once they turn sixteen.

The four missing years in the original cohort sequence (see table 2.1) complicate several of the analyses that we perform. Any measure that depends on a comparison or cumulation across years will be affected by the fact that the original cohort has several two-year gaps and the recent cohort does not. Examples of such measures are rates of job changing from one year to the next, age at first full-time job, and total number of unemployment spells. We use a host of strategies to adjust for this problem, which are discussed on a measure-by-measure basis. In general, we have taken two approaches. Often, we use only the matched twelve years—those years in which there are data for both cohorts—as seen in the fourth column of the table. This matching sacrifices the additional years in the recent cohort in order to attain strict comparability across cohorts. Sometimes, it is also necessary to have equal intervals between paired observations—for example, when rates of job changing are analyzed. In these cases we further restrict our analysis to the eight matched, equal-interval, paired years, as shown in the last column of the table. Throughout the book we identify which version of the data is being used.

## Data Structure and Measures

For each of the years that the two cohorts were followed, rich and detailed information was gathered on demographic characteristics, school enrollment, educational attainment, work history, wages, and job characteristics such as occupation and industry. This type of data is unique because it affords us a window on the complex process by which upward mobility is built over the key stages of the career. It also, however, requires many decisions about how information should be organized and analyzed. Such decisions are described in detail in appendix A and as needed throughout the book, so we discuss only the most general here.

Several alternative measures are commonly used to track individuals over time in labor market studies of longitudinal data: age, work experience, and calendar year. We use either age or work experience as the fundamental dimension along which young workers attain their schooling, enter the labor market, and pursue higher wages. This strategy allows us to compare the two cohorts initially on a standard dimension and then to introduce the effects of other factors, such as education, demographics, work history, and prevailing economic conditions. Calendar year is not an appropriate metric, because, as seen in figure 2.1, eight age groups are captured within any given year—resulting in too much variability in life-cycle stages. Pooling observations by age or experience has the added advantage of smoothing business-cycle effects.

Longitudinal data can be analyzed in two ways. One way is to use the person as the unit of analysis. In this case, each person contributes one observation, with variables that summarize his entire labor market history. These variables may index time, but they do not change over time: for example, highest degree obtained, age at first full-time job, total number of employers, and total amount of wage growth. The second way to analyze these data uses the person-year as the unit of analysis. In this case, each person contributes multiple observations, one for each year (and therefore age) at which he was interviewed. Under this type of analysis, the variables can change over time. For example, educational attainment, working status, and wages all change as the person grows older, and often we wish to model such dynamics and their determinants. We use both approaches in this book, depending on the analysis. For all graphs and tables, the default analysis is one based on person-years; we note all instances in which the analysis is based on persons.

Finally, another complication inherent in the use of longitudinal data is that the same variable may be measured differently over successive interviews. The NLS, for example, has greatly improved and expanded its survey instrument over the years. As a result, the information available for the recent cohort is generally both richer and more detailed than that available for the original cohort. Even within each cohort, some questions changed over time. Much of our effort in cleaning these data was therefore spent on constructing measures that are strictly consistent across all survey years and across both cohorts. If a measure could not be created consistently, we did not use it, in order to retain as rigorous a cross-cohort comparison as possible.

Some of the variables that we use are straightforward, and in these cases, we do not review their construction in detail.[3] Other variables, however, do require elaboration and are reviewed as they are introduced throughout the book, with a detailed technical discussion given in appendix A. For all variables, it is important to keep in mind that these surveys were administered once a year, for a maximum of sixteen years. At each interview, information was gathered both about the respondent's status in the interview week and about his status during the past year (for example, the number of weeks worked). If the respondent missed the previous year's interview, the NLS gathered information on basic variables for the missing year(s). Further details on how we treated missing data are given on a measure-by-measure basis and are also discussed in the next section.

The respondent's working status during the interview week is the most important piece of information for our study, because it tracks entry into the labor force and anchors many of the other variables we use. For both cohorts and for all years, the NLS uses the same standard set of questions from the Current Population Survey (CPS) questionnaire that are designed to ascertain whether a respondent worked in the week of the interview. The questions identify the respondent's main status in the previous week, either working (including temporary layoff or absence), unemployed, or not in the labor market (including primarily in school).

This set of questions on labor force activity also identifies the respondent's main job, or what is commonly known as the "CPS job." The CPS job is identified in the same way across both cohorts in all survey years. Typically, it is the job the respondent held in the week before the interview, but if the respondent held more than one job during that week, the CPS job is defined as the one at which he worked the most hours. For the recent cohort, information is gathered on up to five jobs since the previous interview, but for the original cohort, only the CPS job is identified and tracked. We therefore restrict our focus to the CPS job throughout this book to ensure comparability across the cohorts. All of our job-specific measures, such as hours worked, wages, industry, and occupation, refer to the respondent's CPS job at the time of interview.

## Comparability of the Samples

Any attempt to compare two different data sets must begin with an analysis of comparability. Little research exists on this issue, and so we have conducted a rigorous analysis of comparability between the two NLS cohorts. The following discussion focuses on two questions.[4] First, was the initial sample of each cohort representative of its population, and do the initial samples differ systematically from each other in terms of demographic composition? Second, was there nonresponse bias over the course of each survey panel, and if so, does that bias differ across the two panels? In the course of answering these questions, several other issues arose, which we also discuss.

### Representativeness and Comparability of the Initial Sample

For both cohorts, the initial samples were multistage, stratified probability samples designed to be representative of the noninstitutionalized civilian U.S. population of youth.[5] To test for representativeness, we compared the original cohort's 1966 sample with the 1966 March CPS and the recent cohort's 1979 sample with the 1979 March CPS. The CPS samples were restricted to non-Hispanic white males aged fourteen to twenty-two, to allow us to match our baseline samples.[6] Comparisons were made along a number of dimensions, including demographic, schooling, and work history variables.

In terms of demographic and schooling-related characteristics, both of our samples proved to be quite representative, as expected. This is not the case, however, for work-related measures. Compared with CPS estimates, both of the NLS samples show higher labor force participation rates, unemployment rates, wages, and numbers of weeks worked. This is by now a well-established difference between CPS and NLS estimates, and it has been the subject of detailed research (Freeman and Medoff 1982; Borus, Mott, and Nestel 1978; Bowers 1981; Handcock, Morris, and Bernhardt 2000).

Two main explanations have been proposed. First, the young respondents in the NLS surveys are interviewed directly, but in the CPS surveys, a "proxy" respondent such as the mother or father often answers questions for younger respondents. Proxy respondents may not give accurate answers to work-related questions, especially if their children are working while in school (and it is precisely for students that the differences in estimates are strongest). A second explanation attributes the difference to "rotation group bias" in the CPS sample design: households interviewed for a second time by the CPS tend to report lower employment and unemployment activities than those interviewed for the first time in the rotation (Bowers 1981). Although complete consensus has not yet been reached, our reading of this research area is that the NLS estimates are likely to be more accurate. In any event, we are comparing across two NLS surveys and thus holding the NLS effect constant.

The next question is whether the initial samples of the two cohorts differ in terms of demographic composition. Such differences can confound the analysis of other substantive outcomes if they are not recognized and controlled for. We therefore took the initial samples of each cohort (1966 and 1979) and compared them along a number of dimensions. Two variables, age and education, emerged as problematic. Once we controlled for age and education, no other significant demographic differences were found between the two cohorts' initial samples.

The recent cohort is somewhat older than the original cohort at the time of the first interview (and of course, this difference will persist over time). Given that age is the key determinant of labor force behavior among young workers, any analysis must therefore control for age at the outset, and we do this routinely throughout the book. The recent cohort also has completed fewer years of education than the original cohort in the initial survey year. It turns out that this difference is a function of the timing of the interview windows for the two cohorts. Almost all of the respondents in the recent cohort were interviewed between January and May of 1979, before graduation or the completion of a standard academic year. By contrast, almost all of the respondents in the original cohort were interviewed between October and December of 1966, already well into the next academic year. When we adjusted for this effect, we found no significant differences in years of education.[7]

## Shifting Interview Windows

The problem of different interview windows affects more than just the initial samples—it persists throughout the survey panels. Across the sixteen years, the original cohort was consistently interviewed between October and December (a handful of cases spilled over into

**Figure 2.2    Comparison of Interview Month Between the Two Cohorts**

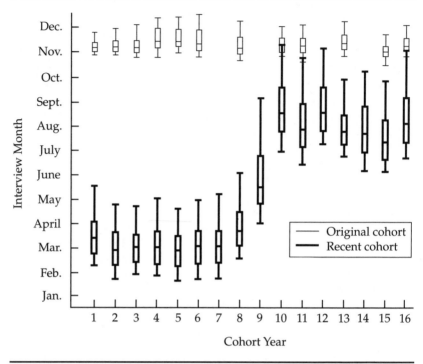

*Source:* Authors' compilation.

January of the next year). The recent cohort, however, had a shifting interview window over the sixteen-year period. The field periods for each cohort are displayed in figure 2.2. This difference complicates any cross-cohort comparisons of education-related variables, especially current enrollment status. The ideal solution to this problem would be to assign the November value of their enrollment status to the recent cohort, thereby matching the modal interview month for the original cohort. This would create a mismatch, however, between the measurement of education variables and the measurement of work-related variables. Imputing all recent cohort variables to their November values is impossible, because the requisite information is often not available. Our solution, therefore, is twofold. First, we adjust the most sensitive variable, current enrollment status, to be congruent across the two cohorts (as described in chapter 3). We also make sure that we control for age, education, and enrollment composition in every analysis or, at the very least, test for such an effect when describing raw percentages or means.

## Trends in Wage Dispersion in the Recent Cohort

In an unpublished but widely cited paper, Peter Gottschalk and Robert Moffitt (1992) benchmark earnings trends in the CPS against those in three major longitudinal data sets for the years 1979 to 1988. They find that the recent cohort (NLSY) had significantly lower variance in reported annual earnings and, in contrast with all other data sets, a negative trend in variance over time. Their finding raises serious questions about the validity of the recent cohort data for research on trends in earnings inequality.

We revisited Gottschalk and Moffitt's comparison of the recent cohort and the CPS, extending the data through 1994 and performing additional analyses to locate the sources of the discrepancy in earnings dispersion trends. The discrepancy between the data sets is explained by two things: model specification and full-time, full-year working status. With a properly specified model, the earnings dispersion trends for full-time, full-year workers are statistically equivalent: both the CPS and NLSY show a general increasing trend in dispersion over time.[8] The difference in trends among those workers who were not employed full-time year-round, however, appears to be real. Current Population Survey respondents who work part-time or part-year (or both) report lower earnings than comparable NLSY respondents, and the bottom tail of their distribution reaches much further down the earnings scale. These differences are already pronounced in the first year (1979), and they grow over time, thus contributing significantly to the growing discrepancy between the two samples.

Regardless of working status, the level of reported annual earnings is higher in the NLSY than in the CPS by about 20 percent at the median. This suggests that the CPS data may be the source of the problem, because errors in earnings reports are more likely to result in underreporting than overreporting. The most likely explanations for such errors are differences in the CPS and NLSY questionnaire (the latter is more detailed) and the use of proxy respondents in the CPS, as neither sample bias nor attrition bias has been suggested as a problem in the NLSY. Readers interested in more details are referred to Handcock, Morris, and Bernhardt (2000).

## Missing Data

Probably the most important issue in comparing these two data sets is the potential bias induced by missing data. In longitudinal surveys, missing data in a given survey year can result either from permanent

**Table 2.2  Attrition and Missed Interview Rates by Cohort**

| Status of Respondent | Original Cohort (N = 2,743) | | Recent Cohort (N = 2,434) | |
|---|---|---|---|---|
| | Percentage | Number | Percentage | Number |
| Never missed an interview | 41.1 | 1,128 | 64.6 | 1,572 |
| Missed at least one interview but did not dropout | 33.1 | 908 | 27.6 | 671 |
| Permanently lost to attrition | 25.8 | 707 | 7.8 | 191 |

*Source:* Authors' compilation.

attrition (respondents who are permanently lost from the panel) or from missed interviews by respondents who come back into the study at some later date.[9] Both types of nonresponse are summarized in table 2.2, and we begin with a discussion of the latter.

## Missed Interviews

Throughout the course of both panels, some respondents temporarily dropped out but then returned to the survey in later years. For these respondents we were able to recover much of the information for the years that were missed. The recent cohort surveys made this recovery process relatively straightforward, because respondents who came back into the survey were asked detailed questions about the intervening years. As a result, we were able to recover virtually all missed years for virtually all temporary dropouts (see appendix A for details on the methods used to do this).

The original cohort surveys were much less thorough in their retrospective questions. Through case-by-case analysis, however, we were able to recover the most important data (for example, measures of employment and education) for most of the missed years. The rules regarding recovery were strictly consistent across years and cohorts and were strictly unbiased.[10] This recovery process took substantial time and effort; but the result is that we have effectively eliminated any bias stemming from recovered information and, as well, have more complete information on each respondent. Table 2.3 presents summaries of recovered person-year observations by cohort and year.

The recovered person-year observations were effectively assigned zero weight by the NLS, so we imputed new weights for them and the rest of the sample to reflect their inclusion. Some of the variables

Table 2.3    Recovered Person-Year Observations, by Cohort

| Panel Number | Original Cohort | Recent Cohort |
|---|---|---|
| Year 1 | — | — |
| Year 2 | 15 | 70 |
| Year 3 | 27 | 58 |
| Year 4 | 32 | 54 |
| Year 5 | 41 | 46 |
| Year 6 | 43 | 75 |
| Year 7 | — | 94 |
| Year 8 | 42 | 127 |
| Year 9 | — | 147 |
| Year 10 | 29 | 124 |
| Year 11 | 66 | 110 |
| Year 12 | — | 127 |
| Year 13 | 48 | 82 |
| Year 14 | — | 59 |
| Year 15 | 58 | 36 |
| Year 16 | — | — |

*Source:* Authors' compilation.

used by the NLS in assigning the original weights were not available, so we had to devise our own weighting frame. Every respondent was available in the initial year of each study, so we divided the respondents into age and education cells based on that year. Within each cell, z-scores for the baseline year weights were used to construct a new weight in the recovered year based on the mean and standard deviation of the same cell in that year. Because adding the new weights changes the total sum of the weights, we renormalized the weights back to their original total. Given the small $N$ of person-years reflected in table 2.3, we believe this has little adverse effect and great benefits in terms of recovering important information.

## Permanent Attrition

Permanent attrition is perhaps the most serious threat to the integrity of a longitudinal panel. Permanent attrition is relatively minimal in the recent cohort, at just 7.8 percent from 1979 to 1994. Attrition is sizable, however, for the original cohort, at 25.8 percent from 1966 to 1981 (see table 2.2).

The difference in attrition between the two cohorts is largely the result of changes in the NLS's retention strategy between the two surveys. In the original cohort, nonmilitary respondents who missed two consecutive interviews were dropped from the sample.[11] In the recent cohort, respondents who missed one or more interviews remained eligible for the survey and were pursued, with great effort, for future interviews. This means that for the NLSY there is no formal definition of attrition, except through death. To make the two cohorts comparable in the use of the two-year "drop" rule, we define anyone in the NLSY cohort who missed the last two interviews (1993 and 1994) to be lost to attrition. This, combined with deaths, results in the 7.8 percent attrition rate for the NLSY.

For both cohorts, the NLS adjusted the sampling weights in successive years to account for attrition bias along the main sampling dimensions (race, region of residence, and family income).[12] Thus if there is no attrition bias, or if bias is limited to the main sampling dimensions, the use of the adjusted weights presents no problem. For the recent cohort, the consensus is that the minimal amount of attrition has not compromised the representativeness of the sample. Findings for the original cohort, however, are mixed, with at least one study concluding that significant attrition bias exists (O'Neill 1982; Parsons 1987; Rhoton 1984; Falaris and Peters 1998). Because our research focuses on several outcome variables not covered in these previous studies, we conducted our own analysis to test for attrition bias in the original cohort.

We divided the original cohort respondents into two categories— those retained through the sixteenth year and those lost to attrition— and examined how these two groups compared on a host of demographic and work history variables.[13] In the first stage of our analysis, we plotted the mean and 95 percent confidence interval for each variable by survey year, broken down by attrition group. Variables that showed a significant difference between attrition groups in at least one survey year were selected for more detailed analysis.

In stage two of our analysis, we systematically examined whether the respondents lost to attrition differed significantly at the time of attrition from those retained. To answer this question we constructed an "artificial" data set to permit an unbiased person-level analysis. Each respondent contributed one observation. For those lost to attrition, we recorded the information on work history and demographic variables for the last year he was observed. For the retained respondents, the year of information used for the analysis was sampled to match the distribution of years among respondents lost to attrition. In this way, we remove any bias in estimates stemming from the longer "survival" of those not lost to attrition.

In table 2.4, we list the variables identified as potentially problematic and their mean or percentages by attrition group. Education

Table 2.4   Demographic and Work History Variables for Original Cohort, by Attrition Status

| Variable | Attrition Status | | Difference Significant |
| --- | --- | --- | --- |
| | Retained | Attrited | |
| Mean years of education completed | 13.0 | 12.4 | * |
| Percentage completing any degree | 77.5 | 70.3 | * |
| Percentage completing college degree | 45.9 | 38.4 | * |
| Mean hourly wage (1999 dollars) | 13.5 | 12.9 | |
| Percentage married | 47.7 | 42.0 | |
| Percentage enrolled in school | 31.8 | 27.1 | |
| Percentage living in South | 30.0 | 29.4 | |
| Percentage living in SMSA | 70.1 | 74.1 | |
| Percentage working | 81.2 | 77.2 | |
| Percentage unemployed | 4.8 | 7.8 | |
| Percentage out of labor force | 14.0 | 15.0 | |
| Cumulative percentage of weeks worked | 65.5 | 63.0 | |
| Cumulative percentage of weeks unemployed | 3.4 | 5.5 | * |
| Cumulative percentage of weeks out of labor force | 31.1 | 31.5 | |
| Cumulative number of weeks worked | 285.4 | 269.0 | |

Source: Authors' compilation.
Note: All means are based on person-level observations. All variables are measured in current year.
*Difference significant at .05 level.

shows the most consistent attrition bias, whether measured in terms of years completed or degrees obtained: those who dropped out of the survey had less education at the time of attrition than those retained. This effect can be seen in figure 2.3, and it does not disappear when controlling for other demographic and work history variables. We therefore consider education to be our "source" attrition variable, as it were, and we control for education in all analyses. In descriptive presentations, we disaggregate by education whenever we find that it significantly alters our substantive findings.

Most of the remaining variables show no significant attrition bias in the aggregate. In particular, our key outcome variable, the respondent's current wage, shows no bias. The lack of bias is quite apparent in figure 2.4, which plots mean hourly wages (in 1999 dollars) by

**Figure 2.3   Education Level of Original Cohort, by Attrition Status**

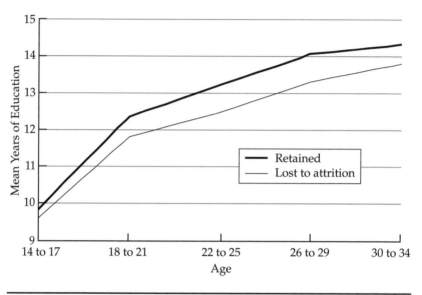

Source: Authors' compilation.

age for both attrition groups. The slight divergence in wages toward the end is not statistically significant, as the number of observations in the attrition group grows quite small in the final years (on the order of twenty observations). Moreover, once we disaggregate by education, all traces of a difference disappear. Thus, to the extent that attrition has an (insignificant) impact on wages by the end of the survey, this impact can be eliminated by controlling for education.

We next fit a series of regression models to further examine the impact of attrition. Specifically, we regressed most of the variables in table 2.4 on (1) age and age squared, (2) dummies for current education, and (3) an attrition dummy indicator interacted with current education. This model specification allows us to test whether there is any residual attrition effect within education groups. Several variables from table 2.4 were excluded from this analysis: cumulative percentage of weeks unemployed or out of the labor force and percentage of those currently unemployed or out of the labor force. These variables are extremely skewed and are thus inappropriate for regression-based models. However, note that the two states of unemployment and out of labor force, when combined, are simply the converse of working: any marked attrition-based differences in these two states should

**Figure 2.4    Hourly Wages for Original Cohort, by Attrition Status
(1999 Dollars)**

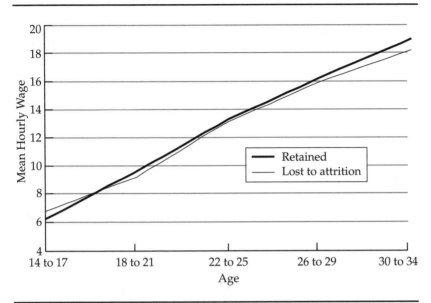

*Source:* Authors' compilation.

therefore show up in our analysis of cumulative percentage of weeks worked and current work status.

The coefficients for the attrition-by-education interaction dummies are shown in table 2.5. There are a few significant effects, but the most important lesson from this table is that we again observe no significant attrition bias in wages. Especially for the demographic variables, the smattering of significant effects for various education groups should not be cause for great concern. These effects turn out to be minor when translated into actual probabilities and quickly disappear when any other controls are introduced into the model.

The work-related variables show somewhat stronger attrition effects, though these are still modest and are largely confined to college graduates. For college-educated respondents lost to attrition, the reduction in cumulative percentage of weeks worked is 9 percent (about 30 weeks out of an average of 385 weeks of work experience). There is also a significant reduction for college graduates in the log-odds ratio of employment. If we use the baseline estimate that 93.9 percent of retained college graduates work, we derive a predicted rate of 83.0 percent for those lost to attrition.[14]

Finally, we took a closer look at education, as the one variable that

**Table 2.5    Estimated Attrition Coefficients for Original Cohort, by Current Education Level**

| Dependent Variable | High School Dropout | High School Graduate | Some College Experience | Bachelor's Degree or Higher |
|---|---|---|---|---|
| log(hourly wage) | .06 | .02 | −.03 | −.05 |
| Enrolled in school[a] | −.68* | −.57 | .00 | .32 |
| Married[a] | −.71* | −.16 | −.33 | −.55* |
| Living in South[a] | −.23 | .05 | −.09 | −.16 |
| Living in SMSA[a] | .12 | .35* | .09 | .66* |
| Cumulative percentage of weeks worked | .38 | −5.57* | −.52 | −9.14* |
| Cumulative number of weeks worked | −12.03 | −12.62 | −9.93 | −30.89* |
| Working[a] | −.12 | −.19 | −.34 | −1.14* |

*Source:* Authors' compilation.
*Note:* All models include age, age squared, and direct education effects, in addition to the education-specific attrition effects.
[a]Discrete variables; results are given as log-odds ratios from logistic regressions.
*Significant at .05 level.

showed consistent attrition bias. Respondents lost to attrition had significantly lower levels of education than respondents who were retained. This results in both an artificially high figure for mean years of education for the retained sample and a significantly higher proportion for those with any degree—including a college degree.

How does this affect our comparison of educational attainment across the original and recent cohorts? In the first two columns of table 2.6, we summarize educational attainment in the ending survey year among thirty- to thirty-six-year-olds for each cohort. The immediate impression is that of a strong decline in the attainment of higher education in the recent cohort. The table shows that a decline in educational attainment is also observed in comparable CPS samples.[15] Thus the question is, how much of the decline in educational attainment in the NLS is an artifact due to attrition bias in the original cohort, and how much is "real," reflecting actual trends in the workforce?

To answer this question, we first made our measure of educational attainment comparable across the NLS and the CPS. For the original cohort, we use raw years of education completed, to match the 1981 CPS coding. For the recent cohort, we use a measure that takes into

**Table 2.6    Comparison of NLS and CPS Educational Distributions, White Men Aged Thirty to Thirty-Six (Percentage)**

| Level of Education | NLS | | CPS | | Change (1994–1981) | |
| --- | --- | --- | --- | --- | --- | --- |
| | Original Cohort in 1981 | Recent Cohort in 1994 | 1981 | 1994 | NLS | CPS |
| High school dropout | 8.6 | 10.5 | 11.0 | 9.5 | 1.9 | −1.5 |
| High school graduate | 30.7 | 33.9 | 34.6 | 36.3 | 3.2 | 1.7 |
| Some college experience | 24.6 | 28.5 | 21.8 | 26.4 | 3.9 | 4.6 |
| Bachelor's degree or higher | 36.1 | 27.1 | 32.6 | 27.8 | −9.0 | −4.8 |
| Mean | 14.0 | 13.5 | 13.7 | 13.6 | −0.5 | −0.1 |

*Source:* Authors' compilation.
*Note:* The 1981 education measure is raw years of education completed. The 1994 measure also uses information on degrees completed; see text for explanation.

account whether or not a respondent actually completed a degree, to match the 1994 CPS coding.[16] Because different measures are being used in each year, one cannot directly infer changes in educational attainment over time from this table; one can, however, observe how well the NLS data are tracking the CPS data.

We then compute the difference between 1981 and 1994 distributions for the NLS and the CPS data. As seen at the bottom of the final two columns of table 2.6, both data sets show a decline in higher-educational attainment over time, but the decline is stronger in the NLS data. In the case of high school dropouts, the NLS trend is in the wrong direction, showing growth rather than decline, but the numbers are quite small. For all other groups, the NLS trends are consistent with the CPS trends. In particular, the decline in the proportion of college graduates is the largest absolute change observed in the CPS data. This is also true in the NLS data, though the decline here is overstated. If we assume that the change in the CPS distribution is "correct," attrition bias accounts for about 0.4 of the 0.5 years' decline in mean education, a proportionately high but substantively small amount.

In summary, there is evidence of attrition bias in the original cohort along a number of dimensions, but with appropriate controls in place, many of these biases become either insignificant or insubstantial. Most important, our primary dependent variable in this book, hourly wage, showed no significant attrition bias in any of our analyses. We routinely control for demographic and work history variables in all wage models, and there is no indication that more complicated models for selection bias are warranted.

The significant attrition effects that are evident in work-related variables after controlling for education are largely confined to college graduates (less than a third of the sample). Nonetheless, this does suggest that we should closely examine any outcome variables that are related to current work status. We do this in chapter 4, which focuses on the rate of job changing. This variable is inherently based on current work status, and we therefore conduct a much more thorough analysis of the impact of attrition on our findings.

Finally, the NLS data are mirroring trends over time in educational attainment, albeit in exaggerated form. This result is encouraging, though it still means that we must control for education in all of our analyses, which we do routinely throughout the book.

## The Vietnam War and the Original Cohort

One of the best-known characteristics of the original cohort data is that 30.1 percent of the respondents served in the Vietnam War at some point during the survey panel. To our surprise, we found little impact of service on attrition. The attrition rate for Vietnam veterans was quite similar to that of the nonveteran sample, and the timing of attrition over the course of the panel is nearly the same. Underlying these two findings is the fact that a majority of the veterans returned to the survey after their military service, and at that point, the veterans behaved much like the general population in terms of their propensity to drop out of the study.

One inescapable effect of Vietnam War service on the survey data was a high rate of missed interviews from 1967 to 1971. The impact on interviewing patterns is significant. Among all respondents not lost to attrition, an average of 0.2 interviews was missed at some point during the sixteen-year panel, for a variety of reasons not related to the war. Veterans, however, missed, on average, an additional 2.5 interviews because of their service in the war.

The other impact is that during these years of military service, the veterans lost valuable experience in the civilian labor market at an early stage in their careers. Yet it appears that they were able to make up much, if not all, of the lost ground. Mark Berger and Barry Hirsch (1983) also compare the civilian earnings experiences of Vietnam veterans and nonveterans between 1968 and 1977. They find that "veterans exhibited longitudinal earnings profiles which were initially lower but steeper than those of nonveterans," resulting in similar relative earnings by the end of the period. Similarly, our analysis of the original cohort shows that by their early thirties, veterans earned an average of $18.62 an hour compared with $18.84 for nonveterans (in 1999 dollars). Veterans were even able to achieve the same cumulative employment rate as nonveterans, between 77 and 78 percent. The one measure on which we do find some disadvantage is length of tenure with current employer. By their early thirties, veterans have an average tenure of fifty months, compared with sixty-three months for nonveterans. This difference of a year, however, is less than the 2.5 years lost, on average, to service in Vietnam—so even on this dimension, veterans were apparently able to catch up with the rest of cohort to a significant degree.

For all analyses reported in this book, we checked the sensitivity of our findings to the inclusion of the Vietnam veterans, and in those few cases in which the effect was substantial, we excluded the veterans and discuss our decision in the text.

# = Chapter 3 =

## The Transition into
## the Labor Market

A DESCRIPTIVE comparison of our two cohorts of young workers—in how they acquire education, make the transition into
the labor market, and accumulate work experience in different industries and occupations—allows a broad overview of how the
labor market has changed over the past three decades. Clearly, one
could write a book on any of these topics alone. Our purpose here is
to lay the groundwork for later analyses and to identify key compositional shifts that will need to be taken into account. Some of the
trends we document will be familiar, such as deindustrialization and
the rising rates of high school graduation. Others are quite novel, especially those indicating greater volatility in the transition from
school to work. In combination, these trends set the stage for the dramatic shift in the wage structure that is our main focus.

### Educational Attainment

Education clearly figures prominently in the early stages of work life.
Schooling and its completion are key markers of the transition into
the labor market, and the type of degree earned has a profound effect
on career options and eventual earning power. Education has also
become more important, as evidenced by the growing earnings gap
between college graduates and the rest of the labor force during the
1980s and 1990s. The age range we observe for the two NLS cohorts,
from sixteen to thirty-seven years old, is well suited for investigating
these changes in education and its effects.

Table 3.1 shows the final highest level of education observed for
our respondents.[1] The fraction of young men who are high school
dropouts has decreased over time, down from 14.6 percent in the
original cohort to 10.1 percent in the recent cohort. This is part of a

42

**Table 3.1    Final Education Level Attained, by Cohort (Percentage)**

| Final Education Level | Original Cohort | Recent Cohort |
|---|---|---|
| High school dropout | 14.6 | 10.1 |
| High school graduate | 30.1 | 42.1 |
| Some college experience | 25.0 | 20.4 |
| Bachelor's degree or higher | 30.2 | 27.4 |
| N | 2,743 | 2,434 |

*Source:* Authors' compilation.
*Note:* All percentages are person based.

long-standing trend in the United States toward the completion of secondary schooling. Youth are now more likely to graduate from high school, an encouraging shift in light of the growing demand for educational credentials in the labor market. The proportion of young adults with some college experience, on the other hand, has declined slightly, as has the prevalence of four-year college degrees, down from 30.2 percent in the original cohort to 27.4 percent in the recent. This may come as a surprise to readers who expected to see a uniform trend toward higher educational attainment over time. It is not an artifact of our samples, as CPS data for men aged twenty-five to thirty-four replicate these findings.[2]

The CPS data for trends in men's educational attainment are summarized in figure 3.1. College attendance and completion rates did indeed rise quite strongly during the late 1970s. During the 1980s, however, rates of postsecondary schooling declined. A number of explanations have been suggested for this downturn. The surge in college attendance during the 1970s coincided with the Vietnam War years, when college deferments provided protection from the draft. This suggests that enrollment may have been temporarily inflated by draft evasion and returned to more stable levels after the war.[3] Other explanations of the decline in attendance during the 1980s point to the stagnant earnings of that decade (translating into a lack of financial resources for college) and the relative decline in the college wage premium (discouraging the pursuit of higher education).[4] In any event, only in the early 1990s do we begin to see an uptick in college attendance again.

The key point is that even in the current economy, close to half of the workforce never goes beyond a high school education, and less than a third attains a four-year college degree. This is a sobering reality check. Policy discussions routinely point out that the educated have fared well under postindustrialism while the less educated have

Figure 3.1    Educational Attainment, Men Aged Twenty-Five to
Thirty-Four, CPS Estimates, from 1940 to 1999

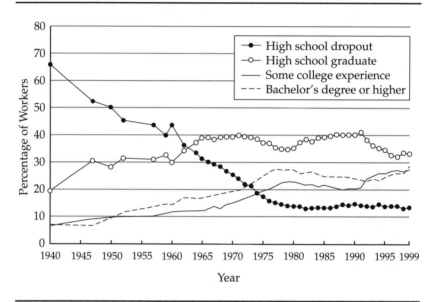

*Source:* Data from the U.S. Census Bureau 2000.

fared poorly. The sense, even when not intended, is that the latter group consists mainly of stragglers who have not yet responded to rising skill requirements. In fact, however, more than two-thirds of workers do not attain four-year college degrees. Trends for less-educated workers are therefore trends for the large majority of Americans.

## The Transition into the Labor Market

The transition from school into the labor market is a complex and tumultuous period for young adults. It is a critical stage for career development, in that choices made early on can significantly constrain the options that are later available. For this reason, a large research literature has tried to identify the elements of a successful transition (Rindfuss, Swicegood, and Rosenfeld 1987; Stone and Mortimer 1998). The process is typically examined by measuring a set of events that mark its key stages. Labor economists focus on indicators such as enrollment, completion of schooling, and success in finding a full-time, year-round job. Demographers often add indicators of household and family formation, such as first marriage and children. Although the ideal sequence is posited to be school completion, employment, marriage, and children, it is widely recognized that this simple pattern rarely describes the transitions that people actually make. Instead, the stages overlap, are longer or shorter than expected, and sometimes change order (Rindfuss, Swicegood, and Rosenfeld 1987).

Working during the high school years is common, though the jobs held are typically part-time and part-year. Interrupted schooling has also become more common. There is substantial heterogeneity in the reasons for returning to school (Light 1994), but in general, reenrollment has been found to pay off for wage growth. As a result, the transition to full-time employment is in many cases not a simple one. Young workers may sometimes have to settle for part-time or part-year work and sometimes for no work at all. Unemployment spells are common among high school dropouts, but even those who complete college may face a period of unemployment as they move into the labor force. In addition, young adults spend a surprising amount of time neither employed nor in school (Klerman and Karoly 1994).

Despite these variations, a general pattern characterizes the aggregate transition into the labor market. We illustrate this pattern in figure 3.2, pooling the two cohorts and ignoring for a moment the longitudinal structure of the data. The graph shows the labor force status of our respondents as they age from sixteen to thirteen-seven years. Their status is classified into four states: exclusive enrollment in school, enrollment combined with labor force participation, exclusive labor force participation, and neither in school nor in the labor force.[5] At the age of sixteen, the overwhelming majority of the sample is enrolled in school. Even at this stage, however, more than half of the students are in the labor force. Not all of those who report labor force participation are working (some are unemployed), and most of those who are working have part-time jobs.[6] Nevertheless, joint school enrollment and labor force participation is the norm, not the exception (for similar findings, see D'Amico 1984; Light 1994). School enrollment drops sharply in the next few years, with less than half of the sample enrolled by the age of twenty and less than a quarter by the age of twenty-five. Labor force participation quickly becomes the dominant state, and by the early thirties, more than 90 percent of the sample is exclusively working or looking for work.[7]

This broad pattern, however, has changed over the past three decades. Young men in the recent cohort are now taking longer to complete their education, as shown in figure 3.3. The plot shows rates of educational completion by age, defining date of completion as the last time a respondent is observed in school. Among those with a high school diploma or less, 14 percent of the original cohort had not yet

**Figure 3.2  Transition into the Labor Force, by Age (Pooled Cohorts)**

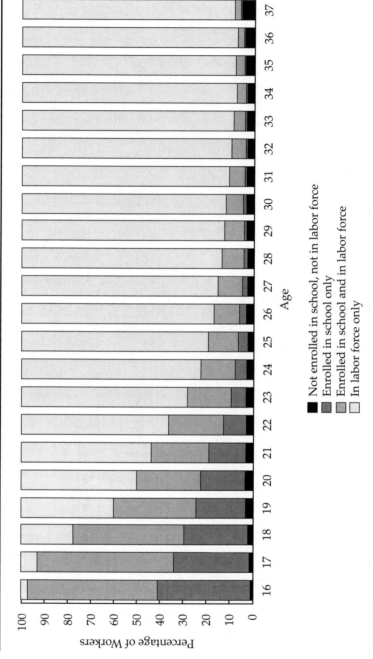

*Source:* Authors' compilation.

completed their schooling by the age of nineteen, compared with 25 percent of those in the recent cohort; on average, the delay in completion is 1.2 years. For those with some college experience or more, 41 percent of individuals in the original cohort had not yet completed their education by the age of twenty-three, compared with 55 percent of the recent cohort; on average, the delay in completion is 1.4 years.[8]

Young men are now also entering the labor force sooner. Among sixteen- and seventeen-year-olds who will stop their education at high school, the labor force participation rate is 63 percent in the original cohort and 69 percent in the recent. This faster transition into the labor force has not paid off in recent years, however.[9] The left panel of figure 3.4 plots the unemployment rate (in the week of the interview) by age. For sixteen- and seventeen-year-olds, unemployment for the recent cohort is almost double that for the original. Although this gap narrows with age, unemployment remains higher for the recent cohort well into the mid-twenties. The right panel of figure 3.4 shows the fraction of high-school-educated respondents working a full year (forty-eight weeks). Between the ages of twenty and thirty, the recent cohort is consistently less likely to hold a full-year job (up to 20 percent less likely), and the majority of this difference derives from higher unemployment rates.

Trends in the greater economy are clearly playing a role here. When the original cohort entered the labor market, the national youth unemployment rate ranged from 6 to 10 percent. The recent cohort, by contrast, faced rates of 11 to 20 percent during the early 1980s, twice as high as those seen by their predecessors. Our data suggest that those with less education bore the brunt of the impact and that the effect on year-round employment lasted well into their mid-twenties.[10] We should point out, however, that not all unemployment is detrimental, because it can result in productive job search (and often does, early in the career).[11] Moreover, as we show later in this chapter, on aggregate the recent cohort does not show lower levels of work experience accumulated over time. Unemployment may have been more prevalent, but because of the earlier entry into the labor force, this has not affected the years of work experience gained.

Our findings to this point suggest that there have been several important changes in the way youth enter the labor market. Young white men in the 1980s and 1990s extended the amount of time they spent in school. Because the net amount of educational attainment has not risen, this suggests that they interrupted their schooling. In an era of corporate restructuring and the externalization of on-the-job training, returning to school between spells of employment becomes a potential strategy for midcourse skill development. If this strategy yields

**Figure 3.4  Transitions to Employment for Respondents with a High School Degree or Less, by Cohort**

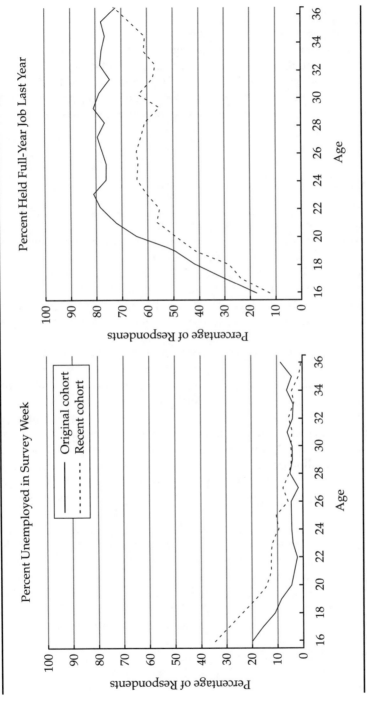

Source: Authors' compilation.

successful outcomes, then the argument for continuous learning in a knowledge-based economy gains strength. Such interruptions may also, however, signal a type of churning that generates few educational credentials and signals an inability to build up continuous tenure with one employer; in this case, the impact would be detrimental. Either way, it is important that we establish whether interrupted schooling has become a more prevalent route into the labor market in recent years.

## Transition Sequences

To investigate the impact of interrupted schooling, we move to a longitudinal person-based analysis, looking at the entire sequence of work and schooling that each individual builds in the early phase of his career. We first define an individual to be in one of three states in each survey year: exclusively enrolled in school, working while enrolled, or not enrolled.[12] The transition sequences then consist of the different ways those stages are ordered over time. Our goal is to classify these sequences into broad categories that reflect alternative pathways in the transition from school to work.

Three distinct pathways emerged from our data. The first captures what we often think of as the traditional route to entering the labor market: completing all schooling in one continuous spell without working and then beginning work.[13] We label this path "exclusive enrollment." The second consists of a single continuous education spell during which the individual worked at least one year; this pathway we label "working while enrolled." The final pathway is defined by those who interrupted their education for at least one year and then returned to school in a subsequent year. These individuals may have been working, unemployed, or out of the labor force during the intervening period, but in all cases they were not in school, so we label this pathway "interrupted enrollment."[14] We analyzed these sequences with and without Vietnam veterans and found that military service did not have a large impact on the pathway distribution, so we include veterans in all findings reported below.

The frequencies of these three pathways are shown in table 3.2. The cohort differences are quite striking. Exclusive enrollment became much less common for all education groups during the 1980s and early 1990s, as compared with the late 1960s and 1970s. Much of the shift has been toward working while in school, and this second pathway has become the modal path for most education groups. Among those in the recent cohort pursuing bachelor's or higher degrees, fully

Table 3.2  Pathways to Educational Attainment, by Cohort (Percentage)

| Final Education Level | Exclusive Enrollment | Working While Enrolled | Interrupted Enrollment |
|---|---|---|---|
| High school dropout | | | |
| Original | 54.7 | 35.6 | 9.7 |
| Recent | 34.7 | 45.1 | 20.2 |
| High school graduate | | | |
| Original | 36.0 | 47.3 | 16.7 |
| Recent | 17.1 | 63.3 | 19.6 |
| Some college experience | | | |
| Original | 16.7 | 38.9 | 44.4 |
| Recent | 5.1 | 44.8 | 50.1 |
| Bachelor's degree or higher | | | |
| Original | 11.7 | 44.9 | 43.5 |
| Recent | 6.5 | 66.1 | 27.4 |

Source: Authors' compilation.
Note: All percentages are person based. See text for definition of pathways.

two-thirds now work while remaining continuously enrolled, an increase of almost 50 percent over their predecessors.

Not only the prevalence, but also the intensity, of working while in school has increased.[15] As shown in table 3.3, the number of years that students work has risen. For example, 10.1 percent of high school graduates in the original cohort worked three or more years while in school, compared with 23.0 percent in the recent cohort. For youth with some college experience, that figure rose from 34.5 to 52.1 percent, and for the most educated group it rose from 47.3 to 66.2 percent.[16]

It is the final pathway—interrupted enrollment—that shows perhaps the most interesting trends over time. As table 3.2 shows, interruptions in education have become more prevalent in the recent cohort for all except the most educated.[17] Yet we should not automatically assume that this signals a shift toward "continuous learning" and skill development. The strongest increase in interrupted enrollment has occurred among high school dropouts, who are twice as likely now to take this path than their earlier counterparts. Although returning to school might be regarded as a good strategy for dropouts, in fact we know that these respondents did not manage even to acquire a high school diploma (since we are looking at final education in the table). The strategy of returning to school does not appear to have paid off for this group.

Note also that interrupted schooling has become the dominant

Table 3.3   Total Number of Years Worked While Enrolled in School, by Cohort

| Final Education Level | 0 Years | 1 to 2 Years | 3 or More Years |
|---|---|---|---|
| High school dropout | | | |
| Original | 58.4 | 38.7 | 2.8 |
| Recent | 42.5 | 50.6 | 6.8 |
| High school graduate | | | |
| Original | 37.7 | 52.3 | 10.1 |
| Recent | 19.6 | 57.4 | 23.0 |
| Some college experience | | | |
| Original | 21.1 | 44.4 | 34.5 |
| Recent | 8.8 | 39.1 | 52.1 |
| Bachelor's degree or higher | | | |
| Original | 14.3 | 38.4 | 47.3 |
| Recent | 7.3 | 26.6 | 66.2 |

*Source:* Authors' compilation.
*Note:* All percentages are person based.

pathway for those with some college experience—an important trend, because these are individuals pursuing associate's degrees, certificates, additional credits, and the like. Here we may in fact be seeing evidence of the "lifelong learning" movement, in that much of public policy during the past decade has focused precisely on boosting the educational attainment for subbaccalaureate workers. This may also explain why interrupted schooling has not become more common for workers who eventually obtain lucrative four-year college degrees—it simply is not necessary.

The upshot of our sequence analysis is that there is now greater volatility in the labor market transition for those without a college degree, involving more moves back and forth between school and work, and less volatility for the most educated. Given that the wage gap between college graduates with four-year degrees and the rest of the labor force has grown, this finding would suggest that the strategy of interrupted schooling is not necessarily linked to higher wage payoffs.

## Other Dimensions of the Transition

We next turn to several other dimensions of the transition into the labor market: the accumulation of work experience, industrial and occupational location, marriage, and wages.

## Work Experience

Work experience consistently ranks at the top of the list of factors that employers consider when hiring, because it captures information about the acquisition of general skills needed to function effectively in the workplace (National Center on the Educational Quality of the Workforce 1995). Along with education, experience is the strongest predictor of wages, and as is the case with education, the wage returns to experience appear to have increased in recent years.

We have identified several trends that might affect the rate at which young men in recent years have been able to accumulate work experience. The recent cohort was more likely to work while in school but also more likely to be have been unemployed, to have worked part-year, and to have interrupted the chain of schooling and work. These are conflicting trends, and we find that on average, they essentially balance out over time. The top panel of figure 3.5 shows the growth in mean work experience by age for the two cohorts. Both cohorts show a steady and nearly identical progression toward more labor market experience.[18] By his mid-twenties, the typical young man in our sample had around seven years of work experience, and by his mid-thirties, around fifteen years. These are only averages, of course, but the important point is that we are fully observing the first decade and a half of labor market experience for these cohorts. For white men, roughly three-quarters of lifetime wage growth occurs during the first ten years in the labor market (Murphy and Welch 1990). Our window of observation for these cohorts thus covers the key period for wage determination and eventual success in the labor market.

Although the two cohorts do not differ in the average amount of work experience they accumulated over time, we might expect that the recent cohort would have more variable work experience, given its more volatile and differentiated paths into the labor market. The bottom panel of figure 3.5 shows that this is indeed the case. The variance of experience has increased markedly in the recent cohort, especially by the early to middle thirties. This is an important finding: because experience is a key determinant of earnings, any changes in the dispersion of experience is likely to have a strong impact on the dispersion of earnings.

## Industry and Occupation Shifts

After the transition to the labor force has been made, job stability and wage growth depend increasingly on the occupations and industries in which young adults are employed. The early working years are a

**Figure 3.5   Work Experience, by Age and Cohort**

Mean Experience

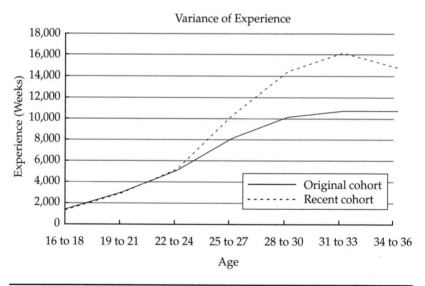

Variance of Experience

*Source:* Authors' compilation.

time for exploring different career options and making decisions about which occupation to pursue. The context for such decisions, however, has changed dramatically over the past thirty years, with the shift from an economy based on mass production to one based on services. The general figures are well known but worth repeating. Between 1972 and 1996, the percentage of nonfarm jobs in goods-producing industries dropped by nearly one-third, from 32.1 to 20.4 percent, and the decline in manufacturing was especially marked, falling by 41 percent during this time period (Meisenheimer 1998). Four out of five Americans now work in the service sector, and the impact on what Americans do in the workplace and the careers they pursue has been profound (Macdonald and Sirianni 1996). Wages in the service sector are more unequal and often lower than in goods-producing industries, in part because of the lower rate of unionization (Freeman and Medoff 1984).

Table 3.4 shows the industry and occupation distribution for workers in their middle to late thirties, broken down by cohort and education.[19] The age range captures the final years we observe for our sample of workers and thus gives a sense of the industrial and occupational niches into which they have settled. The trend toward deindustrialization in the U.S. economy since the early 1970s is quite evident here. Focusing first on workers with no more than a high school education, we find a 34 percent decline in manufacturing employment. These traditionally unionized industries typically offer better-paid entry-level jobs, more-stable employment, and good benefits for workers without a college education. Such opportunities have clearly declined for the recent cohort. On the flip side, the recent cohort is depending more heavily on jobs in business services and retail trade, where employment increased by 35 percent.[20] Both of these industry groups lie at the low end of the service sector and account for a significant portion of total job growth in recent years (Plunkert 1990; Ilg 1996). They typically offer low wages, high turnover, and poor career prospects—think of sales clerks, janitors, food preparation workers, and the like. Well into their mid-thirties, dropouts and high school graduates in the recent cohort are relying on these industries for a living.

Turning to the occupational breakdowns, it is clear that less educated workers still depend on manual labor for jobs. Two-thirds of these workers in the recent cohort still work in laborer and craft occupations by the time they are thirty to thirty-seven years old. This proportion may eventually decrease with age, but manual labor continues to serve as a mainstay of employment for those without college degrees. The trend for these workers, however, is toward service occupations, both at the low end (sales, service, and clerical workers) and at the high end (managers, professionals, and technicians). The latter increase is surprising, given that we are focusing on those with at best a high school diploma, but industry breakdowns show that it

Table 3.4   Industry and Occupation Distribution for Workers Aged Thirty
to Thirty-Seven, by Education and Cohort (Percentage)

| Category | High School Degree or Less | | Some College Experience or More | |
|---|---|---|---|---|
| | Original Cohort | Recent Cohort | Original Cohort | Recent Cohort |
| Industry | | | | |
| Construction, mining, agriculture, and fishing | 19.8 | 24.6 | 9.0 | 8.2 |
| Manufacturing | 38.0 | 25.2 | 22.4 | 21.7 |
| Transportation and communication | 10.0 | 10.4 | 9.6 | 7.0 |
| Wholesale and retail trade | 15.4 | 19.1 | 13.8 | 13.7 |
| Finance, insurance, and real estate | 2.2 | 1.5 | 8.2 | 8.8 |
| Business services, personal services, entertainment, and recreation | 6.1 | 9.9 | 6.2 | 13.1 |
| Professional services | 3.0 | 4.9 | 19.5 | 19.8 |
| Public administration | 5.4 | 4.4 | 11.2 | 7.7 |
| Occupation | | | | |
| Laborers, foremen, and craft workers | 73.2 | 66.6 | 21.7 | 19.0 |
| Sales, clerical, and service workers | 13.8 | 15.7 | 21.9 | 22.1 |
| Managers, professional and technical workers | 12.9 | 17.7 | 56.4 | 58.9 |

Source: Authors' compilation.
Note: All percentages are person based.

has occurred mainly in retail trade, where such occupations are not generally well paid. Others have also found that a significant part of the growth in managerial occupations has been driven by low-wage retail industries and thus generates less wage growth than might be expected.[21]

Not surprisingly, those who attend or complete college are much more likely to be working in high-wage service industries—professional services, public administration, and the finance sector—for both cohorts. These are not growth industries, however, even for college-educated workers. The fraction employed in these industries has stagnated. Growth has instead been strongest at the lower end of the service sector, driven by the doubling of employment in business services. The trends in the occupational distribution present a similar message. Although professional, managerial, and technical jobs have increased by 4.5 percentage points across the two cohorts, a proportionate increase of 8 percent, this is not nearly as strong a gain as one might expect from overall labor force trends. For example, between 1983 and 1993, total U.S. employment in executive, administrative, and managerial occupations grew by 28.8 percent; in professional occupations, by 34.7 percent; and in technical and related support occupations, by 27.7 percent (Rosenthal 1995). These aggregate trends obscure marked differences by race and sex. Closer inspection of CPS data shows that occupational upgrading over the past three decades has been stronger among white women, and to some extent among nonwhite workers, than among white men (though the latter still dominate well-paid occupations).[22]

In sum, the past three decades have seen a shift away from goods-producing jobs and toward service jobs for young white men. In general, however, growth has been concentrated at the lower end of the service sector rather than in the professional, high-tech, and financial sectors more commonly associated with postindustrialism in the popular press. This can be expected to have an impact on both the level of and dispersion in wages, because unionized manufacturing industries continue to pay better than low-end service sector industries, and wage inequality has typically been higher in the service sector.

## Marriage Patterns

A complex set of changes in the process of household and family formation has also unfolded over the years that we observe these two cohorts. Age at first marriage has risen, divorce has become more common, and average family size is shrinking. It is largely beyond the scope of this study to examine these trends in detail, but it would also be unwise to ignore them entirely. Changes in family structure are likely to influence a number of the economic changes we are interested in, particularly job stability and wages.

From a labor market standpoint, marital status is perhaps the best single indicator of these processes. Almost all of the men in our samples make the transition into marriage at some point during the sixteen years that we observe them. The "marriage premium" in wages is well established, though what it represents is the subject of lively debate (Daniel 1995; Korenman and Neumark 1991). Marriage also tends to lead to more job stability. If marriage rates differ between the two cohorts, it will be important to take this into account in our analyses.

**Figure 3.6   Percentage Married, by Age and Cohort**

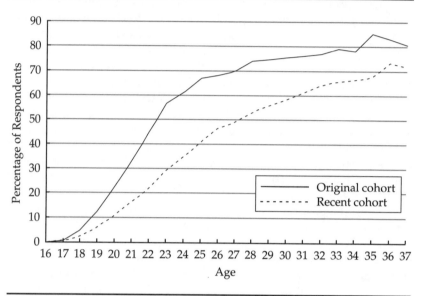

*Source:* Authors' compilation.

The fraction of men who are currently married at each age is shown in figure 3.6. The cohort differences are substantial. The gap in marriage rates is largest during the mid-twenties: by the age of twenty-five, about 68 percent of the men in the original cohort are married, compared with just over 40 percent in the recent cohort. Although the discrepancy narrows with age, marriage rates remain about 15 percent lower for the recent cohort well into their thirties. Overall, the original cohort is married for about 50 percent of the person-years we observe them, whereas the recent cohort is married for about 39 percent of those person-years. These are large differences that persist during most of the years in the survey panel, and they occur in all education groups. In all of our model-based analyses in this volume, we therefore routinely control for marital status.

## Wages

A major part of this book is devoted to analyzing trends in wages and long-term wage growth, but here we give a brief introduction. First, it is worth restating why we focus on wages in this analysis, as there are other ways to measure monetary outcomes in the labor market, such as annual earnings and household income. Each of these measures represents a different mix of job and personal characteristics, so the choice of measure depends on the goal of the analysis. Our primary interest is in the impact that the restructured labor market of the 1980s and 1990s has had on the job opportunities an individual faces over his life course, so we would prefer an outcome measure that captures the characteristics of the jobs available. For this reason, the hourly wage is the most appropriate outcome measure for our analysis. Annual earnings are confounded by hours and weeks worked and the possibility of different jobs having been held during the year. Household income is affected by changes in family structure and household composition in ways that take us well beyond the scope of this analysis. Hourly wages, though not a pure measure of the demand side of the market, are still the best indicator we have of the economic opportunities available to young adults.

Trends in hourly wages across our two cohorts are shown in figure 3.7. Median hourly wages rise more than threefold from the late teens to the mid-thirties, and as noted earlier, this represents nearly three-quarters of the total wage growth these workers will attain over their lifetimes. The cohort differences illustrate patterns now well known to researchers. Wage growth has stagnated and become more unequal for the recent cohort. These differences become more pronounced as the young workers age and settle into their long-term wage trajectories. By the mid-thirties, the median worker in the recent cohort is earning over 20 percent less than his predecessor in the original cohort. At the same time, the right panel of figure 3.7 shows that the variance in wages for the recent cohort has increased. For a brief period in the late teenage years, the recent cohort's wages are slightly less variable than the original. This is largely a function of earlier full-time entry into the labor market in the original cohort. The trend quickly reverses after the college years, however, and by the mid-thirties, wage dispersion is twice as large in the recent cohort. These dispersion measures are based on the variance of logged wages; to give a sense of what this means in terms of real wages, the 90:10 real wage ratio in final wages is 2.9 in the original cohort and 3.5 in the recent.

The combination of stagnation and polarization means that wages have fallen for practically all workers, but they have fallen much more for those at the bottom than for those at the top. Workers without a college degree have taken the greatest losses, but what might come as a surprise is that in the recent cohort even those with a college degree did not fare all that well.

In table 3.5 we see that young white men with a high school diploma or less saw their real wages decline by 20 percent in recent years. Even those with some college experience saw declines of 17

**Figure 3.7  Trends in Hourly Wages, by Age and Cohort (1999 Dollars)**

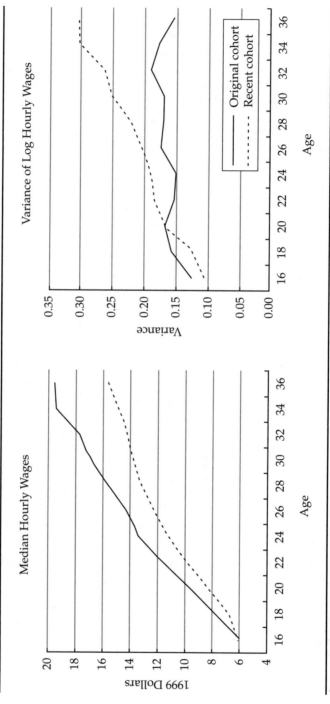

**Table 3.5  Medians and Variances of Hourly Wages for Workers Aged Thirty to Thirty-Seven, by Cohort**

| Education | Median Hourly Wage (1999 dollars) | | | Variance in Log Hourly Wage | | |
| --- | --- | --- | --- | --- | --- | --- |
| | Original Cohort | Recent Cohort | Percentage change[a] | Original Cohort | Recent Cohort | Difference[b] |
| High school dropout | 12.81 | 10.35 | −19.2 | .16 | .17 | .02 |
| High school graduate | 16.36 | 12.93 | −21.0 | .15 | .20 | .06 |
| Some college experience | 17.98 | 14.91 | −17.1 | .16 | .26 | .10 |
| Bachelor's degree or higher | 20.01 | 18.42 | −8.0 | .15 | .27 | .12 |
| All workers | 17.27 | 13.61 | −21.2 | .17 | .25 | .09 |

*Source:* Authors' compilation.
[a]Percentage change in median hourly wages from the original cohort to the recent cohort.
[b]Variance in log hourly wage of recent cohort minus that of original cohort.

percent. The rising demand for skill has evidently been quite selective since workers with college credits and even associate's degrees have not been sheltered from the deterioration in wages. Only college graduates with four-year degrees have escaped the larger losses, but their wages have still declined by nearly 8 percent, on average.

The upshot is that the college wage premium relative to high school graduates widened from 1.22 in the original cohort to 1.42 in the recent, an increase of almost 16 percent. These kinds of trends, evident in virtually every data set, have prompted much talk of the growing importance of education and skill in the postindustrial economy. It is important to recognize, however, that the "college premium" is rising not because college graduates earn more than previous generations but rather because those without a college degree are earning significantly less.

## Summary

This chapter gives an initial overview of how these two cohorts of young white men made the transition from school into the workforce. The original cohort entered the labor market in the late 1960s, at the tail of the economic boom. The recent cohort entered the labor market in the early 1980s, after the onset of corporate restructuring. We observe the first decade and a half of labor market experience for these young adults, a critical period for wage growth and eventual success. If indeed a leaner, restructured labor market is emerging in this country, then the recent cohort has been the first to experience it in full strength.

Our first look at the two cohorts reveals many of the broader trends that have characterized the U.S. economy during the past three decades. Although young men are now increasingly more likely to complete high school, the attainment of postsecondary education fell slightly in the 1980s. Even in the current economy, roughly half of the workforce never goes beyond high school, and more than two-thirds never attains a four-year college degree. This point is worth remembering as we explore trends in wage growth later in this volume.

The transition to the labor force has changed noticeably. Youth are now taking longer to complete their schooling, are significantly more likely to work while in school, and are returning for additional education in greater numbers. This does not necessarily signal the advent of a "lifelong learning" strategy to enhance skill development. For some workers, interrupted schooling does indeed indicate the pursuit of associate's degrees, certificates, and other forms of subbaccalaureate education. For others, however, it merely signals greater volatility and churning in the transition to the labor market. This is especially true for workers with no postsecondary education, for whom greater interruptions to schooling have been accompanied by more unemployment and greater difficulty in finding a full-year job. The upshot can be seen in how much work experience these young adults acquire over time: whereas mean levels of experience are about the same for the two cohorts, the variability in experience is substantially higher in the recent cohort by the time they reach their mid-thirties.

Once out of school, workers in the recent cohort are less likely to rely on goods-producing jobs and more likely to hold service sector jobs. This shift mirrors economy-wide trends: job growth has been concentrated at the lower end of the service sector, with poor wages and career prospects, rather than in the professional, high-tech, and financial sectors more commonly associated with postindustrialism in the popular press.

Finally, wage attainment has deteriorated. Median real wages in the early to late thirties declined by 21 percent from the original cohort to the recent cohort. The decline was concentrated among less educated workers, but even college graduates with four-year degrees did not fare well; and, of course, wage inequality has increased significantly in recent years. This is not, then, a story of the rich getting richer and the poor getting poorer; rather, nearly everyone is losing some ground, with those at the bottom losing the most.

Clearly, we want to know much more about the actual dynamics that have generated these descriptive trends. A key component is the process of job search and job changing, perhaps the main activity of youth in the early stages of their careers. We already have broad evidence that the transition into the labor market has become more volatile, but has job stability in particular changed? What are the consequences of job changing? Is there evidence that churning between dead-end, low-wage jobs has increased in the new economy? Over the long term, what happens to the wage trajectories that these young workers build? Finally, how do all of these dynamics differ for less educated low-wage workers? These questions are the focus of the remaining chapters of the book.

# = Chapter 4 =

## Rising Job Instability

Whe the *New York Times* ran its eight-part series on the downsizing of America several years ago, the response was overwhelming (Louis Uchitelle and N.R. Kleinfield. March 3, 1996. "On the Battlefield of Business, Millions of Casualties." *New York Times*, 11). Flooded with letters, the newspaper set up an Internet site to accommodate the need for more information and for people to share similar experiences of being reengineered and restructured. Other media followed suit, reporting on downsizing in their local communities but also commenting on the *Times* articles themselves. The series clearly captured a strong anxiety in the national psyche about increasing job insecurity, an anxiety that had built up during the numerous layoffs of the early 1990s.

Some of the immediate fear has receded in the current strong economy and tight labor market. Yet traces remain, and if anything, a tacit acceptance of the end of lifelong employment appears to have set in. In early 1999, *Newsweek* magazine ran a special issue entitled "Your Next Job," a sort of worker's guide to the new millennium. The article focused on the "new Nomads"—computer programmers, managerial consultants, and independent contractors who hop from project to project and employer to employer, shape their own destinies, and in the process reap high-tech rewards (McGinn and McCormick 1999). The common theme of this and other articles is that the employment relationship has become more tenuous, characterized by weaker commitments between firms and workers, and that workers need to embrace rather than resist the new flexibility.

While the perception of increased job stability is widespread, empirical documentation of this "fact" remains elusive. We therefore take up the issue in this chapter, by analyzing trends in stability and tenure for young adults over the past three decades.

There are a number of reasons to be concerned about a rise in instability for young adults, in particular. Job stability has—at least

64

historically—played a critical role in the process of career formation. Job changing early in the career is often beneficial, as young workers "shop" for the job that best matches their needs and qualifications. Over time, however, sticking with one employer becomes more beneficial. Workers can hone their skills and acquire new ones on the job. They gain access to company-provided training, consistent wage growth, full-time benefits, and internal career ladders and promotions into higher-level occupations. This is especially critical for the majority of Americans who do not attain four-year college degrees. Job changing thus becomes increasingly costly as workers stay with one firm for longer periods of time. The skills that workers learn on the job tend to be employer specific, and these are lost when that employer is left. The generalized skills that were acquired during formal schooling may have become outdated and no longer yield as high a payoff on the open market. The possibility of promotions into higher-level jobs and vesting for pensions are lost as workers find themselves starting again at the bottom rung of the career ladder.

This picture may be outdated, however, stemming from the days of internal labor markets and a strong manufacturing sector in which tenures of twenty or more years were not uncommon. The new economy may operate according to different rules, so that success in the labor market no longer depends on strong ties with one employer. (We explore this possibility in later chapters.) Nevertheless, there is a priori reason for concern. Roughly two-thirds of lifetime job changes occur during the formative years of labor market experience, when long-term relationships with employers are established (Topel and Ward 1992). This is precisely the stage of the life cycle observed for our two NLS cohorts, so any rise in instability that we find has potentially strong implications for long-term wage attainment.

## The Instability Debate

After close to a decade of research on the topic, no consensus yet exists on whether instability has increased, by how much, and for whom. On the one hand, there is not enough evidence to warrant claims that the "Great American Job" is dead ("Jobs in an Age of Insecurity" 1993); on the other, some decline does seem to have occurred. Judging its strength is made difficult, however, by data and measurement problems, sensitivity to time span studied, and differences in how the significance of results is interpreted.[1]

The primary sources of cross-sectional data on job stability are the Current Population Survey and the Displaced Worker Survey. Kenneth Swinnerton and Howard Wial (1996), using the CPS, find evidence of an overall decline in job stability, whereas Francis Diebold, David Neumark, and Daniel Polsky (1997) and Henry Farber (1998), using the same survey data, do not. Changes in the wording of the CPS tenure question and in nonresponse rates over time hamper the building of synthetic age cohorts and duration analysis and make it difficult to resolve the different findings. Adding recent CPS data and making better adjustments for changes in wording and other data problems, Neumark, Polsky, and Daniel Hansen (1997) do find a modest decline in the first half of the 1990s among older workers with longer tenures. Similarly, using the Displaced Worker Survey, Farber (1997) finds a mild rise in involuntary job loss during the 1990s, but changes in wording and time windows make analysis difficult here, as well.

Longitudinal data sets permit more direct measurement of moves between employers, and research on the Panel Study of Income Dynamics (PSID) initially appeared to provide consistent evidence of a general increase in the rate of job changing (for example, Rose 1995; Boisjoly, Duncan, and Smeeding 1998). Several other papers find no such overall trend, however, and the disagreement hinges, once again, on how one resolves the problem of measuring year-to-year job changes (Polsky 1999; Jaeger and Stevens 1999). Employers are not uniquely identified in the PSID, so a job change must be inferred using several different questions about length of tenure, and these questions have changed over the years (see Brown and Light 1992). Different assumptions have led to different findings. This measurement problem does not plague the National Longitudinal Surveys, because they provide unique employer identification codes that are consistent over time. This makes the NLS the best source of data available for the analysis of trends in job stability.

Another key problem is that the field has so far focused on trends in instability for all workers. Less attention has been given to specific groups in the labor market, which may mask different trends for different groups of workers. Researchers who have differentiated their analyses in this manner have come up with surprisingly consistent results. Less educated workers, black workers, older men with long tenures, and youth do seem to have experienced an increase in job instability, though the results differ from one study to another according to whether the 1990s are included in the analysis and whether the analysis is restricted to involuntary job loss (for example, see Neumark, Polsky, and Hansen 1997; Jaeger and Stevens 1999; Polsky 1999; Monks and Pizer 1998). This suggests that researchers should engage more carefully in group-specific analyses, which we do here by focusing on young adults in depth.

## Measures and Data

The NLS data have a distinct advantage for this research area because, unlike other data sets, they provide unique employer identification codes that are consistently recorded.[2] We can therefore unambiguously measure whether an employer change occurred over a given time span. Note that employer changes are different from job changes: the latter can occur without the former, as when a worker is promoted or moved to another division within the same company. For simplicity's sake we use the more intuitive term "job change" throughout this book, but it should be understood that we are referring to a separation from an employer rather than a change in jobs with the same employer. Employer separation is the right measure for our purposes, because it directly signals changes in the employment relation that are the focus of theoretical debate.

Our measure of job stability is a straightforward one: we take all the individuals who were working in a given year and calculate the fraction who were still working with the same employer two years later. We call this the "two-year job separation rate." For example, a separation rate of .45 means that 45 percent of the individuals working at time $t$ were working with the same employer two years later, at time $t + 2$.

To ensure that this measure is constructed comparably across the two cohorts, we focus on tracking the respondent's main "CPS" employer and construct the change statistics on the basis of two-year, rather than one-year, intervals. The two-year interval is necessary to accommodate the four missing years in the original cohort survey. There are six two-year intervals for each cohort, and they are evenly spaced across the survey time span.[3] This matching strategy allows us to conduct a rigorous and controlled comparison of job instability across cohorts, but the reader should remember that as a result, we are not counting all recorded jobs and job changes for the respondents. For example, our analysis later in this chapter of the number of accumulated employers is an underestimate in absolute terms, and it provides a lower-bound estimate of the relative difference between the two cohorts.

To be eligible for this analysis, the respondent had to have been working for pay in the first year of the interval and not missing in the last year. In addition, we dropped person-year observations outside the sixteen-to-thirty-four age range to ensure adequate sample sizes within age groups.[4] The resulting sample sizes and mean number of observations contributed by respondents are given at the top of table 4.1. The table also shows the independent variables used in the anal-

**Table 4.1    Characteristics of Sample for Job Change Analysis, Overall and by Cohort**

| Characteristic | Pooled Sample | Original Cohort | Recent Cohort |
|---|---|---|---|
| Number of persons | 4,616 | 2,340 | 2,276 |
| Number of person-years | 18,077 | 8,811 | 9,266 |
| Mean number of observations per person | 3.9 | 3.8 | 4.0 |
| Two-year separation rate | .494 | .464 | .527 |
| Age range (years) | 16 to 34 | 16 to 34 | 16 to 34 |
| Mean age (years) | 24.9 | 25.0 | 24.8 |
| Mean work experience (months) | 82.1 | 80.2 | 84.2 |
| Enrolled in school (percentage) | 22.0 | 18.9 | 25.3 |
| Current education (percentage) | | | |
|    Less than high school | 16.4 | 16.5 | 16.4 |
|    High school graduate | 39.2 | 34.8 | 44.0 |
|    Some college experience | 23.0 | 24.8 | 20.9 |
|    Bachelor's degree or higher | 21.4 | 23.9 | 18.7 |
| Current tenure (percentage) | | | |
|    One year or less | 40.1 | 40.2 | 39.9 |
|    One to three years | 29.9 | 28.8 | 31.2 |
|    Three or more years | 30.0 | 31.0 | 28.0 |
| Living in the South (percentage) | 29.2 | 29.7 | 28.2 |
| Married (percentage) | 49.9 | 60.3 | 38.4 |
| Industry (percentage) | | | |
|    Construction, mining, and agriculture | 14.2 | 13.6 | 14.8 |
|    Manufacturing, transportation, and communications | 34.3 | 37.1 | 31.2 |
|    Wholesale and retail trade, business services | 31.1 | 26.1 | 36.6 |
|    Finance, insurance, and real estate, and professional services | 15.7 | 17.3 | 14.0 |
|    Public administration | 4.7 | 5.9 | 3.4 |
| Professional, managerial, and technical occupations (percentage) | 26.4 | 28.4 | 24.2 |
| Finished with education (percentage) | 59.8 | 58.9 | 60.9 |

*Source:* Authors' compilation.
*Note:* All quantities based on person-years, unless otherwise described, and all are weighted.

ysis. All the covariates are measured identically in the two cohorts, and all are time-varying; that is, they are measured at year $t$ for any comparison of employers across year $t$ and year $t + 2$.

Finally, because the job instability field has been fraught with data and measurement problems, we conducted a series of analyses to validate the NLS data as a source of sound information on job stability.[5] A major challenge in this field has been to reconcile the three main data sources on job instability (the CPS, the PSID, and the NLS) and to gain a thorough understanding of the limitations of each. Papers by Neumark, Polsky, and Hansen (1997) and David Jaeger and Ann Stevens (1999) have made considerable headway on this task for the CPS and the PSID. We undertook this task for the NLS data, finding strong agreement between NLS and PSID estimates of instability but less with the CPS estimates over time—the latter echoes some of the findings of Jaeger and Stevens (1999). As the potential bias associated with permanent attrition is always a key problem for longitudinal data, we also conducted an extensive attrition analysis. Even under the most conservative assumptions, we find that the effect of attrition on our instability estimates appears to be small; several adjustments are discussed in the next section.

## Trends in Job Instability

In figure 4.1 we begin with a simple visual exploration of our data, asking whether young adults in the recent cohort have experienced greater job instability than those in the original cohort. Before we discuss specific results, it is worth noting the generally high rate of job changing evident throughout the graphs. The job separation rates often exceed 0.5, meaning that more than half of the workers in a particular group left their current employers within the next two years. Part of this is clearly a function of the high mobility rates of young adults (Light and McGarry 1998; Klerman and Karoly 1994). In their study of young men, Robert Topel and Michael Ward (1992) find that two-thirds of all new jobs end within the first year. The structure of the American labor market contributes, as well. Although most workers eventually settle into long-term jobs (Hall 1982), a high degree of job mobility extends well beyond the late teens and early twenties.

Job changing has apparently become more prevalent. The first panel of figure 4.1 shows the aggregate difference between the two cohorts. Without any adjustments having been made, we find that 46.4 percent of the original cohort and 52.7 percent of the recent cohort had left their current employer two years later. This translates into a 13.6 percent proportionate increase in the rate of job changing

Figure 4.1 Cohort Differences in Job Separation Rates

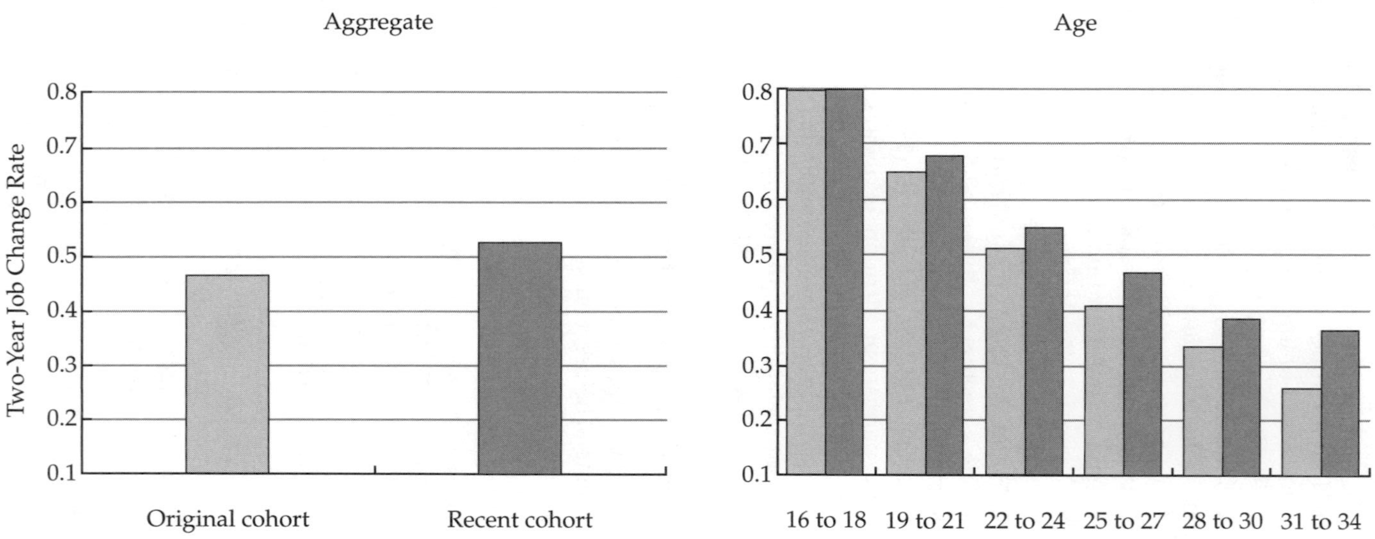

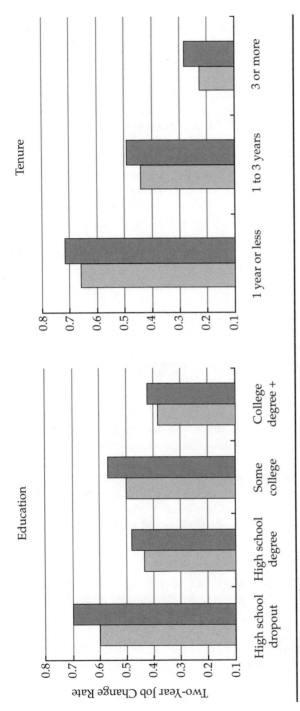

Education

Tenure

Two-Year Job Change Rate

High school
dropout

High school
degree

Some
college

College
degree +

1 year or less

1 to 3 years

3 or more

*Source:* Authors' compilation.

among young workers in recent years. The remaining panels of figure 4.1 illustrate some of the important ways in which this cohort difference is patterned.[6] The "Age" panel illustrates the well-known fact that age is one of the central determinants of job instability. Young workers entering the labor market show a high level of job shopping, which declines markedly as they begin to form permanent attachments to employers. The recent cohort, however, has a clear disadvantage in attaining employment stability, especially at later ages. The same pattern holds for the effect of tenure on job stability. In general, the longer a worker stays with his current employer, the less likely he is to leave that employer, suggesting that when a good match is found, stable employment results. Higher rates of separation are evident throughout the tenure distribution for the recent cohort, however, not just during the early years.[7]

Finally, education also has a strong impact on job changing, as we might expect. It is important to note that here we are looking at the final level of education reached by the respondents (so as not to confound level of education with enrollment). High school dropouts have the highest separation rate and are clearly at the greatest disadvantage; rates for the other education groups are generally lower.[8] The main message from this graph, however, is that the recent cohort consistently shows a higher rate of job changing across all education groups.

We thus have preliminary evidence that job instability has, in fact, increased during the 1980s and early 1990s for young adult men. The problem with taking these types of simple descriptives much further, however, is that all of these dimensions (age, education, tenure) change simultaneously as the cohorts are surveyed over time, making it difficult to judge the magnitude of the increase in the rate of job changing. We therefore move directly to modeling the separation rates to determine whether there has been a secular increase in the rate of job changing, net of these compositional shifts.

## The Model

Let $Y_{ijt}$ indicate whether individual $i$ in job $j$ in year $t$ has left that job by year $t + 2$. We specify a logistic regression model of the following form:

$$\text{logit}[P(Y_{ijt} = 1 \mid X_{ijt}, J_{ijt}, U_{it}, C_i, \phi_i)]$$
$$= \theta_o X_{ijt} + \theta_1 J_{ijt} + \theta_2 U_{it} + \theta_3 C_i + \phi_i,$$

where $P(Y_{ijt} = 1 \mid X_{ijt}, J_{ijt}, U_{it}, C_i, \phi_i)$ is the probability that an individual in job $j$ in year $t$ has left that job by year $t + 2$, given that they have characteristics $X_{ijt}$, $J_{ijt}$, $U_{it}$, $C_i$, and $\phi_i$ and that logit($p$) = log[$p \div$ $(1 - p)$] is the log-odds of the probability $p$.[9] Here $X_{ijt}$ represents time-varying characteristics of the respondent, $J_{ijt}$ represents time-varying characteristics of the job, including tenure, $U_{it}$ represents the local unemployment rate in the individual's labor market in year $t$, and $C_i$ represents a cohort indicator variable, coded zero for the original cohort, one for the recent cohort. Finally, we include a random individual-specific effect (ISE), $\phi_i$, to capture unmeasured characteristics of the individual that are stable over the sample period. Because the main objective of this term is to reflect the longitudinal nature of the sample, we adopt a simple specification, modeling it as independent of the other regressors (Heckman and Singer 1984).[10] The estimate of the cohort difference was robust to this, and other, specifications of unobserved heterogeneity.[11]

Throughout our analysis, we discuss the estimated effects in their exponentiated form, so that we can talk in the more intuitive language of the effect of a given variable on the odds of job-changing. These odds are defined as the probability of leaving an employer divided by the probability of staying with the employer.

## Findings

Table 4.2 presents the results of several versions of the above model. In model 1, we begin with a basic specification. Reflecting the patterning observed in figure 4.1, the odds of job changing clearly and strongly decline with age, tenure, and accumulated work experience, as young workers begin to form permanent attachments to employers. The odds of job changing for a youth with long tenure (three or more years), for example, are roughly half the odds for a youth with short tenure (one year or less). Higher national unemployment has the effect of slightly lowering the odds of a job change: when job prospects worsen, the incentives for staying with the current employer increase.[12] Workers without a high school diploma are significantly more at risk of leaving their current employers than are high school graduates. This also holds for workers with some college experience, though current enrollment plays a role in this result. College graduates, on the other hand, are significantly less likely to change jobs.

The difference between the two cohorts remains strong in this model, even with these controls in place: the adjusted odds of a job change are 43 percent higher for the recent cohort. We consider this our best baseline estimate of the increase in job instability experienced by young white men in the 1980s and early 1990s as compared with their counterparts in the late 1960s and 1970s. There are several rea-

**Table 4.2  Logistic Regression Estimates for Two-Year Job Separations**

| | Model 1 | | Model 2 | | Model 3 | | Model 4 | | Model 5 | |
|---|---|---|---|---|---|---|---|---|---|---|
| Variable | $\hat{\beta}$ | exp($\hat{\beta}$) | $\hat{\beta}$ | exp($\hat{\beta}$) | $\hat{\beta}$ | exp($\hat{\beta}$) | $\hat{\beta}$ | exp($\hat{\beta}$) | $\hat{\beta}$ | exp($\hat{\beta}$) |
| Intercept | 1.544*** | 4.68 | 1.173*** | 3.23 | 1.436*** | 4.20 | 1.839*** | 6.29 | 0.930*** | 2.53 |
| | (.052) | | (.060) | | (.067) | | (.070) | | (.069) | |
| Recent cohort [original cohort] | .358*** | 1.43 | .244*** | 1.28 | .176*** | 1.19 | .156* | 1.17 | .373*** | 1.45 |
| | (.052) | | (.052) | | (.052) | | (.079) | | (.067) | |
| Age | -.146*** | .86 | -.063** | .94 | -.037 | .96 | -.109*** | .90 | -.060 | .94 |
| | (.021) | | (.022) | | (.023) | | (.021) | | (.034) | |
| Age squared | .005*** | 1.00 | .002 | 1.00 | .001 | 1.00 | .004*** | 1.00 | .003 | 1.00 |
| | (.001) | | (.001) | | (.001) | | (.001) | | (.002) | |
| Current education [high school graduate] | | | | | | | | | | |
| Less than high school | .558*** | 1.75 | .542*** | 1.72 | .478*** | 1.61 | .497*** | 1.64 | .747*** | 2.11 |
| | (.069) | | (.069) | | (.068) | | (.068) | | (.101) | |
| Some college experience | .393*** | 1.48 | .205*** | 1.23 | .208*** | 1.23 | .349*** | 1.42 | .088 | 1.09 |
| | (.057) | | (.060) | | (.061) | | (.058) | | (.091) | |
| Bachelor's degree or higher | -.127* | .88 | -.234*** | .79 | -.151* | .86 | -.145* | .86 | -.295*** | .74 |
| | (.064) | | (.065) | | (.071) | | (.066) | | (.087) | |
| Current tenure [one year or less] | | | | | | | | | | |
| One to three years | -.747*** | .47 | -.725*** | .48 | -.702*** | .50 | -.726*** | .48 | -.807*** | .45 |
| | (.042) | | (.042) | | (.042) | | (.042) | | (.059) | |
| Three or more years | -.859*** | .42 | -.842*** | .43 | -.811*** | .44 | -.833*** | .44 | -.954*** | .38 |
| | (.055) | | (.056) | | (.056) | | (.055) | | (.072) | |

| | (1) | | (2) | | (3) | | (4) | | (5) | |
|---|---|---|---|---|---|---|---|---|---|---|
| Work experience | -.008*** (.001) | .99 | -.006*** (.001) | .99 | -.006*** (.001) | .99 | -.008*** (.001) | .99 | -.008*** (.001) | .99 |
| Local unemployment rate | .008 (.007) | 1.01 | .009 (.007) | 1.01 | -.009 (.007) | 1.00 | 0.008 (.007) | 1.01 | .016 (.010) | 1.02 |
| Currently enrolled in school | | | .447*** (.054) | 1.56 | .402*** (.055) | 1.50 | | | | |
| Living in the South | | | .105* (.052) | 1.11 | .085 (.051) | 1.09 | | | | |
| Married | | | -.342*** (.045) | .71 | -.297*** (.045) | .74 | | | | |
| Industry [retail and wholesale trade, business services] | | | | | | | | | | |
| Construction, mining, agriculture | | | | | .115 (.066) | 1.12 | -.037 (.082) | .96 | | |
| Manufacturing, transportation, communication | | | | | -.763*** (.051) | .47 | | | -.927*** (.070) | .40 |
| FIRE | | | | | -.202** (.066) | .82 | -.198* (.088) | .82 | | |
| Public administration | | | | | -1.334*** (.107) | .26 | -1.456*** (.116) | .23 | | |
| Professional, managerial, technical occupations | | | | | -.147** (.053) | .86 | | | | |

(Table continues on p. 76.)

**Table 4.2** *Continued*

| Variable | Model 1 β̂ | Model 1 exp(β̂) | Model 2 β̂ | Model 2 exp(β̂) | Model 3 β̂ | Model 3 exp(β̂) | Model 4 β̂ | Model 4 exp(β̂) | Model 5 β̂ | Model 5 exp(β̂) |
|---|---|---|---|---|---|---|---|---|---|---|
| Interaction: cohort with industry | | | | | | | | | | |
| Recent cohort in high-level services | | | | | | | −.043 (.124) | .96 | | |
| Recent cohort in traditional industries | | | | | | | .241** (.091) | 1.27 | | |
| Individual heterogeneity: standard deviations | 1.087*** (.036) | | 1.080*** (.036) | | 1.025*** (.035) | | 1.029*** (.035) | | 1.259*** (.054) | |
| Change in −2 log likelihood | −2133*** | | −137*** | | −427*** | | −459*** | | −734*** | |

*Source:* Authors' compilation.

*Note:* Dependent variable is two-year job separation. Standard errors are identified in brackets. Contrast categories are identified in parentheses. Age is rescaled to age − sixteen. Work experience is measured in months. Model 5 is fit for a subsample of respondents; see text for full explanation. For model 4, change in −2 log likelihood is relative to model 1, for model 5 it is the change relative to the null model for the subsample.

***significant at .001, **significant at .01, *significant at .05.

sons why the adjusted estimate is likely to be more accurate.[13] We know that the cohorts' differences in age and education, as well as the prevailing unemployment rates, will affect their relative job stability. In addition, the delayed labor force entry of the Vietnam veterans means they reach employment stability at a later age, artificially dragging down the overall stability of the original cohort. Controlling for all of these variables thus provides a clearer picture of whether there have been any changes in job stability net of these expected effects.

With the cohort difference still strong after these controls, the next question is what additional factors play a role. In model 2, we examine the impact of some other demographic changes. Enrollment in school raises the odds of a job change, an outcome that is not surprising given that jobs held during schooling are often temporary and short lived.[14] Living in the South is associated with higher levels of job instability, whereas marriage has a stabilizing effect. Because the two cohorts differ along these dimensions, the variables have a compositional effect on the cohort difference in job instability: the odds of a job change are now 28 percent higher for the recent cohort—still highly significant but clearly of a lower order of magnitude. Most of this reduction is driven by lower marriage rates in the recent cohort and its longer periods of college enrollment.

In model 3, we ask whether the economy-wide shift toward the service sector has played a role. Service industries as a rule are more unstable than the public sector and the goods-producing and traditionally unionized industries (excepting construction, where the nature of work is inherently transient). We therefore expect the young workers in the recent cohort to be at a clear disadvantage. Mirroring the economy-wide trend, they are less likely to be employed in the public sector and more likely to be employed in the service sector, especially in low-end, high-turnover industries such as retail trade and business services. Controlling for these compositional shifts further reduces the cohort difference: the job change odds are now 19 percent higher for the recent cohort, about half of the baseline estimate.

In these first three models, all of the variables are constrained to have the same effect for both cohorts, so that we are capturing the impact of compositional shifts in the variables, not changes in their impact. We did test whether the rise in job instability for the recent cohort was particularly pronounced for those with less education. Surprisingly, we found no such differential—the rise in instability has been felt by all education groups, consistent with James Monks and Steven Pizer's (1998) finding for a similar sample.

There is, however, a further twist to the industry story. In model 4, we fit an interaction between the cohort effect and the industry effect. The cohort dummy now captures the cohort difference in job instability within the baseline industries of retail and wholesale trade and business services. The first interaction term indicates that the cohort difference is similar within finance, insurance, and real estate and professional services. The second interaction term, however, shows a significantly stronger cohort difference in industries that historically have been unionized. Thus not only are youth in the recent cohort suffering from greater reliance on the "unstable" service sector, but they are also not benefiting as much when they are employed in traditionally stable industries such as manufacturing. What we are most likely identifying here, albeit indirectly, is the shedding of employment and declines in unionization in the goods-producing and to some extent the public sectors.[15] Figure 4.2 highlights these findings, showing the prevalence of industry shifting among job changers in each cohort and the prevalence of shifts between the goods-producing sector and the service sector. Although a person in the recent cohort who changes jobs is more likely to change industries, especially in his late twenties and early thirties, he is not much more likely than someone from the original cohort to make the shift between the goods-producing and the service sector. Thus not all of the increased volatility in job changing can be linked to the process of deindustrialization. A significant part stems from increased volatility within sectors.

Finally, we ask whether the greater instability of the recent cohort is simply a function of the more volatile transitions to the labor market that we documented in chapter 3. For example, it may be that once the transition to work has been completed and the recent cohort reaches its mid-thirties, the difference in job instability disappears. This would indicate a new labor market that is more turbulent initially but eventually provides the type of job stability that past generations of workers enjoyed. In model 5 we reestimate model 1 for workers after they have completed their schooling. Specifically, we include observations from individuals only at the point at which they are never again enrolled in school and their education level never increases. The focus, therefore, is on the experience of the young workers once they have permanently entered the labor market. The results from model 5 are consistent with those from the full sample in model 1, and the estimated cohort difference remains strong and significant.[16] Thus the increased job instability we have found does not disappear once the young workers "settle down" and is therefore not just a legacy of churning in the labor market early on—it apparently is a general feature of the postindustrial labor market.

**Figure 4.2  Of Those Who Changed Jobs . . . .**

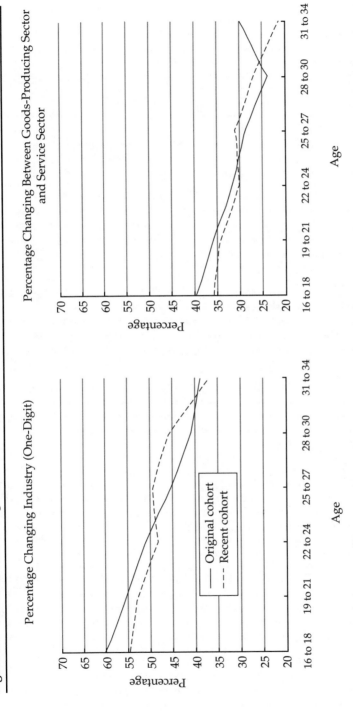

Percentage Changing Industry (One-Digit)

Percentage Changing Between Goods-Producing Sector
and Service Sector

—— Original cohort
- - - Recent cohort

*Source:* Authors' compilation.

## A Closer Look

We have so far examined a general measure of job instability, simply asking whether or not a worker had left his current employer two years later. More questions could be asked. For example, if a job separation occurred, was it voluntary or involuntary? Does a history of instability lead to more instability? Do the answers to these questions differ by cohort?

Several studies have differentiated between rough measures of voluntary and involuntary job separations (for example, Farber 1997; Polsky 1999). Although there is no agreement on whether job instability has risen as a whole, it is generally acknowledged that the rate of involuntary job separation has increased over the past several decades. Unfortunately, our data set does not permit an accurate and consistent measure of the reasons for leaving employers, because the original cohort has high and biased missingness on that variable for much of the survey time span.[17]

We can, however, pursue another strategy and look at where these young adults ended up two years after leaving their employers. There are three possibilities: the worker may have a new employer, he may be unemployed, or he may have left the labor force altogether. Of these three outcomes, the latter two are probably more likely to signal an involuntary separation (through layoffs, firing, and the like) as opposed to a voluntary quit. This is not necessarily the case, however, as workers may drop out of the labor force to return to school, and unemployment may simply indicate time spent searching for a better job, especially among young adults. Nevertheless, it is probably true that involuntary terminations are more prevalent among workers who are not employed two years later.

In table 4.3, we focus on workers who report that they were working in year $t$ and examine their destination state in year $t + 2$. To minimize education-related voluntary quits, we also restrict the sample to those who have completed their schooling. Given the two-year time span, multiple unemployment spells or exits from the labor force could have occurred during the interim.[18]

The first two columns of the table simple reiterate what we have already shown, that the recent cohort is less likely than the original to stay with the same employer and more likely to move to a new one. The difference in the first column becomes more pronounced with age and signals a decline in the recent cohort's ability to establish long-term relationships with employers. The third and fourth columns indicate that the recent cohort has also experienced an increased likelihood of unemployment and exits from the labor force.

Table 4.3   Breakdown of Two-Year Job Separation Rate, by Destination,
Cohort, and Age (Percentage)

| Age and Cohort | Destination | | | |
| | With Same Employer | With New Employer | Unemployed | Out of Labor Force |
| --- | --- | --- | --- | --- |
| 20 to 24 | | | | |
| Original | 50.8 | 44.0 | 3.4 | 1.8 |
| Recent | 46.8 | 44.9 | 6.1 | 2.2 |
| Percent difference | −4.0 | +.9 | +2.7 | +.4 |
| 25 to 29 | | | | |
| Original | 63.8 | 32.7 | 2.3 | 1.2 |
| Recent | 58.3 | 36.1 | 3.8 | 1.8 |
| Percent difference | −5.5 | +3.4 | +1.5 | +.6 |
| 30 to 34 | | | | |
| Original | 72.8 | 24.2 | 2.1 | 0.9 |
| Recent | 64.3 | 29.9 | 3.3 | 2.5 |
| Percent difference | −8.5 | +5.7 | +1.3 | +1.6 |

*Source:* Authors' compilation.
*Note:* Sample is restricted to those who have permanently entered the labor market.

These increases are proportionately large, but in absolute terms they do not approach the magnitude of the employer-to-employer shifts. With age, the recent cohort is more likely to find new employers after changing jobs (the cohort difference in the second column rises with age). Even by their thirties, they are more likely to become unemployed or exit the labor force than the original cohort. Given that we are looking at workers only after they have finished their schooling, these findings suggest a greater prevalence of involuntary job loss, because unemployment and exits from the labor force are more prevalent for the recent cohort. This evidence also signals greater disruption in the continuity of employment and earnings for the recent cohort.

In light of this evidence it is natural to ask whether higher levels of job instability have become chronic in recent years. Although a certain amount of "job shopping" can be good, chronic instability can be harmful, engendering unproductive cycling from one job to the next. Figure 4.3 confirms this intuition, showing that the greater the number of prior job changes, the greater the risk of leaving one's current job.[19] There is no evidence that this relationship has become more pronounced in recent years: the cohort difference is quite similar throughout.[20] We also performed a more nuanced analysis, along the lines of Farber (1994), who finds that job changes in the preceding

**Figure 4.3    The Effect of Prior Job Changes on Current Job Changes, by Cohort**

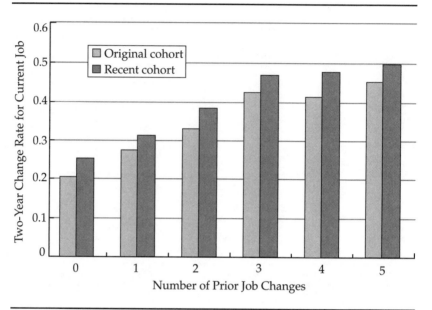

*Source:* Authors' compilation.

year have a stronger effect than those further removed in the past and that the increased risk of a job change is concentrated in the first six months on the job. Using the models from table 4.2, we tested for and replicated this pattern of effects but, again, did not find it to be more pronounced for the recent cohort.

Although chronic job instability in itself has not become more intense in recent years, greater numbers of workers are experiencing its effect. As a result, the typical worker in the recent cohort has accumulated more employers than his counterpart in the original cohort. Figure 4.4 shows the distribution of the total number of CPS employers accumulated over the entire survey span, at the point of the last interview.[21] The last interview typically finds our young workers in their early to middle thirties, with about twelve years of work experience and about five years of tenure.[22] For both cohorts, the modal pattern is similar: about half of workers had accumulated four or five employers.[23] There has been a strong rightward shifting of the distribution in recent years, however. Substantially fewer workers in the recent cohort have stable job histories: only 11 percent report a total of one or two employers, compared with 16 percent in the original co-

**Figure 4.4    Total Number of Employers Accumulated by Final Interview, by Cohort**

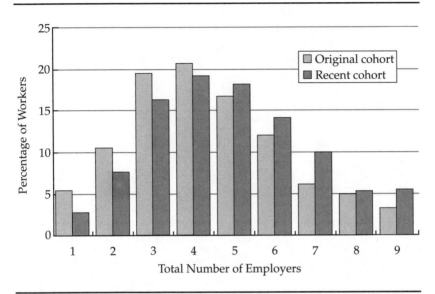

*Source:* Authors' compilation.
*Note:* Percentages are person based.

hort. On the other end, there are now substantially more workers with unstable job histories. The fraction reporting a total of seven or more employers has risen from 15 percent in the original cohort to 21 percent for the recent.

## Changes in Tenure

When job instability rises, it is inevitable that tenure will become shorter on average; each time an individual leaves an employer and starts with a new one, the tenure clock is reset to zero. Indeed, some of the research that has tested for an increase in job instability has taken the strategy of looking for changes in tenure distributions. So the question is not whether tenure has declined in recent years but, rather, by how much. In this section, we examine how much the length of stay with an employer (tenure) has been affected by the higher rate of job separations in the recent cohort.

We continue to use the strictly matched version of the data from the previous section.[24] Thus the original cohort is observed between 1967 and 1980, and the recent cohort between 1980 and 1993, in roughly two-year intervals. Because both of the NLS data sets record

**Figure 4.5   Median Tenure by Cohort**

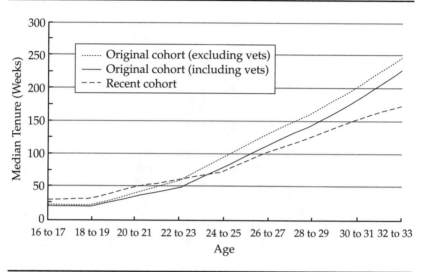

Source: Authors' compilation.

starting dates of the respondent's main job and uniquely identify the employer of that job, we are able to accurately measure the distribution of continuous tenure with an employer at a given point in time.

Figure 4.5 shows how the median tenures of the two cohorts have been affected. Early on, the recent cohort actually had somewhat longer tenures than the original cohort, which is in part a result of their earlier labor force participation during those ages. After the mid-twenties, however, their greater job instability begins to make itself felt in shorter tenures, with a substantial gap by the early thirties. When we exclude the Vietnam veterans from the original cohort, the difference becomes even stronger—again, because those serving in Vietnam lost several years of labor market participation and are therefore several years behind others in their cohort in terms of building a long-term relationship with one employer. One can think of the two lines for the original cohort as bounds of a sort: the true median line probably lies somewhere in between them. We investigated whether the distributions of tenure differed in other ways (for example, the variance) but found no significant differences, net of the change in the median.

Finally, in figure 4.6 we plot the full tenure distribution for workers in their mid-thirties.[25] Viewed in this way, the nature of the cohort differences becomes quite clear: 35 percent of the original cohort but 45 percent of the recent cohort had tenures of two years or less. Con-

**Figure 4.6    Tenure Distribution of Workers Aged Thirty-Three to Thirty-Seven by Cohort**

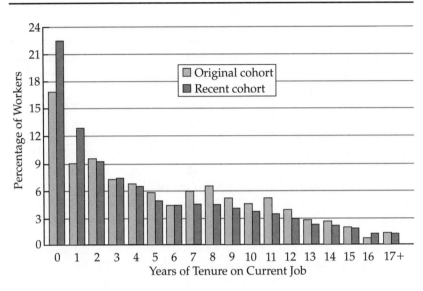

*Source:* Authors' compilation.

versely, 41 percent of the original cohort but only 32 percent of the recent cohort had tenures of seven years or more. This graph depicts only tenure to date, not how long the jobs will eventually last. As Robert Hall (1982) points out, using data from the 1978 CPS, 27.7 percent of the jobs held by thirty- to thirty-four-year-old workers will eventually last twenty or more years. Nonetheless, the key point here is that the recent cohort is several years behind the original cohort in establishing long-term employment relationships. Even if the two co-horts suddenly became identical in their rate of job changing, this relative difference in tenure length would persist over time: to make up the lost ground, the recent cohort would actually have to become more stable. Given the results from our models in the previous section, there is no reason to expect convergence of these distributions in the future; the higher job instability for the recent cohort persisted throughout the observation period, affecting them well into their mid-thirties.

## Summary

In this chapter, we have identified a marked increase in job instability among young white men during the 1980s and early 1990s, as compared with workers of the same age in the late 1960s and 1970s. The robustness of this finding to different controls is striking. It does not disappear, for example, once the young workers "settle down," and is therefore not just a legacy of job churning early in the career. It is also not limited to less educated workers. Some variation does exist, but the dominant theme is that the rise in instability has been felt across the board. Few groups have escaped it, whether defined by age, education, work experience, or strength of attachment to employers.

After taking into account basic differences in composition between the two cohorts, we estimate that the odds of a job change are 43 percent higher for the recent cohort. This means that, all else being equal, a twenty-four-year-old high school graduate in the recent cohort with a year or less of tenure had a .63 probability of changing employers, compared with .55 for the original cohort. This translates in a 16 percent increase in job instability. Later in his career, a thirty-four-year-old high school graduate in the recent cohort with three or more years of tenure still had a .21 probability of changing employers, compared with only .16 for the original cohort. This represents an even stronger increase (34 percent) in job instability. Our findings therefore suggest that public perceptions of rising job instability may not be so far off base, at least for those who entered the labor market during the late 1970s and early 1980s.

Some of the increase is associated with changes in demographics. Lower marriage rates in recent years have contributed to rising instability, though it is unclear which is cause and which is effect. So has the trend toward longer school enrollment, especially during the college years. The shift in population density toward southern states has also led to higher rates of job instability, perhaps reflecting the lower rates of unionization in the South.

The shift of the U.S. economy to the service sector has also played a role, as the young workers in the recent cohort are less likely to be employed in the public and manufacturing sectors and more likely to be employed in the service sector, especially low-end, high-turnover industries such as retail trade and business services. In addition, however, there has been a decline in job security within industries. This decline has been especially pronounced in manufacturing, at a time when many young men still depend on this sector for employment. Thus not only are youth in the recent cohort suffering from greater reliance on the "unstable" service sector, but they are also not benefiting as much when they are employed in traditionally stable industries such as manufacturing. What we are probably identifying here are the declines in unionization and shedding of employment in the goods-producing and public sectors.

Job instability is not necessarily a bad thing, especially early in the career when workers "shop" for the best job. We have some evidence, however, that the rise in instability has been at least partly harmful to the young workers in the recent cohort. First, we know that the greater the number of past job changes, the greater the risk of leaving one's current job, so the recent cohort is especially prone to future instability, by virtue of its higher past instability. Second, not only did these youth shift between employers more frequently, they also became unemployed and dropped out of the labor force more often. Because the pattern extends into midcareer, it signals a worrisome disruption of continuity in employment and earnings. Third, rising job instability has taken a toll on tenure in the recent cohort. Among workers in their mid-thirties, the fraction with two years of tenure or less rose from 35 percent in the original cohort to 45 percent in the recent cohort. Conversely, the fraction with tenures of seven or more years fell from 41 percent in the original cohort to 32 percent in the recent.

At first glance, then, there is reason for concern. We have not yet addressed the key issue of the wage consequences of job instability, but we know that at least historically, attaining stability by the onset of midcareer is important. Access to training, benefits, and promotions is contingent on staying with one employer, where track records can be built and firm-specific skills can be gained. This is especially true for workers who do not have specialized skills in high demand— and again it is worth remembering that three-quarters of Americans do not attain a four-year college degree. A small number of professionals and software designers may well embrace the greater mobility between firms as a mechanism for greater control over what they do and when they do it. For the majority of workers with fewer resources and fewer skills, however, the increase in instability is more likely to represent greater disruption in work and family life and a stunting of career development.

# = Chapter 5 =

## The Short-Term Consequences
## of Instability

O NE OF the empirical "facts" to emerge from labor economics is that changing jobs early in the career is highly beneficial, yielding more short-term wage growth than staying put with one employer. It is important to appreciate the influence of these early years. The majority of lifetime wage growth occurs during the first ten years in the labor market. For white men, the figure is roughly three-quarters (Murphy and Welch 1990). So to a large and sobering extent, what happens early in workers' careers determines where they will end up over the long run; trajectories of upward mobility are set in a relatively short time window.

This is also the period when we see the majority of job changes, and these job changes pay off well. Topel and Ward (1992) estimate that the typical job change results in a 12 percent increase in quarterly wages, as compared with a quarterly increase of 1.8 percent when staying with the same employer. Altogether, transitions to new jobs account for about 40 percent of early wage growth. Thus job shopping is a key mechanism by which workers escape low-paying jobs and make the initial jumps up the income ladder that are so critical to later success. If we want to understand the process by which inequality is generated, this is clearly the place to look.

As time progresses, however, sticking with one employer becomes more valuable, and the returns to job changing decline, as does the frequency of job changing itself. Dynamically, the picture is one in which "transitions to higher wage jobs stabilize employment" (Topel and Ward 1992, 472). Though the causal chain is difficult to disentangle, a number of different factors are likely to be operating. Workers may find they have reached the highest-paying job available, given their skills and qualifications, and decide that future moves are unlikely to yield much payoff. Credentials gained several years ago may have become outdated in a labor market flush with newly minted graduates. Nonmonetary benefits, such as health insurance, pensions, residential stability, and characteristics of the job itself, may increase in importance as workers get older and build families. Firms and workers may have invested in specific training that makes the continued presence of the worker more valuable to the firm and a separation more costly to the worker. Even beyond such investments, firms may provide incentives to retain productive, well-matched workers.

In sum, from the standpoint of wage growth, the ideal story suggests an optimal progression of initial job shopping followed by stable employment with one firm.[1] This means that, broadly speaking, two variables drive wage growth over the career: early job changing and then long tenures (Moore, Viscusi, and Zeckhauser 1999). The impact of these variables depends, in turn, on other factors. Voluntarily quitting tends to pay off better than being fired, and within firms, promotions yield greater wage growth than staying put. The well educated gain more than the less educated from switching employers; in fact, this is where the education wage differential is most pronounced (Bartel and Borjas 1981). Women gain less than men, which accounts in significant part for the diverging gender gap over the life cycle (Loprest 1992). Some industries and occupations reward job mobility more than others: in unionized manufacturing industries, stability and long tenures may actually be more beneficial throughout. Finally, although it is generally true that switching jobs early on does not impede wage growth (Gardecki and Neumark 1998), there is growing evidence that a history of many employers has long-term negative effects (Light and McGarry 1998; Keith and McWilliams 1995). This raises the important question of whether employers' perceptions of workers' histories, apart from real differences in productivity and performance, contribute to the impact of job instability (Ghez 1981).

The upshot is that there is considerable heterogeneity in the way that young workers build wage growth over the early part of their careers. Audrey Light and Kathleen McGarry (1998) show that at the very least, there are three types of wage change/job change paths.[2] Some workers are relatively immobile throughout their careers and nevertheless attain solid wages. Others follow the dynamic described earlier, shopping to locate well-paying and more stable jobs as they age. Finally, there are workers who fail to reap the gains from job shopping and remain stuck in low-wage, unstable trajectories throughout their lives.

The question for us is how these dynamics play out for the two cohorts in our study. We have seen in the previous chapter that young men experienced an increase in job instability during the 1980s and early 1990s. It is difficult to judge that increase a priori, however, because, as we have seen, more-frequent job changes and shorter tenures are not necessarily a bad thing. The real question is this: what happens to wage growth as a result? For example, it is possible that the very nature of career development has changed in recent years. The recent cohort might be changing jobs more frequently and accumulating less firm-specific tenure but nevertheless be able to capture consistent wage growth over time. Alternatively, these workers may gain less now from job changing. In this case, there would be true cause for concern, given that more of them are changing jobs in the first place. Thus our appraisal of the rise in job instability must in the end focus on wage outcomes. This chapter investigates how the returns to changing and not changing jobs have changed over the last thirty years.

The relationship between wages and job mobility is the topic of considerable debate in labor economics, yielding different behavioral theories such as the mover-stayer model and variations on sorting and job-matching models (for example, Burdett 1978; Jovanovic 1979). We do not attempt to engage these theoretical debates in our analyses. Our goal is simply descriptive, to establish whether the association between job stability and wage outcomes has changed in recent years. We obviously draw on the existing literature in structuring our analyses, but we avoid the type of behavioral conclusions that would require theoretical modeling.

## Measures and Data

To link wage changes with job changes in a rigorous manner, we continue to use the data set from the previous chapter, which contains only strictly comparable years for the two cohorts. Recall our measure of a job change. If an individual was working in a given year, we ask whether he was working for the same employer two years later. Our measure of a wage change follows a similar logic. For any two years $t$ and $t + 2$ that were used to compute whether or not a job change occurred, we compute the corresponding wage change: $(\ln)\text{wage}_{t+2} - (\ln)\text{wage}_{t}.$[3] We are therefore measuring wage changes across a series of two-year spans, with each change representing one observation. Because these wage changes are pooled in our analyses, individuals may contribute more than one observation.[4]

Several substantive points about this measure should be stressed. First, it is a relative measure, by intent. Calculating the absolute increase or loss in wages from time $t$ to time $t + 2$ would result in a measure that largely reflects the absolute pay level of an individual: high-wage workers would generally receive larger wage gains than low-wage workers. In this chapter, however, we are more interested in the dynamics of wage growth, the steep upward slopes early in the career that can raise even low initial wages to a middle-class income. Technically, our outcome measure can be restated as $\ln(\text{wage}_{t+2} \div \text{wage}_t)$. This ratio simply tells us the percentage increase in wages that occurred over the two-year time span. For example, a ratio of 1.05 indicates a 5 percent increase, regardless of the starting wage level. In the discussion that follows, we loosely refer to "wage gains" and "the returns to job changing," but the reader should always remember that ours is a relative measure, analogous to the percentage increase in wages. In fact, as we will see, the relationship between the two measures is direct.

Second, by necessity, the sample consists of workers who were employed and receiving wages in both years—this is a subset of the sample from chapter 4, which also included workers who either had become unemployed or had left the labor force by year $t + 2$ (and were therefore not receiving earnings in the second year). The result is that we are here focusing on workers during the more stable phase of their early careers, where employment is more continuous and less likely to be interrupted with unemployment or schooling. Nevertheless, as demonstrated in chapter 4, even for this sample the rate of job instability was higher for the recent cohort.

Finally, we again dropped person-year observations outside the sixteen-to-thirty-four age range to ensure adequate sample sizes within age groups. Observations in which the respondent was self-employed or working without pay in either year $t$ or year $t + 2$ were also excluded. The resulting sample sizes are given in table 5.1, as well as descriptives for all variables. Covariates are measured identically in the two cohorts, and all are time-varying. Most are measured at year $t$ for any year $t$ versus $t + 2$ comparison; others are lagged to capture information from the previous two-year comparison; and one covariate captures future information from the next two-year comparison. All analyses are weighted.

## Education and the Returns to Job Changing

We begin with a simple description of the immediate wage returns to changing and not changing jobs across the two cohorts. Figure 5.1 shows the median change in log wages among less educated workers

Table 5.1    Characteristics of Sample for Wage Change Regressions

| Characteristic | Value |
|---|---|
| Unweighted N (for models 1 and 2), | |
|    Number of persons | 3,491 |
|    Number of person-year observations | 15,319 |
|    Mean number of observations contributed by each person | 4.4 |
| Weighted percentage | |
|    Original cohort | 53.8 |
|    Recent cohort | 46.2 |
|    Changed jobs current period | 42.1 |
|    Did not change jobs in preceding period | 51.6 |
|    Did not change jobs in next period | 58.3 |
|    Part-time worker | 13.7 |
|    Married | 52.1 |
|    Construction, mining, agriculture, and fishing | 13.3 |
|    Manufacturing, transportation, and communications | 35.5 |
|    Wholesale and retail trade, business and personal | 30.3 |
|    Finance, insurance, and real estate, and professional services | 15.7 |
|    Public administration | 5.2 |
|    Professional, managerial, and technical occupations | 27.3 |
|    Currently enrolled in school | 20.8 |
| Weighted mean | |
|    Difference in log wages | .107 |
|    Years of tenure | 2.185 |
|    Years of tenure squared | 12.455 |
|    Residualized years of experience | .025 |
|    Residualized years of experience squared | −.120 |
|    Number of previous jobs | 3.465 |
|    Local unemployment rate | 6.583 |
|    Previous (ln) wage (for model 3, restricted sample) | 2.429 |

Source: Authors' compilation.

(those with a high school diploma or less) and among more educated workers (those with some college experience or college degrees). First note that, in general, these graphs mirror the age dynamic that has been documented by previous research. Early in the career, job changing pays off more than staying with an employer—in fact, these wage gains are substantially higher than any experienced later on. Summarizing across both of the cohorts and disregarding education for the moment, during the first three years in the labor market the median increase in real wages is 25.5 percent for job changers and 14.5 percent for nonchangers. After roughly the first decade in the labor market, there is less to be gained from switching employers, and wage growth as a whole slows down. For those with at least ten years of work experience, the median increase in real wages is 1.3 percent for job changers and 2.4 percent for nonchangers. What is being reflected here is the well-known shape of the age-earnings profile, which slopes steeply upward in the early stages of the career and then slowly reaches a plateau of small, incremental wage gains. In line with this shift, the rate of job changing as a whole slows down, and workers begin to stay with one employer for longer spells.[5]

The striking message from these graphs, however, is that less educated workers in the recent cohort have failed to capture wage growth precisely when it is most critical: in the early stages of job search and job changing. This is most apparent during the first decade in the labor market, though the difference persists throughout. By contrast, when these young workers stay with the same employer, there is little difference in the wage gains captured by the two cohorts. In fact, the recent cohort benefits more from staying with the same employer after just a few years in the labor market, because the returns to job changing decline so steeply at that point.

Workers with more education have fared better. Their wage gains have increased in recent years, with a median two-year increase in real wages of $1.49 for the recent cohort as compared with $1.34 for the original. Educated workers, however, have seen these gains across the board, both when changing jobs and when settling with one employer. The corresponding losses for less educated workers have been stronger and concentrated almost exclusively among job changers: in real terms, the median gain of changers in the recent cohort was $0.64, as compared with $1.60 for the original cohort. There was little difference among nonchangers ($0.57 as compared with $0.78). When coupled with our findings from the previous chapter that the recent cohort has also seen an across-the-board increase in the rate of job changing, this trend is cause for concern.

Finally, we should point out that the term "wage gain" is something of a misnomer. It is true that few workers experience wage losses over time, if no adjustments are made for inflation (Altonji and Devereux 1999). In terms of real wages, however, significant numbers of workers do see declines from one year to the next. To illustrate this surprising but well-documented point (Moore, Viscusi, and Zeckhauser 1999), we calculate whether workers had a fall or a jump in real wages over any given two-year time span. We use deflated wages, and to allow for measurement error, we include only decreases and increases of more than 10 percent in our calculation of falls and jumps, respectively. Almost half of the workers in our sample experienced at least one wage fall during the period studied, and

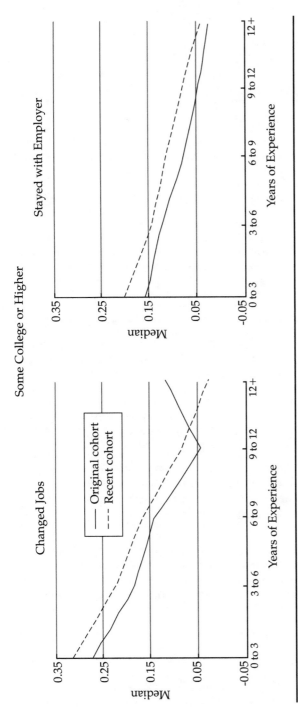

Some College or Higher

Changed Jobs

Stayed with Employer

Original cohort
Recent cohort

Median

Median

Years of Experience

Years of Experience

0.35  0.25  0.15  0.05  -0.05

0 to 3   3 to 6   6 to 9   9 to 12   12+

0 to 3   3 to 6   6 to 9   9 to 12   12+

*Source:* Authors' compilation.

Table 5.2    Cohort Differences in Wage Changes, by Education and Job Change Status

| Education and Job Change Status | Type of Wage Change[a] | | |
| --- | --- | --- | --- |
| | Fall | No Change | Jump |
| High school diploma or less | | | |
| Did not change jobs | | | |
|   Original cohort | 15.8 | 43.5 | 40.7 |
|   Recent cohort | 13.2 | 47.6 | 39.2 |
| Changed jobs | | | |
|   Original cohort | 23.2 | 19.4 | 57.3 |
|   Recent cohort | 28.9 | 23.1 | 48.0 |
| Some college or four-year degree | | | |
| Did not change jobs | | | |
|   Original cohort | 14.5 | 41.9 | 43.6 |
|   Recent cohort | 12.4 | 38.4 | 49.2 |
| Changed jobs | | | |
|   Original cohort | 24.1 | 19.4 | 56.5 |
|   Recent cohort | 24.0 | 19.2 | 56.9 |

Source: Authors' compilation.
[a]Based on percentage wage change, defined as $(\text{wage}_{t+2} - \text{wage}_t)/(\text{wage}_t)$ using deflated wages. Falls and jumps are less than and greater than, respectively, 10 percent of the wage at time $t$.

the majority experienced at least one wage jump. Within any given two-year time span, 18.8 percent of wage changes are falls, a smaller proportion than the 47.5 percent that are jumps, but still substantial. Both of these percentages are higher among job changers, as one might expect, given that their wage outcomes are more likely to be volatile than, for example, in the case of within-firm promotions.

As shown in table 5.2, however, these broad patterns differ by education and by cohort. For less educated workers—the group that has taken disproportionate hits when changing jobs—the prevalence of real wage losses has increased in recent years, from 23.2 percent to 28.9 percent. No other group has seen an increase. Behind the overall deterioration in wage gains, then, lies a substantial increase in real wage losses.

## Model-Based Analysis

To understand the factors associated with these trends, we turn to a series of regressions predicting the two-year difference in (ln) wages.

These regressions are meant not to establish a causal link but instead to examine the robustness of the visual message from the graphs and to test whether compositional differences are driving our findings. Table 5.3 gives the results of three models, all of which focus on the differential returns to changing and not changing jobs, by cohort and education group. We show both the raw coefficients and the percentage wage gains that are predicted by the model, because the latter are easier to interpret.[6]

Model 1 controls for a basic set of covariates: tenure, experience, industry, local unemployment rate, hours worked, school enrollment, and marital status. All work in the expected direction and have similar effects across both cohorts.[7] Even with these compositional shifts held constant, the patterning observed in the graphs remains significant. Less educated workers in recent years have seen dramatically lower wage growth when they change jobs (increases of 5.7 percent compared with 16.4 percent for the original cohort), to the point that staying with one's current job yields a greater payoff. On the other hand, the cohort differential for nonchangers is insignificant (increases of 10.8 percent versus 10.2 percent for the original cohort). For workers with at least some college experience, however, wage gains are larger than there were in the past, regardless of whether they changed jobs or not.

In model 2, we also control for the number of previous job changes.[8] The logic here is that the greater instability of the recent cohort might be confounding the effects we are trying to identify. In fact, controlling for past instability has only minor effects. Less educated workers in the recent cohort still have significantly lower wage increases when they change jobs (4.4 percent compared with 17.1 percent for the original cohort). Thus the detrimental trend in wage growth is not a function of more unstable work histories.[9]

Finally, we ask whether our results are explained by the wage path that the young workers are building in this early phase of their career. In model 3, we control for the deflated (ln) wage that directly preceded the current wage change: formally, $(\ln)\text{wage}_{t-2}$. To fit this model we had to redefine our sample somewhat. A significant number of observations (about 20 percent) did not have a valid value for the previous wage; these were generally younger workers who had not worked in previous years. In this model, therefore, we are focusing on older, more experienced, better-educated workers with longer tenures and greater stability.

Here the results are more attenuated, so that among less educated workers there is no longer such a strong cohort difference in the returns to job changing (though it is still evident and in the same direc-

**Table 5.3  Wage Change Regression Results**

| Variable | Model 1 | | | Model 2 | | | Model 3[a] | | |
|---|---|---|---|---|---|---|---|---|---|
| | Estimate | Signif. | Predicted Gain[b] | Estimate | Signif. | Predicted Gain | Estimate | Signif. | Predicted Gain |
| High school diploma or less | | | | | | | | | |
| Did not change jobs | | | | | | | | | |
|   Original cohort (constant) | .155 | *** | 10.2 | .217 | *** | 11.1 | .312 | *** | 6.6 |
|   Recent cohort | .005 | | 10.8 | −.016 | | 9.3 | .023 | | 9.1 |
| Changed jobs | | | | | | | | | |
|   Original cohort | .055 | *** | 16.4 | .053 | *** | 17.1 | .023 | | 9.0 |
|   Recent cohort | −.042 | *** | 5.7 | −.063 | *** | 4.4 | −.027 | | 3.8 |
| Some college or more | | | | | | | | | |
| Did not change jobs | | | | | | | | | |
|   Original cohort | .002 | | 10.5 | .004 | | 11.6 | .019 | | 8.6 |
|   Recent cohort | .017 | | 12.1 | .000 | | 11.1 | .055 | ** | 12.6 |
| Changed jobs | | | | | | | | | |
|   Original cohort | .030 | ** | 13.6 | .034 | *** | 15.0 | .034 | ** | 10.3 |
|   Recent cohort | .037 | ** | 14.4 | .024 | | 13.8 | .071 | *** | 14.4 |

| | | | |
|---|---|---|---|
| Number of previous job changes | | −.019 *** | −.008 ** |
| Number of previous job changes for recent cohort | | .008 * | −.003 |
| Previous (ln) wage | | | −.076 *** |
| | | | |
| Adjusted $R^2$ | .047 | .051 | .046 |
| Adjusted $R^2$ using smoothed wages | .267 | .298 | .264 |
| $N$ (weighted) | 18,229 | 18,209 | 14,584 |

Source: Authors' compilation.

Note: Dependent variable is two-year change in log wages. All models have the following controls: years of tenure and its square, years of experience and its square, the local unemployment rate, marital status, hours worked, current enrollment, industry, and occupation. \*\*\*significant at .001, \*\*significant at .01. \*significant at .05.

[a]Model 3 is estimated only for respondents with a valid value for previous (ln) wage; see text for explanation.

[b]Predicted percentage gain in wages from time $t$ to time $t + 2$. Predicted value is evaluated at variable means for all covariates and is then converted by exponentiating and subtracting 1.

tion as before). Some of this difference may derive from the restricted sample being used in this model. We suspect, however, that there is a substantive effect operating as well. Disadvantage accumulates over time, so that low returns to job changing early in the career pile up and begin to generate a low-wage path. That path, in turn, leads to low wage gains in the future.[10]

The explained variance for these models, though statistically significant, is quite low. This is because there is a certain amount of variability in short-term wage changes that inherently cannot be explained (because of measurement error, for example). One solution to this problem is to smooth raw wages of such short-term variability, and we do this using a mixed-effects model described in appendix D.[11] Refitting our models with these smoothed wages results in much higher $R^2$ values, as shown at the bottom of table 5.3. Thus, we are in fact explaining a significant amount of the systematic variability in wage gains with our models. The reason we present coefficients estimated on raw wages is that they are more accurate: invariably, the smoothed wages also smooth the effects of covariates (though the patterning of effects is identical).

In sum, the benefits of job shopping have changed. Traditionally a key mechanism by which young men generate early wage growth and set themselves on a path toward upward mobility, this strategy no longer appears to work for less educated youth. The majority of these young workers have seen marked declines in the returns to job changing during the 1980s and early 1990s, and an increasing number now experience real wage losses instead. By contrast, those with college backgrounds have done somewhat better, with greater short-term wage gains than were seen in the past.

The devaluing of high school graduates and dropouts in the labor market has been focused almost exclusively at the point of job changing: on-the-job wage gains have not deteriorated. This may reflect greater flexibility on the part of employers in adjusting the wages of new hires (as opposed to tenured workers), and it may also reflect differential sorting among changers and nonchangers that we have not captured with the control variables in the models. For example, it is well established that wage returns differ depending on the reason for a job change and whether or not workers are promoted within firms (Polsky 1999; Baker, Gibbs, and Holmstrom 1994). We do not have consistent data on these variables across both cohorts. Nevertheless, the ability of our models to identify a strong patterning of returns to changing and not changing jobs indicates that we are successfully tapping the basic dynamic of early career wage growth.

## Moves to Stable Jobs

The story emerging from these data is that the traditional career dynamic of a gradual movement toward higher-wage, stable jobs has collapsed in recent years for workers without college experience. So far, we have assembled several pieces of evidence: greater job instability and lower returns to job shopping. Both of these analyses, however, have focused on isolated two-year wage changes.

With a wider time window we can begin to look at the kinds of trajectories that these young workers are building, trajectories defined by both wage and job mobility. A full exploration of this long-term wage growth is taken up in the next chapter. We can, however, make a preliminary stab in this direction by asking whether movement toward more-stable jobs is paying off for workers who entered the labor market in the 1980s and 1990s. Previous research has established that "jobs that yield higher wage growth tend to survive, and sluggish wage growth is associated with impending mobility" (Topel and Ward 1992, 457; see also Bartel and Borjas 1981). The causal chain of this dynamic is complex and difficult to disentangle. Still, even a descriptive analysis of this relationship and how it has changed in recent years can be revealing.

As before, we use a model that predicts the wage change from time $t$ to time $t + 2$. This time, however, we look both forward and backward and record the stability of both the future job and the past job. Specifically, we look to the job in the "next period" (at time $t + 2$) and measure whether that job will be stable or short lived (that is, changed by time $t + 4$). Although this may seem a short span in which to assess a job's stability, it is, in fact, a good indicator, because even by their mid-thirties about half of all workers' jobs last less than two years. Similarly, we look at the respondent's job in the "prior period" (time $t - 2$) and measure whether that job was stable or short lived (that is, different from the time $t$ job). The question, then, is how these two covariates affect the size of the current wage change. The results are given in table 5.4. Note that we control for the usual demographic variables as well as past job instability (the number of previous job changes made). We also control for whether the respondent changed jobs in the current time period.[12] The goal here, then, is to isolate and focus on pathways of job mobility over time, controlling for aging effects and overall differences in job stability.

The baseline comparison group consists of observations in which the respondent changed jobs in all periods—the previous period, the current period, and the following period—and received a predicted increase in wages of 7.9 percent.[13] By comparison, workers who did

**Table 5.4  Wage Change Regression Results Using Prior and Next Job Changes**

| Variable | Estimate | Significance | Predicted Change in Wages[a] |
|---|---|---|---|
| Changed job in either prior or next period or both (constant) | .185 | *** | 7.9 |
| Did not change job in prior period | | | |
| High school or less | | | |
| Original cohort | −.027 | | 5.0 |
| Recent cohort | −.004 | | 7.5 |
| Some college or four-year degree | | | |
| Original cohort | −.044 | * | 3.2 |
| Recent cohort | .001 | | 8.0 |
| Did not change job in next period | | | |
| High school or less | | | |
| Original cohort | .085 | *** | 17.4 |
| Recent cohort | .030 | ** | 11.1 |
| Some college or four-year degree | | | |
| Original cohort | .091 | *** | 18.1 |
| Recent cohort | .088 | *** | 17.8 |
| Did not change current job | −.027 | *** | |
| Number of previous job changes | −.017 | *** | |
| Adjusted $R^2$ | .056 | | |
| Adjusted $R^2$ using smoothed wages | .303 | | |
| N (weighted) | 18,244 | | |

*Source:* Authors' compilation.
*Note:* Dependent variable is two-year change in log wages. The model also controls for the following variables: number of previous job changes, years of tenure and its square, years of experience and its square, the local unemployment rate, marital status, hours worked, industry, occupation, and currently enrolled. ***significant at .001, **significant at .01. *significant at .05.
[a]Predicted percentage increase in wages from time $t$ to time $t + 2$. Predicted value is evaluated at variable means for all covariates and is then converted by exponentiating and subtracting 1.

not change jobs in the prior period see lackluster wage growth. Thus there is no benefit to stability in the immediate past, confirming our general sense that job shopping yields a greater payoff early in the career. There is also a similar penalty for current stability, as shown in the lower portion of the table.

The impact of future stability is different. To wit, being on a path toward a more stable job pays off remarkably well: all such workers experienced significant increases in wages compared with those moving to short-lived jobs. The magnitude of the returns is quite substantial. Again, however, less educated workers in recent years are not garnering as large a return as in the past. Their average wage gain of 11.1 percent stands in contrast to the 17.4 percent gain captured in the original cohort, a substantial decline of about a third.

The traditional dynamic, that stabilization brings with it the attainment of solid wages, has weakened for this group of workers.[14] Thus we need to qualify the conclusions drawn in the previous section. On average, at any given point in time, it is true that the deterioration in wage gains for less educated youth stems from their inability to fully capture the returns to job shopping. Yet when we look at the sequencing of job changes, it becomes clear that they also have failed to capture fully the returns to eventual stability. This indicates that we are probably looking at processes both in the external and in the internal (firm) labor market.

## The Inequality of Wage Gains

So far we have focused on the average returns to job changing and seen stark differences by education group. This has given us some insight into the recent growth of "skill-based" inequality. We know, however, that there is more to the economy-wide rise in inequality than growing education differentials—the rise has occurred within education groups as well. This suggests that we should also examine the variability in the returns to job changing. This measure has been neglected in previous research, yet Michael Moore, Kip Viscusi, and Richard Zeckhauser (1999) have shown that the variability in overall wage growth is generated by a systematic unfolding of wage change paths that are permanent and not simply random noise.

Figure 5.2 plots the variances of the observed two-year wage changes by education, experience, and job change status, for both cohorts. It should come as no surprise that generally speaking, a job change results in more variable wage outcomes, especially once workers begin to differentiate themselves after several years in the labor market. Switching employers can result in substantial wage gains, but it can also result in wage losses—partly because the open market is more competitive than that internal to firms and partly because reasons for leaving a job differ and therefore have different consequences (see, for example, Stevens 1996). Staying put with one employer is unlikely to generate such polar outcomes, because the flexibility of

**Figure 5.2 Variance of Change in Log Wages**

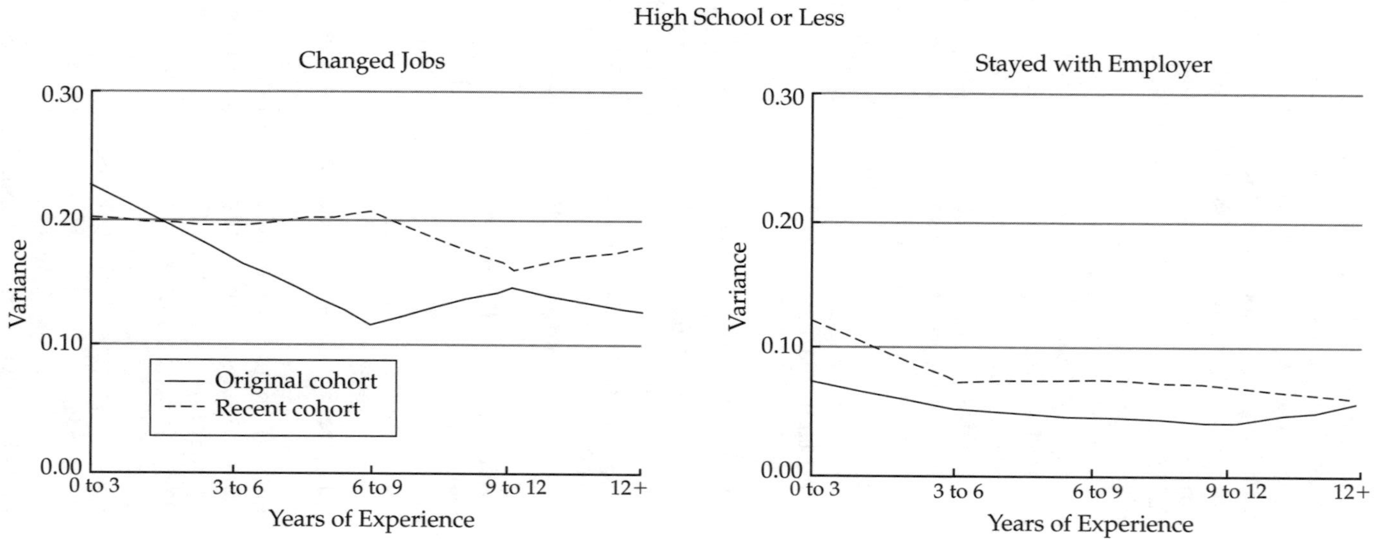

High School or Less

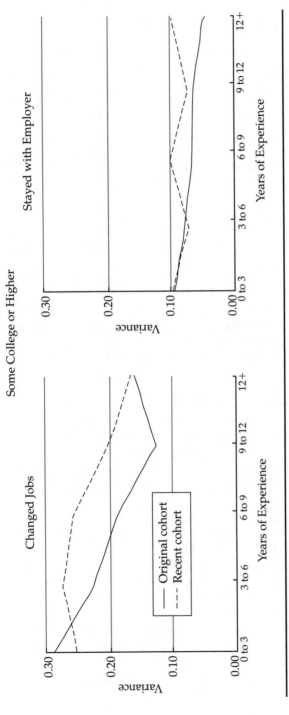

Some College or Higher

Changed Jobs                    Stayed with Employer

Variance                        Variance

0.30                            0.30

0.20                            0.20

0.10                            0.10

0.00                            0.00

0 to 3   3 to 6   6 to 9   9 to 12   12+        0 to 3   3 to 6   6 to 9   9 to 12   12+

Years of Experience             Years of Experience

—— Original cohort
- - - Recent cohort

*Source:* Authors' compilation.

wage setting on the part of employers is more constrained, by either implicit or formal contracts.

On both fronts, however, the recent cohort has clearly seen increased variability. Although the increase is most apparent among job changers, in fact it is just as strong, if not stronger, among nonchangers. If we focus on workers with at least three years of labor market experience (in order to hone in on the period of differentiation), we find that the variance for job changers increased by 26.3 percent and for nonchangers by 36.9 percent (these numbers do not differ appreciably by education). Thus the early career is generating more unequal and more uncertain wage outcomes for the recent cohort than it did in the past.

To render the increase in variance more tangible, we take a closer look at the distributions of wage changes using relative distribution methods. A natural way to compare the wage change distributions across the two cohorts is to overlay them, comparing the fraction of each group observed at each wage-gain level (again, using deflated wages). The relative distribution is essentially the density ratio between the two distributions as one moves along the earnings scale. In the discrete version of the relative distribution, we take the wage-gain distribution of the original cohort and divide it into deciles, each containing 10 percent of respondents. The relative distribution then measures the ratio of the fraction of the recent cohort to the fraction of the original cohort in each of these original cohort deciles. If the two distributions are the same, then the relative distribution will take the uniform value 1 throughout—10 percent of recent cohort respondents fall into each of the deciles of the original cohort. Alternatively, there could be relatively more or less of the recent cohort in some deciles. In this case, the value of the relative distribution will rise above 1 or fall below 1. For example, a value of 1.2 means that 12 percent of the recent cohort fell into that decile, compared with 10 percent of the original cohort. This represents a 20 percent greater probability of falling into that wage-gain decile for the recent cohort (additional details of the method can be found in appendix C).

In figure 5.3, we again focus on workers with at least three years of experience. We adjust for the median difference in wage gains between the two cohorts (because we have already documented that difference) and form the relative distribution of the two cohorts. The effect is like lining up the two distributions to match the medians, which isolates remaining differences in the shapes of the distributions. Because there are no marked differences by education or job change status, we do not disaggregate along these dimensions.[15] We

**Figure 5.3    Relative Density of the Change in Log Wages**

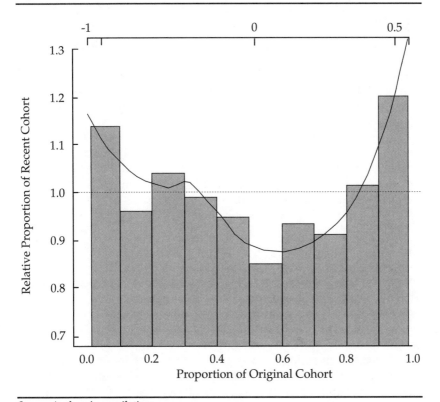

*Source:* Authors' compilation.
*Note:* Analysis based on median-matched wages.

have graphed both the discrete version of the relative distribution (shaded bars) and the continuous version (solid line).

The picture is clear. Inequality in wage gains has risen substantially for the recent cohort. If there had been no changes in median wage gains, then, as this figure indicates, the relative frequency of both very high and very low gains would have increased. For example, the percentage of workers with wage gains in the bottom decile of the distribution would have increased by 14.2 percent, and the increase in the top decile would have been 22.5 percent. However, we know that there has also been a downshift in median gains for less educated workers. The net effect of these two trends is that many young adults in the new economy will be lucky to experience any of the high and even mid-level wage gains that their predecessors enjoyed.

Again, this polarization has occurred among both well educated and less educated workers and among job changers and nonchangers alike. What we are seeing is an across-the-board increase in the inequality and uncertainty of wage gains. Because the link to eventual wage growth is so strong, we can expect that this rise in inequality will make itself felt in the long-term paths of upward mobility that these young workers are building.

## Summary

On average, the majority of lifetime wage growth occurs during a worker's first ten years in the labor market. To understand how inequality is generated, we need to focus on this formative period during which trajectories of upward mobility are effectively set.

Traditionally, these trajectories have had a distinctive character. At first, changing jobs is a key mechanism by which workers escape low-paying jobs and make the initial jumps up the income ladder that are so critical to later success. Then gradually, staying with one employer becomes more valuable, and the frequency of job changing declines. Although this may be the optimal progression—job shopping followed by stability—the paths that workers actually take show a wide range of patterns. The result is a considerable amount of heterogeneity and inequality in wage outcomes.

Because job changing is so strongly implicated in wage growth, it is natural to ask whether the rise in job instability has played a role in the wage distribution shifts of the past thirty years. We find that less educated workers in the recent cohort (those with a high school diploma or less) have failed to capture the returns to job changing precisely when it is most critical: in the early stages of job search. This is most apparent during the first decade in the labor market, though the difference persists throughout. By contrast, when these young workers stay with the same employer, we find little difference in the short-term wage gains captured by the two cohorts. The devaluing of high school graduates and dropouts in the labor market has been concentrated at the point of job changing, and there has been a significant rise in actual wage losses. Workers with college credits or college degrees have fared better. Their short-term wage gains have risen slightly in recent years, both when they do and when they do not change jobs.

These trends remain largely undiminished even after controlling for a host of other factors, such as demographic characteristics, industrial and occupational shifts, and the worker's record of past instability. With all controls in place, we predict a 17.1 percent return to job changing for less educated workers in the original cohort but only a 4.4 percent return in the recent cohort. In our sample, more than half of the recent cohort held a high school diploma or less by the end of survey, when respondents were in their mid-thirties. So for a substantial portion of the workforce, the value of one of the key routes to upward mobility, job shopping, has apparently collapsed, suggesting that a long-term deterioration in worker welfare may be under way.

These results stem from analyses that focus on isolated two-year intervals only. A more complex picture emerges when we begin to look at longer stretches of the paths that the young workers are building. All else equal, being on a path toward a more stable job pays off remarkably well: all workers experienced significant incremental gains in wages compared with those who moved to short-lived jobs. This clearly illustrates the joint progression of job and wage mobility. Here too, however, high-school-educated workers in recent years are not garnering as large a return as in the past. When moving toward a stable job, their average wage gain of 11.1 percent stands in contrast to the 17.4 percent gain captured in the original cohort, a substantial decline of about a third. Thus the traditional dynamic, that stabilization brings with it the attainment of solid wages, has also weakened for this group of workers.

Finally, trends in average wage gains are only part of the story. When we focus on the inequality of wage gains, we find that the recent cohort has clearly seen increased variability on all fronts, rising by roughly 25 to 35 percent. Thus the early career is generating more unequal and more uncertain wage outcomes than it did in the past. What is more, we found this shift among both educated and less educated workers and among both job changers and nonchangers. Given the importance of the early career, we can expect that polarization will also characterize long-term wage growth, regardless of education.

Wage growth (or the lack of it) early in the career can cascade into long-term changes in wage trajectories, so that a little inequality early on is likely to generate greater inequality down the line. Moreover, the incidence of job changing has increased at precisely the same time that the returns to it have changed. So it is not entirely clear how the isolated wage changes we have examined here are put together to generate long-term wage growth. The next chapter takes up a detailed analysis of the full mobility trajectories that these young workers build during the sixteen years that we see them.

# = Chapter 6 =

## Declines in Long-Term Economic Mobility

W E HAVE now documented a series of marked differences between the two cohorts of young workers—in terms of smooth entry into the labor market, the likelihood of early unemployment, the amount of job instability experienced, and the short-term returns to job changing. These findings strongly suggest that we should expect to see a cumulative impact on wages over time.

This chapter focuses on the long-term profiles of wage growth that these young workers achieve over the sixteen-year survey period. Wage growth is perhaps the most fundamental measure of a successful career, and it lies at the heart of the concept of economic mobility. When Americans talk of upward mobility, they are implicitly referencing the attainment of an income that will support a new range of lifestyle choices and new opportunities for themselves and their children. Although other indicators of mobility, such as attainment of a professional occupation or a college degree, may also be a part of the picture, these status markers would have less meaning in the absence of the greater earnings they typically command. By comparing long-term wage growth across the two cohorts, we are therefore directly measuring trends in upward mobility over the past three decades.

Previous research on changes in the wage structure has relied largely on cross-sectional data. The findings of this literature are now well known. Since the mid-1970s, average wages have stagnated, and wage inequality has grown (Levy and Murnane 1992; Mishel, Bernstein, and Schmitt 2001). These cross-sectional findings, however, do not directly translate into mobility terms. They are equally consistent with a scenario in which young workers start in low-wage jobs but by adulthood have moved to high-wage jobs, or one in which some youth get stuck in a cycle of low-wage jobs while others experience dramatic wage growth over their careers. It is obviously critical that we know which scenario holds, and only longitudinal data can tell us this.

We therefore begin our analysis by asking the key question of this book, namely, has upward mobility changed for the recent cohort? In particular, has it become more unequal? We answer this question by comparing wage trajectories across the two cohorts. The primary analytic question is whether permanent or transient effects are at work here. Have the trends documented in previous chapters cumulated into permanent changes in lifetime wage growth, or have they simply added some short-term volatility to the process? We find that wage growth has both stagnated and grown more unequal in the recent cohort and that these are permanent, long-term changes that will persist over the life course. The bottom line, for the public and policy makers alike, is that there has been a marked deterioration in upward mobility, one that threatens the meaning of prosperity in postindustrial America.

Identifying the factors that explain this trend is a complex task, because we want to understand how the entire wage profile is generated over the career. Small differences in single wage changes can cumulate into substantial differences over time. The amount of job changing will matter, and its impact will, in turn, depend on the acquired skills and experience of the worker as well as the opportunities afforded by occupational and industrial location. In sorting out the different forces at work, we pay close attention, of course, to the role that education has played; but we also pursue other effects that have been harder to pin down in cross-sectional research. In particular, the previous chapters suggest that rising job instability may offer a key explanation for the recent deterioration in the wage structure. Chapter 5 indicates that the immediate gains from changing employers have declined, especially for high-school-educated workers, and that the distribution of gains has become more unequal. We also know from chapter 4 that young men in the recent cohort are changing jobs more often. The joint effect of these short-term changes on long-term wage growth is still unclear, however, and testing for such a link constitutes the primary goal of this chapter.

We end by decomposing the overall changes in wage growth between the two cohorts, pulling out the impact of changes in composition and in rewards. We do this by, in effect, putting the recent cohort through the original economy. Had the economic conditions of the original cohort been repeated, would the recent cohort's lower levels of human capital, less favorable industry and occupational distributions, and higher job instability have produced essentially the same outcome? Or does the stagnation and polarization in economic mobility derive from the fact that the rules of the game have shifted, that the rewards for skills and stability have changed and become more unequal?

## Measures and Data

Throughout this chapter, we use the twelve-year matched files for the two cohorts.[1] We do so because one of the key variables we focus on is the cumulative number of employers reported by the respondents over time, and this must be constructed in an equivalent way across the cohorts. We also restrict the sample to workers sixteen years of age and older and to person-years in which paid employment is reported. The resulting sample sizes for the original and recent cohorts are reported in the top portion of table 6.1. As in previous chapters, we focus on hourly wages rather than yearly earnings because the latter are confounded by hours and weeks worked and the number of jobs held during the year.[2]

We use two measures to capture the effects of job changing: one captures job instability over the long term, the other instability over the short term. The long-term measure is the total number of different CPS employers the young workers had reported by their last interview. As always, we count only the main CPS employers in each year to ensure comparability across the cohorts. This means that we are underestimating the count of all employers a respondent has ever worked for. Because our interest here is in the relative difference in job stability between the cohorts, not the absolute number of employers, the CPS-based measure provides an accurate indicator. Note that this long-term measure is person specific. It does not vary over time but rather indexes instability over a worker's entire job history.

The short-term measure of instability is based on years of tenure with the current employer. Although tenure is typically thought of as time spent with an employer, it can also be interpreted as time spent since the last job change, so that someone with only six months of tenure, for example, is someone who has recently made a job change. In contrast to the cumulative number of employers, tenure varies over time for each person. We can therefore use it to see how recent job changes affect long-term wage growth. We modify the raw tenure measure by taking its complement: twenty years minus tenure. We chose the value of twenty because it just exceeds the maximum years of tenure observed in the samples. Taking the complement has no effect on our tenure coefficient estimates except to change their sign. This sign change is useful, however, because it means that the measure tracks recent job changes directly: the larger the measure, the

Table 6.1    Characteristics of Samples for Wage Profile Regressions, by Cohort

| Characteristic | Original Cohort | Recent Cohort |
|---|---|---|
| Unweighted N | | |
| Number of persons | 2,623 | 2,376 |
| Number of person-year observations | 18,520 | 18,857 |
| Number of complete person-year observations[a] | 17,994 | 18,085 |
| Mean number of observations contributed per person | 6.86 | 7.61 |
| | | |
| Weighted percentage | | |
| High school dropout | 18.0 | 17.1 |
| High school graduate | 34.4 | 43.8 |
| Some college experience | 24.2 | 20.4 |
| Bachelor's degree or higher | 23.3 | 18.7 |
| Currently enrolled | 35.4 | 27.3 |
| Part-time worker | 15.7 | 17.6 |
| Married | 58.1 | 40.4 |
| Goods-producing industry | 50.7 | 45.3 |
| Low-end service industry | 26.6 | 36.7 |
| High-end service industry | 22.7 | 18.0 |
| Blue-collar occupations | 49.3 | 48.8 |
| Sales, service, and clerical occupations | 22.2 | 26.2 |
| Professional, managerial, and technical occupations | 28.5 | 25.0 |
| | | |
| Weighted mean | | |
| Log real wage (1999 dollars) | 2.53 | 2.39 |
| Cumulative number of CPS employers at last interview | 4.93 | 5.24 |
| Age (rescaled to age − sixteen) | 9.46 | 9.58 |
| Age squared[b] | −15.84 | −14.78 |
| Years of experience | 7.20 | 7.73 |
| Years of experience squared | 71.41 | 81.76 |
| Years of tenure | 2.71 | 2.69 |
| Tenure squared | 17.38 | 16.93 |
| Local unemployment rate (percentage) | 5.97 | 7.64 |

Source: Authors' compilation.
[a]These are the observations used in all regression analyses.
[b]Age squared is residualized so that it is orthogonal to age, and thus it may be negative.

more recent the job change. If the coefficient on this measure is positive, it represents a wage benefit, and if negative, a wage penalty. This helps to highlight a key feature of the cohort changes we document here: it is not that the benefits to high tenure have increased but rather that the penalties for low tenure have increased. For the remainder of the chapter, we refer to this variable as the "tenure complement."

As discussed in chapter 2, we use age or experience, rather than calendar year, as our index of time. Both measures have the advantage of smoothing over business cycle effects because observations with the same ages or experience are pooled across multiple survey years. The descriptives for the variables used in the wage profile regressions are given in the lower portion of table 6.1. The variables are measured identically in the two cohorts and all vary over time, except for the total number of jobs reported in the last interview. Occupation has been collapsed into three categories: blue collar; service, sales, and clerical; and professional, managerial, and technical. Industry has also been collapsed into three categories: goods producing (manufacturing, construction, mining, transportation and communication, agriculture),[3] low-end service (wholesale and retail trade, business and personal services, entertainment), and high-end service (finance, insurance, and real estate, professional services, and public administration). Education is collapsed into four categories: high school dropouts, high school graduates, those with some college experience, and those who attained a four-year college degree. All analyses use the modified weights provided by the NLS (see the discussion on missed interviews in chapter 2).

## Trends in Long-Term Wage Mobility

To start, we look at changes in wages across the two cohorts, treating our data set as if it were a simple cross-sectional sample. In figure 6.1, we see several strong trends by final years of education completed. In general, the wages of high school dropouts show little growth as they age, whereas both high school graduates and those with some college experience show a steady moderate rise. College graduates start out slowly but have the steepest slopes, with sustained growth well into their late thirties. In all four education groups, however, the recent cohort lags behind. Among high school dropouts, even the meager wage gains achieved by the original cohort are not attained in the recent cohort—the median worker in this group did not manage to double his wages over twenty years. High school graduates and those with some college experience also show sharp declines relative to the original cohort, with the discrepancy growing larger over time. Recall that these three education groups, rather than being a small set of stragglers, are the majority of the population, constituting nearly 70 percent of the recent cohort. College graduates in the two cohorts are much closer in their wage attainment, but even here the median worker in the recent cohort is consistently below his predecessor in the original cohort, by 5 to10 percent.[4]

In figure 6.2, we plot the trends in log wage dispersion by age. For the original cohort, there is little trend over time, in any of the education groups. For the recent cohort, by contrast, only high school dropouts show relatively constant variance over time. All other education groups show a marked increase in wage variance as they age, with slightly larger increases among the two college-educated groups. A growing fraction of the rising wage dispersion in this cohort is thus within education group. This trend, found also in other studies, suggests that a substantial portion of the growth in inequality is not driven by changes in the education premium.

In short, our cross-sectional evidence tallies with the findings from previous research: young workers in recent years have seen a marked stagnation and polarization in their wages. As we argue at the outset, this potentially signals a deterioration in wage mobility among young workers. A conclusive statement about trends in mobility requires that we shift to an analysis of longitudinal wage profiles. Each individual worker builds his own distinctive wage trajectory as he grows older. Some of those trajectories are steep, with substantial wage increases each year, and others are flat, with little wage growth over time. To understand what has happened to the mobility paths of young workers in recent years, we must base our analysis on these profiles. For example, it could be that during the 1980s and 1990s, short-term fluctuations in wages became more prevalent as job instability rose. This is the argument made by Gottschalk and Moffitt (1994), Moffitt and Gottschalk (1995), and Ann Stevens (1996). Workers' wages in the recent cohort might show more variability from one year to the next, but the overall spread of their wage trajectories would otherwise remain unchanged. This scenario could account for the greater wage variation in figure 6.2 without indicating any greater inequality in the life chances of the young workers.[5]

Alternatively, it could be that the long-run, permanent growth in wages has, in fact, become more polarized and unequal in recent years—that there are more workers with steep wage trajectories, more workers with flat wage trajectories, and correspondingly fewer workers with mid-level wage growth. Initial evidence along these lines has been shown in previous research (Duncan et al. 1996; Haider 1997). This scenario is much more troubling. The trajectories that we are measuring for the two cohorts cover as much as the first sixteen years of wage growth, and we know that the majority of lifetime wage gains are made during this period. If we find greater permanent

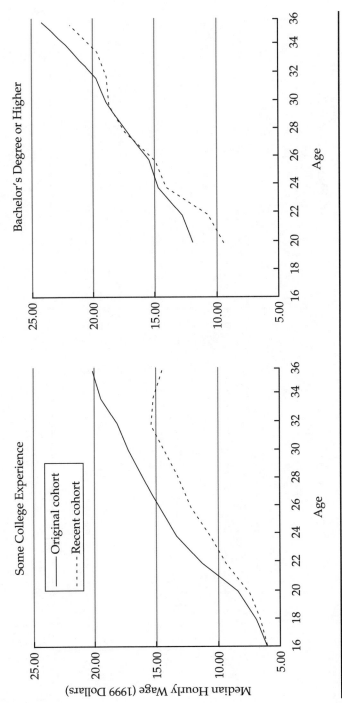

Some College Experience

Bachelor's Degree or Higher

Original cohort
Recent cohort

Median Hourly Wage (1999 Dollars)

Age

25.00
20.00
15.00
10.00
5.00

16  18  20  22  24  26  28  30  32  34  36

*Source:* Authors' compilation.

**Figure 6.2   Trends in the Variance of Hourly Wages**

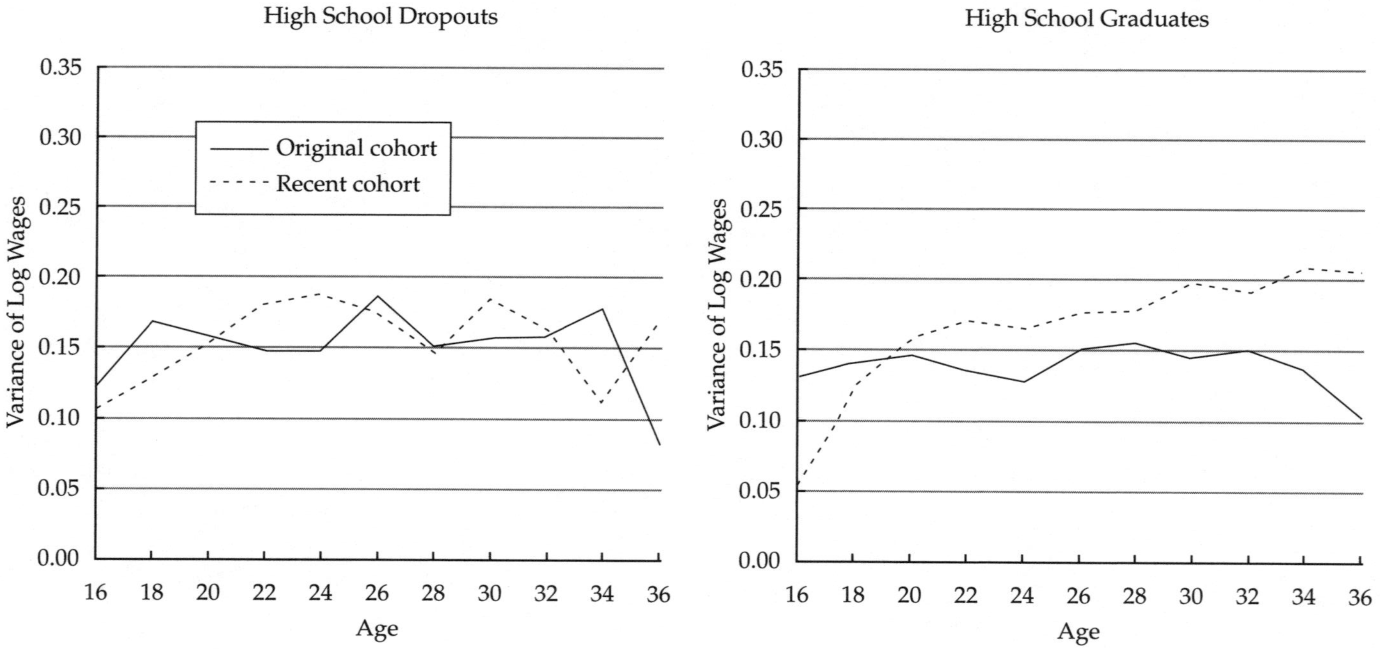

High School Dropouts

High School Graduates

Variance of Log Wages

Age

Original cohort
Recent cohort

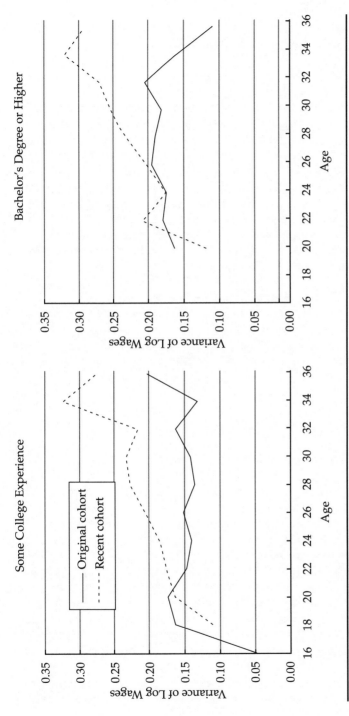

Some College Experience

Bachelor's Degree or Higher

Variance of Log Wages

Age

Original cohort
Recent cohort

*Source:* Authors' compilation.

inequality in this time span, then we are effectively documenting a lifetime of greater inequality in economic mobility.

## The Model

Evidence for these two scenarios can be found by comparing the wage growth trajectories of the two cohorts and asking whether these trajectories have become more unequal in recent years, net of any short-term variability in wage growth. The model we use employs a set of fixed effects to capture the average curve of the wage profile, a set of random effects to isolate the heterogeneity in permanent wage gains among individuals, and a residual term to represent the transitory components of wage change within each individual profile.

The permanent and transitory components of wage profile heterogeneity are specified as follows. We start with a fixed-effect model based on a quadratic specification:

$$y_{it} = \beta_0 + \beta_1 age_{it} + \beta_2 age_{it}^2 + e_{it},$$

where $y_{it}$ is the log of the real wage of individual $i$ in year $t$ and $\beta_0$, $\beta_1$, and $\beta_2$ are the fixed-effect parameters. This part of the model is used to capture the average wage profile. The residual $e_{it}$ is then decomposed into a permanent component $(p_{it})$ and a transitory component $(u_{it})$:

$$e_{it} = p_{it} + u_{it},$$

where we model the permanent component as

$$p_{it} = b_{0i} + b_{1i} age_{it} + b_{2i} age_{it}^2.$$

Thus $p_{it}$ is a random quadratic curve representing the deviation of the individual-specific wage profile from the average wage profile.

Figure 6.3 presents a schematic understanding of the model being estimated. The top panel shows what an average wage trajectory looks like. Wages start out low when the worker is young, rise steeply during the pivotal ages of job search when work experience is gained and skills are developed, and then eventually reach a plateau. In later years, the worker typically holds a long-term job with one employer, and wages grow incrementally through small but consistent yearly increases.

In terms of our model, this trajectory is the average trajectory across all workers, and it is estimated with the fixed-effect parame-

**Figure 6.3    An Intuitive Explanation of the Mixed-Effects Model**

The Average Profile of Wage Growth, Fixed-Effects Parameters

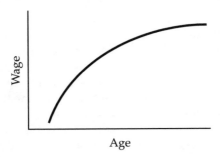

The Deviation of Individual Profiles from the Average Profile:
Permanent Variance

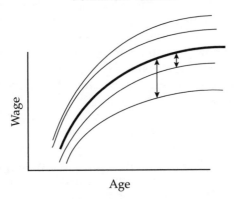

The Remaining Short-Term Fluctuation in Wages: Transitory Variance

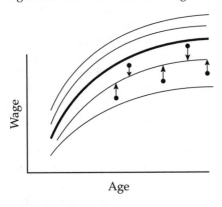

*Source:* Authors' compilation.

ters. To approximate the curvature of this average profile, we estimate a quadratic in age.[6] This allows us to identify the initial wage level (the intercept), the slope upward (the linear age term), and then the plateauing in the older age ranges (the squared age term).

In the middle panel, we recognize that in fact different workers have different long-run trajectories: some are higher and steeper, while others are lower and flatter. Moreover, as we have seen, these differences become more pronounced as young workers differentiate themselves in the labor market. It is the variation in these trajectories that is of interest to us: specifically, whether the fanning out of the individual profiles has become more pronounced and significant in recent years. Because these profiles represent the permanent and long-run shape of individual workers' wage growth, we call the total variation across these profiles the "permanent variance."

Finally, in the bottom panel, we recognize that from one year to the next, individual workers will experience short-term fluctuations around their long-run trajectory. Reasons for such fluctuations include job changes within and between firms, business cycle effects, returning to school part-time, and so forth. Because any systematic gains or losses from these effects are eventually captured in the wage profiles, we therefore call the residual variation around the permanent profiles the "transitory variance."

In the analysis that follows, we estimate this model separately for the original and recent cohorts. The key question is whether the recent cohort has seen an increase in the permanent variance, the transitory variance, or both when compared with the original cohort. A significant increase in the permanent variance indicates that the mobility paths of young workers have become more unequal in recent years.

Table 6.2 shows the estimates of this model fitted separately within each cohort. We start with the fixed effects, given in the top part of the table. To illustrate the combined effect of the three fixed terms, figure 6.4 shows the predicted average wage profile for each cohort. The "typical" profiles for the two cohorts start off at fairly similar wage levels (the intercepts are not significantly different), but the rate of wage growth is much lower for the recent cohort (the linear age terms are significantly different), and this is what drives their long-term wage attainment. By the time they reach the age of thirty, their wages are 20 percent below those of their predecessors. Thus, the fixed-effects parameters are effectively recovering the stagnation in overall wage growth documented in figure 6.1.

These are the average wage trajectories for the two cohorts. How much do individual workers deviate from the average trajectories?

Table 6.2    Results from Baseline Mixed-Effects Models for Each Cohort

| Variable | Original Cohort | Recent Cohort | Significance of Cohort Difference |
|---|---|---|---|
| Coefficients of fixed effects | | | |
| Intercept | 1.7276 | 1.7690 | |
| Age[a] | .1271 | .0902 | ** |
| Age squared | −.0038 | −.0023 | ** |
| Variance components | | | |
| Fixed effects | .1098 | .0637 | ** |
| Random effects | .1878 | .2157 | ** |
| Permanent | .1095 | .1331 | ** |
| Intercept | .0765 | .0900 | ** |
| Age | .0306 | .0405 | * |
| Age squared | .0025 | .0028 | |
| Transient | .0783 | .0826 | ** |
| Total | .2976 | .2795 | |

*Source:* Authors' compilation.
[a]Age is rescaled to age − sixteen.
**Difference significant at $p < 0.01$ level; *Difference significant at $p < 0.05$ level.

The lower part of the table gives the estimated variance components for each cohort.[7] The amount of variance "explained" by age (the fixed effects) is significantly smaller for the recent cohort, and the residual variation (the random effects) is significantly larger. Most of the gain in residual variation derives from an increase in the permanent variance for the recent cohort: this variance component is 22 percent larger in the recent cohort, and the difference is statistically significant, indicating that the permanent, long-run wage profiles of young workers have become significantly more unequal in recent years. The transitory variances also differ significantly between the two cohorts, indicating that the amount of short-term, year-to-year wage fluctuation has increased as well, but the magnitude of that increase is much smaller, less than 6 percent.[8]

In short, the evidence clearly shows that wage growth over the long run has become more unequal, not simply more noisy. In order to pinpoint where this increased inequality is coming from, we can examine the variances for each of the three random effects. The intercept and linear random effects are considerably larger for the recent cohort, and the differences are statistically significant. The quadratic random effect is not significantly different between the two cohorts. Thus, the increased inequality for the recent cohort is being driven by increased variance in both the level and spread of the profiles.[9]

To get a more intuitive feel for the relative contributions of the

**Figure 6.4    Mean Estimated Wage Profiles from the Baseline Model, by Cohort**

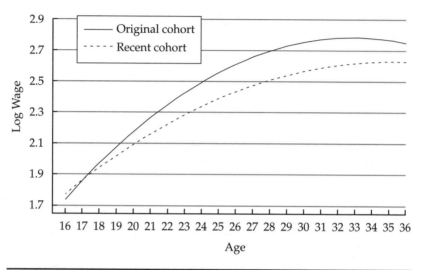

*Source:* Authors' compilation.

permanent and transitory components to the changes in wage dispersion, we can plot the estimates of these components by cohort and age.[10] These are shown in figure 6.5. Note that for both cohorts, the permanent variances increase with age while the transitory variances decline with age. As we might expect, short-term wage fluctuations are substantial in the teenage years and the early twenties but become much less important by the mid-thirties. At that point, the permanent, long-run variability in wages takes over in importance.

The main message from these graphs, however, is that, starting at around age twenty-four, the recent cohort experiences progressively stronger growth in the permanent variance, and by the mid-thirties the difference is quite pronounced. No such difference is seen in the transitory graph.

How have these two trends in mean and variance altered the structure of mobility? Using this model we can predict the permanent wage gains that a young worker might expect to make by the time he reaches the age of thirty-six.[11] Figure 6.6 shows the distribution of these permanent wage gains for the two cohorts, and their relative distribution.[12] In the top panel, the stagnation and polarization of wage growth for the recent cohort is again immediately evident. The baseline model estimate for the median worker in the original cohort

**Figure 6.5 Permanent and Transitory Variances from Baseline Model, by Cohort**

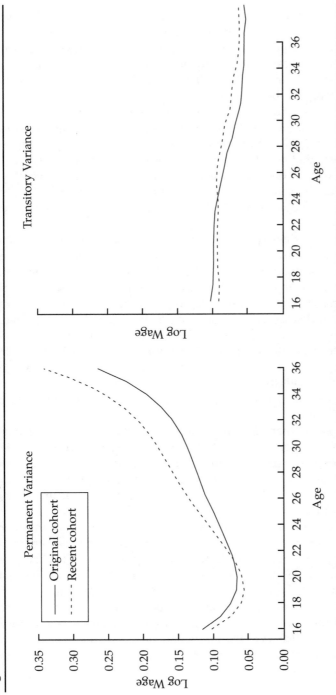

*Source:* Authors' compilation.

is an hourly wage increase of 277 percent, that is, between the ages of sixteen and thirty-six his wages had nearly tripled. In real 1999 dollars, this is a gain of about $9.96 an hour. By comparison, the median worker in the recent cohort saw an increase of 234 percent—in real dollar terms, a gain of only $7.90 an hour. Thus, median wage growth over the long run has dropped by 21 percent.

Things have also worsened for workers at the bottom of the distribution. A stark illustration of this point is the percentage of workers who saw no growth in wages whatsoever from sixteen to thirty-six. We estimate that about 1.3 percent of the original cohort saw either no wage growth or declining wage growth over the entire twenty-year period. For the recent cohort, this number jumped to 5.7 percent—a dramatic increase, given the extreme lack of upward mobility being tapped here.

The relative density graph in figure 6.6 is a good way to quantify the decline and polarization in wage growth (appendix C contains a description of these methods). Nearly 25 percent of the recent cohort had wage gains that would have put them in the bottom decile of the original cohort's distribution. Moreover, in the central three deciles of the original distribution—what used to be the heart of middle-class wage growth—there are now 40 percent fewer workers in the recent cohort. Once we get to the top decile, there is near parity in the fractions of the two cohorts: these workers have managed to hold their ground. The majority of young adults in recent years, however, have fallen far behind, with a big pileup at what used to be the bottom of the distribution.

The upshot, then, is a marked deterioration and polarization in wage growth over the past three decades. Because we were able to isolate long-term trends from short-term fluctuations, there is only one conclusion to be drawn: the structure of economic mobility in this country has been fundamental transformed, to the detriment of the majority of the workforce.

Why has this occurred? Up to this point, we have not introduced any explanatory variables. From previous research, we know that part of the explanation lies in the changing returns to education and experience as well as changes that have taken place in the industrial and occupational structure. As the field has only recently moved to the analysis of longitudinal data sets, however, few researchers have looked at the effects of job changing (but see Gottschalk and Moffitt 1994; Stevens 1996). We therefore start our "explanation" with a descriptive look at the relationship between job instability and wage growth over time.

**Figure 6.6    Predicted Real Wage Growth from Age Sixteen to Thirty-Six, by Cohort**

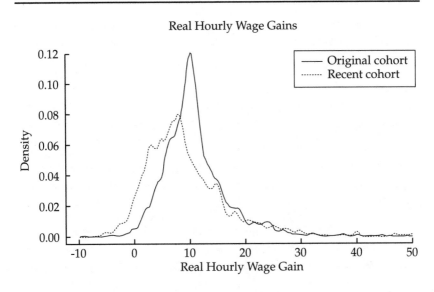

Real Hourly Wage Gains

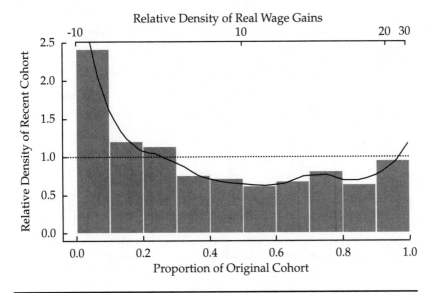

Relative Density of Real Wage Gains

*Source:* Authors' compilation.

## Basic Patterns in Long-Term Job Stability

From previous chapters, we know that job instability has grown significantly in the recent cohort, especially among workers in their mid-thirties. As a result, the total number of employers accumulated over time has increased. We also have seen that the immediate wage returns from a job change have declined and become more unequal, especially for less educated workers.

What about the impact on wage growth over the long term? Ultimately, it is the cumulative sequence of job changes that matters, and we address its effects shortly in a model-based setting. It is worthwhile to take a quick descriptive look, however, to get a feel for the association between job changes and long-term wage attainment.

In figure 6.7 we plot median wages, by experience, for those who did and did not report a job change in the period preceding the wage observation. We residualize wages for age and experience. By doing so, we isolate how each person is doing relative to what we would expect, given their age and experience. If they are doing as well as expected, the residualized wage will equal zero. If the value is above or below zero, it represents, in percentage terms, how much better or worse than expected the wage is for someone of this age and experience.

The comparison is quite striking. Among workers who did not recently change jobs, median wages look pretty similar for the two cohorts, regardless of experience level. Among workers who did recently change jobs, however, we see a strong wage penalty in the recent cohort, especially as work experience is accumulated. A worker in the original cohort who had twelve or more years of experience and who had just changed jobs was earning about 10 percent less than his counterpart who stayed put with the same employer. This penalty has more than doubled in the recent cohort, to 25 percent.

Do these short-term job instability effects differ by education level? The answer to this question can be found in table 6.3, which uses the wage reported at the last interview.[13] In the models that follow we try to isolate these short-term effects using tenure as our indicator (again, very short tenures mean a job change has recently occurred), so we use that measure here to establish its baseline effects. We categorize tenure into two periods, zero to four years and more than four years.[14] Focusing on the bottom line of the table, where the wage differences are shown, we can see that the growing penalty for short tenures is largely confined to less educated workers, more than doubling, from 14 percent to about 30 percent. Among college graduates, by contrast,

**Figure 6.7   Wage Differences Between Workers Who Did and Did Not Change Jobs Last Period**

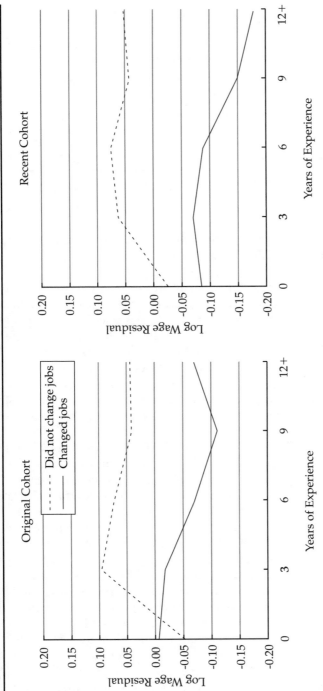

*Source:* Authors' compilation.

**Table 6.3    Final Log Hourly Wage, by Tenure, Cohort, and Education**

| Tenure | No College Degree | | Bachelor's Degree or Higher | |
|---|---|---|---|---|
| | Original Cohort | Recent Cohort | Original Cohort | Recent Cohort |
| Zero to four years | 2.69 | 2.39 | 2.89 | 2.87 |
| Four or more years | 2.83 | 2.69 | 3.06 | 3.02 |
| Low-tenure penalty | −0.14 | −0.30 | −0.17 | −0.15 |

*Source:* Authors' compilation.
*Note:* Sample is respondents aged thirty or older. Wages are in 1999 log dollars.

the penalty has remained fairly stable at 15 to 17 percent. It is important to understand that what we are showing is truly a penalty: wages in the higher-tenure groups have not risen.

The fact that job instability is harmful later in the career has been well documented. But why is it even more detrimental now than in the past? A number of explanations are possible. From the perspective of labor economics, it could be argued that employer-specific skills have become more important in the new economy, and so workers who never stay long with one employer lose out in terms of wage growth. Although plausible, this explanation goes against the argument of many articles in the popular and business press that stress the growing importance of generalized, as opposed to firm-specific, skills.

Another interpretation is that workers who change jobs are more likely to have unstable work habits and poor skills. This is a selection bias argument, in which the emphasis is on unobserved heterogeneity in the workers: we may not have measured the latent traits that make for job instability, but employers recognize them, and the wage penalty is the signal of that recognition. To explain the increased size of the penalty for the recent cohort, however, one would have to argue that these recent job changers are more problematic than were job changers in the past. If job instability had fallen, the argument that the remaining unstable workers were more problematic might be plausible. Job instability has risen, however, and this is not consistent with a simple argument for increased adverse selection.

A more realistic argument might be that these rising penalties reflect what has happened on the demand side of the labor market: the growth of low-wage jobs in the retail trade and business services industries that are frequently characterized by high turnover, the lack of career ladders, and unstable work hours. The cycle of bad pay and frequent job changes shown for the recent cohort may, at least in part, be tied to the expansion of this sector of the economy.

## Factors Driving the Trends in Wage Mobility

We cannot conclusively adjudicate among these alternative interpretations, but we can make a start by examining whether the effects of job instability on wages remain significant once other variables are controlled for. To do this, we take the baseline mixed-effects model (table 6.2), add our two measures of job stability, and then step in a series of other explanatory variables. Again, the two job change variables capture long-term instability (as measured by total number of jobs accumulated at final interview) and short-term stability (as measured by the tenure complement).

We are interested in two features of these expanded models. The fixed effects are of interest because they allow us to ask which variables have become more or less important in recent years, whether job instability matters, and if so, whether its effects are comparable in magnitude to those of other variables. Given the random-effects specification, the fixed-effects coefficients for the variables that change over time should be interpreted as "within-person" effects: they represent the impact on the individual's wage profile. For example, higher education may yield a greater "kick" for the recent cohort and more strongly bump up the wage profile when a college degree has been attained. Working in the low end of the service sector, on the other hand, may yield a negative shock, moving the wage profile downward. The only variable that cannot be interpreted in this manner is the total number of employers accumulated. This variable does not change over time and so it can only move the entire profile up or down; it does not have an impact in any one year.

In addition to the fixed effects, we are also interested in how the new explanatory variables affect our estimates of the permanent variance. For example, if changing returns to education explain why the recent cohort's profiles have become more unequal, then controlling for this variable will more strongly reduce the permanent variance of the recent cohort than that of the original cohort. If we are able to eliminate fully the cohort differences in permanent variance, we will have identified a plausible explanation for rising inequality in upward mobility.

Finally, we should also explain how we have specified the effect of education. The typical approach in wage regressions is to use high school graduates as the baseline comparison group; successive dummy variables then pull out the higher wages for more-educated workers. If we were to use this approach in our data, we would undoubtedly find that the returns to a college degree have "risen" substantially in the recent cohort. This is true, but only in a relative sense. As is clear in figure 6.1, college graduates in the recent cohort did not gain ground in absolute terms—they simply lost the least, while less educated workers lost more. This point has not received nearly enough attention in all the talk about the growing importance of skill in the global economy. To cement it firmly throughout, we take the simple expedient of making college graduates the baseline comparison group. Wages for college graduates have moved the least across the two cohorts and therefore provide a steady target. Dummy variables for less educated workers will then pull out the strong absolute declines in wages experienced by these groups.

## Fixed-Effects Results

With that in mind, we now begin to add variables to the baseline model presented in table 6.2. We start by adding controls for work experience to the model, focusing on the impact of job instability. The results are given in model 1 of table 6.4. The effect of long-term instability, as measured by the total number of employers, is significantly negative for both cohorts, and the difference between them is not statistically significant. Each additional employer exacts about a 1 percent penalty in wages. This is not a large effect, but for the top 10 percent of job changers, who have had nine or more jobs, the impact will become pronounced. The effect of recent job changes, as measured by the tenure complement, is also significantly negative for both cohorts, but this time the recent cohort is significantly more penalized. The coefficients do not at first glance look large, but in fact they are substantial when multiplied by years of tenure. For example, compare a recent job changer (someone who has not yet accumulated any tenure) with a worker who has accumulated ten years of tenure. The difference in their wages will be the value of the coefficient times the tenure complement (20 − 10). Using this comparison, the low-tenure wage penalty is about 6 percent in the original cohort but 15 percent in the recent. In this model, then, the short-term effects of job instability are stronger than the long-term effects.

When we control for education (model 2), the penalties for long-term instability are reduced by nearly 50 percent. This drop in the coefficient indicates a relatively strong correlation between long-term instability and education. The penalty is still significantly negative for both cohorts, though for the recent cohort its significance is only borderline. The impact of short-term instability, by contrast, is not affected when we control for education; it remains as strong as before.

The education effects are also interesting. In both cohorts, less educated workers have substantially lower wages than college graduates. The direct wage penalty for high school dropouts has not changed much across the two cohorts. High school graduates, however, have gone from a 3 percent penalty in the original cohort to a 13 percent penalty in the recent. Moreover, for both groups the "lack of skill" penalty grows with years of work experience, a process that has accelerated in the recent cohort. For high school dropouts, wages fall behind by about 1 percent for each year of experience in the original cohort but by almost 3 percent a year in the recent. For high school graduates, the rates are 1.7 and 2.5 percent a year, respectively. What we are seeing here is a clear cumulation of disadvantage over time. The coefficients for workers with some college experience are significant only for the main effects, not for the interactions—here there is simply a flat penalty rather than one that grows with experience.

In model 3 we introduce a range of other covariates. First note that they do not appreciably change our estimates of the job instability penalties. Whatever is generating these penalties, it must be fairly widespread and not simply a function of industrial and occupational shifts or lower rates of marriage among job changers. Among the education variables, only one change occurs with the introduction of the new variables: the penalty for those who have some college experience declines by about a third in both cohorts. The drop is largely explained by the frequency of part-time work and enrollment among this group. Still, the penalty for those with some college credits remains significantly higher in the recent cohort.

Turning to the block of new variables that we have entered, perhaps the most striking finding is that almost all of them have the same effects for both cohorts. The strongest impacts come from the industry and occupation variables. Our reference group comprises blue-collar workers in the traditional goods-producing sector. In both cohorts, this continues to be a relatively privileged position in terms of wages. Working in the low end of the service sector will typically bring in about 14 percent less, and even working in the higher end of the service sector tends to reduce relative wages by about 10 percent for these young men. The occupation effects are, by comparison, much smaller. Sales and clerical workers make about 3 percent less, while professional, technical, and managerial workers make about 3 percent more.

The industry penalties are comparable in magnitude to the penal-

**Table 6.4  Results from Full Mixed-Effects Regression for Each Cohort**

| Variable | Model 1 Original Cohort | Model 1 Recent Cohort | Signif. | Model 2 Original Cohort | Model 2 Recent Cohort | Signif. | Model 3 Original Cohort | Model 3 Recent Cohort | Signif. | Model 4 Original Cohort | Model 4 Recent Cohort | Signif. |
|---|---|---|---|---|---|---|---|---|---|---|---|---|
| Intercept | 1.910 | 2.096 | ** | 2.075 | 2.329 | ** | 2.303 | 2.608 | ** | 2.277 | 2.457 | ** |
| Age | .094 | .034 | ** | .083 | .026 | ** | .063 | .004[a] | ** | .063 | .003[a] | ** |
| Age squared | −.003 | −.002 | ** | −.003 | −.002 | ** | −.002 | −.001 | ** | −.002 | −.001 | ** |
| Experience | .049 | .076 | ** | .055 | .089 | ** | .046 | .083 | ** | .047 | .085 | ** |
| Experience squared | −.002 | −.002 | | −.001 | −.001 | | −.001 | −.001 | | −.001 | −.001 | |
| Education [bachelor's degree or higher] | | | | | | | | | | | | |
| High school dropout | | | | −.190 | −.204 | | −.151 | −.172 | | −.117[b] | .016[a] | |
| High school graduate | | | | −.027[a] | −.127 | ** | −.056 | −.131 | ** | −.022[a] | .060[a] | |
| Some college experience | | | | −.181 | −.264 | ** | −.118 | −.179 | ** | −.084[a] | .013[a] | |
| Education × experience | | | | | | | | | | | | |
| High school dropout × experience | | | | −.011 | −.029 | ** | −.013 | −.030 | ** | −.014 | −.032 | ** |
| High school graduate × experience | | | | −.017 | −.025 | ** | −.012 | −.022 | ** | −.013 | −.025 | ** |
| Some college × experience | | | | .003[a] | −.003[a] | | .001[a] | −.005[b] | ** | .000[a] | −.008 | ** |
| Currently enrolled | | | | | | | −.076 | −.097 | | −.076 | −.096 | |
| Part-time worker | | | | | | | −.068 | −.040 | ** | −.068 | −.040 | ** |
| Married | | | | | | | .054 | .039 | | .054 | .039 | |
| Local unemployment rate | | | | | | | −.006 | −.008 | | −.006 | −.008 | |

| | | | | | | | | |
|---|---|---|---|---|---|---|---|---|
| Industry [goods producing] | | | | | | | | |
| Wholesale and retail trade, business services | | | | | −.137 | −.142 | −.137 | −.142 |
| Finance, insurance, and real estate, professional services, public administration | | | | | −.109 | −.102 | −.109 | −.102 |
| Occupation [craftsman, operatives, and kindred] | | | | | | | | |
| Sales, service, and clerical | | | | | −.025 | −.030 | −.025 | −.030 |
| Professional, technical, and managerial | | | | | .034 | .035 | .034 | .034 |
| Cumulative number of employers at last interview | −.014 | −.009 | −.009 | −.005[b] | −.009 | −.005[b] | −.009 | −.005[b] |
| Tenure complement | −.006 | −.015 ** | −.008 | −.016 ** | −.009 | −.017 ** | −.008 | −.009 |
| No college degree × tenure complement | | | | | | | −.002 | −.010** |
| Permanent variance component | .107 | .123 ** | .101 | .103 | .091 | .091 | .091 | .091 |

*Source:* Authors' compilation.

*Note:* Age is rescaled to age − sixteen. Unless otherwise indicated, parameter estimates are significant at $p < .01$ level.

[a] Parameter estimate significant at $p < .1$.

[b] Parameter estimate is not significant.

** Cohort estimates are significantly different at $p < .01$ level.

* Cohort estimates are significantly different at $p < .05$ level.

ties for low tenure and education. The fact that these effects are the same for both cohorts means that industry contributes to cohort wage differences only through changes in the mix of available jobs. That helps to simplify the story. We know from table 6.1 that the fraction of person-years spent in the relatively privileged goods-producing sector has dropped from 51 percent in the original cohort to 45 percent in the recent, while the person-years spent in the low end of the service sector has risen from 27 to 37 percent. Given that wages in the latter sector are lower than in the former, this compositional shift will have a negative effect on the wages of the recent cohort.

Up to now, we have kept the job instability and education effects separate. However, we have seen several pieces of evidence that there is an interaction between education and job instability. In model 4, we add a simple interaction term that allows workers without a college degree to have a different penalty for short-term instability (the tenure complement). This term is insignificant in the original cohort. In the recent cohort, by contrast, the interaction term is large and highly significant. In magnitude, the instability penalty for the reference group, college graduates, is not different between the two cohorts. The coefficient of $-0.008$ means that a college graduate who has just changed jobs is likely to earn about 8 percent less than a person with ten years of tenure. Because the interaction term is not significant for the original cohort, this will be the penalty for all the other education groups as well. For less educated workers in the recent cohort, however, the penalty for recent job changes is more than doubled by an additional $-0.012$, raising the total wage drop to a hefty 20 percent under this scenario.

The upshot is as follows: all of the rising penalty for job instability that we have documented in the recent cohort has been borne by less educated workers. Moreover, the interaction term in model 4 erases the significance of the direct education effects in both cohorts.[15] What this means is that the lack of a college degree has, indeed, contributed to the worsening labor market position of less educated workers over the past three decades, but it has done so through two distinct mechanisms: declining returns to work experience and greater penalties for short-term job instability.

We conclude by illustrating how the instability effects might play out for a typical high school graduate. In figure 6.8, we plot predicted profiles for high-school-educated workers with different employment histories. Three employment histories are shown. The first represents a worker with a very stable history, who has had a total of three employers over the fifteen years, with the last job change occurring in the fifth year of his career. The second represents a worker with mod-

Figure 6.8  Predicted Wage Profiles for High School Graduates, by Number of Employers at Final Interview

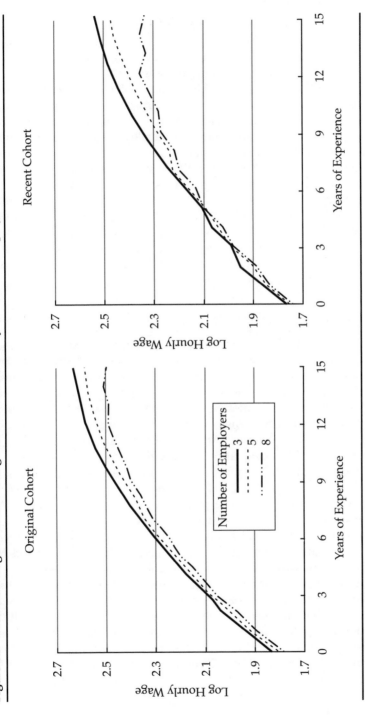

Source: Authors' compilation.
Note: Analysis is person-based.

erate stability, who has had a total of five employers, with the last change occurring in the eighth year. The third represents a worker with high instability, who has had a total of eight employers, with the last job change occurring in the fourteenth year.

In both cohorts, the effects of instability accelerate over time. This is because the tenure effect is cumulative. As soon as a worker changes jobs, the tenure clock starts again. Early in the career the impact of this cycle is not so large, because stable workers have not yet had the time to accumulate significant wage benefits. A worker who is still changing jobs later in his career, however, falls further behind, because the stable workers are now beginning to gain the rewards of stability. The important message from these figures is that the cumulation of disadvantage for workers with unstable jobs has been exacerbated in the recent cohort. In the original cohort, the worker who had had eight employers was earning about 13 percent less by the end of the survey period than the worker who had had only three employers; that penalty has grown to about 20 percent in the recent cohort.

## Permanent Variance Results

To this point, we have focused on explaining cohort differences in average wage growth for less educated and more educated workers. The next question is whether we are also able to explain the growing inequality of wage growth across the two cohorts.

More precisely, the question is whether we observe any reductions in permanent variance when we add more variables to the baseline wage growth model and, if so, whether these reductions affect the cohort difference in inequality. The permanent variances for that initial model are shown in table 6.2. If we now move through each of the more complicated models and track their effects in the last row of table 6.4, we see that the permanent variances are successively reduced with each new block of variables. More important, however, by the time we reach model 2, the cohort difference in permanent variance has become insignificant. This is largely driven by the fact that the permanent variance for the recent cohort has fallen steeply.

Substantively, what we are seeing is that job instability and education explain more variance in the recent cohort than in the original cohort—in fact, these two effects explain all of the rising inequality in long-term wage growth in the recent cohort. Additional reductions in the permanent variance are evident in model 3, but this time by similar amounts for both cohorts. Overall, our explanatory variables have reduced the permanent variance of the original cohort by 17 percent and that of the recent cohort by 32 percent.

In sum, we have done a good job of explaining the two main changes in the structure of economic mobility over the past three decades: the greater inequality in upward mobility and the declining mobility of less educated workers. In identifying the various effects that played a role, however, we have not yet established whether changes in composition or changes in returns have been more important.[16] This is a key question, because changes in returns indicate the emergence of a truly new labor market, one in which the rules of the game have shifted and education and job search, for example, are now being rewarded very differently than in the past.

## Decomposing the Changes in Long-Term Wage Growth

In this section, we try to separate changes in composition and changes in returns for our explanatory variables. What have been the effects of each on the overall distribution of wage growth? Which variables, jointly or singly, account for the dramatic growth in the bottom tail of this distribution evident in figure 6.6? For this analysis we focus on the wages reported at the last interview, for workers who are at least thirty years old.[17]

Our approach is to build a counterfactual distribution by putting the recent cohort through the economy of the original cohort and comparing these predicted wages with those they actually received in the recent economy. In spirit, this is similar to the classic Blinder-Oaxaca regression decomposition, but our approach differs because it is fully distributional. To build the counterfactual distribution, we start by computing hypothetical final wages for workers in the recent cohort, using the estimated coefficients from model 4 for the original cohort. In effect, we are giving workers in the recent cohort the returns to their attributes they would have gotten if they had been in the original economy. We then add back the estimated permanent and transient wage components for each individual from our mixed-effects model, thus preserving the full variation in individual wages. The counterfactual distribution is thus:

$$\hat{y}_{ikt}^{r} = X_{ikt}^{r}\,\beta_k^o + p_{it} + u_{it}$$

where $X$ and $\beta$ are vectors of covariates from the recent cohort and coefficients from the original cohort, respectively, and $p$ and $u$ are the permanent and transient variance components for individual $i$.

Comparing this counterfactual distribution with the actual observed wage distribution for the recent cohort isolates the changes in returns between the old and new economy. Comparing the counter-factual distribution with the original cohort's wage distribution iso-lates the changes in population (and job) composition between the two cohorts.[18]

We use relative distribution methods to make the two comparisons. These methods make it possible to predict more than just the mean shifts; they enable us to see the nature of the distributional shifts asso-ciated with changes in composition and changes in returns. In addi-tion, they form a precise decomposition of the overall distributional change in long-term wage growth. A more detailed technical discus-sion of the decomposition methods is given in appendix D.

Once we have isolated the effects of changes in returns, we can look more closely at their sources. Our job here is made easier by the fact that the only important changes in returns are associated with the education-mediated variables. By varying one set of coefficients at a time, we can compare the impact that the education-related experi-ence and job instability effects have had on the wage distribution.

With respect to the compositional shifts, on the other hand, there are several that matter. We list these variables in table 6.5, showing the direction of the compositional change (in mean value) and the impact this change would have on wages (based on the coefficients for the original cohort in table 6.4). For example, the distributions of both education and job stability have changed in the recent cohort, both in ways that will bring higher wage penalties: the fraction of college graduates has declined, the total number of employers has risen, and the distribution of tenure has shifted downward. In addi-tion, marriage rates have fallen, part-time work has risen, and unem-ployment rates are higher. What is remarkable about the composi-tional changes listed in table 6.5 is that all of them would have the predicted effect of lowering wages. Viewed from this light, anything but wage stagnation in the recent cohort would have been extremely surprising.

We begin by taking the relative distribution of the observed final wage distributions for the two cohorts, recent to original. This is shown in figure 6.9. It looks very much like the relative distribution of permanent wage gains shown in figure 6.6, with striking increases in the bottom tail. By the time of their last interview, 22 percent of the recent cohort reported wages that would have put them in the bottom decile of the original cohort's distribution. There are also relatively more of them in the second and third deciles, and the net result is that the median wage for the recent cohort now falls at about the thirtieth percentile of the original cohort's distribution. By contrast, the wages for the middle three deciles—what used to be the heart of the middle

Table 6.5  Observed Compositional Shifts and Their Predicted Impact on the Recent Cohort's Wages

| Explanatory Variable | Observed Compositional Shift Across the Two Cohorts | Predicted Impact on the Recent Cohort's Wages |
|---|---|---|
| Percentage college graduates | − | − |
| Cumulative number of employers at last interview | + | − |
| Tenure | − | − |
| Percentage part-time workers | + | − |
| Percentage married | − | − |
| Percentage in goods-producing industries | − | − |
| Percentage in service industries | + | − |
| Percentage in service, sales, and clerical occupations | + | − |
| Percentage in professional, managerial, and technical occupations | − | − |
| Local unemployment rate | + | − |

*Source:* Authors' compilation.

class—have eroded significantly. This is not a pure downshift, however, because there is a slight rebound in the top decile, composed of workers who have managed to hold their ground.

The middle and right panels show the decomposition of this overall relative distribution into a composition effect and a returns effect. The results are quite remarkable. Compositional changes have led to a downshift in the recent cohort's wage distribution, as expected (middle panel). It is a fairly gentle downshift, though, raising the fraction in the second and third deciles by about 20 percent, with slightly smaller increases in the first and fourth deciles. Thus compositional shifts are not driving the rush to the bottom of the wage distribution.

Rather, virtually all of the growth in the bottom decile, and nearly half in the second and third deciles, is driven by changes in the returns to education and job instability (right panel). This indicates a true shift in the reward structure of the new economy: job instability and education below a college degree are now increasingly penalized.

Throughout figure 6.9, entropy statistics are shown. These statistics measure how different the two underlying distributions are from each other, where zero represents equivalence. Although the entropy statis-

**Figure 6.9 Composition and Returns Effects on the Relative Distribution of Final Wages**

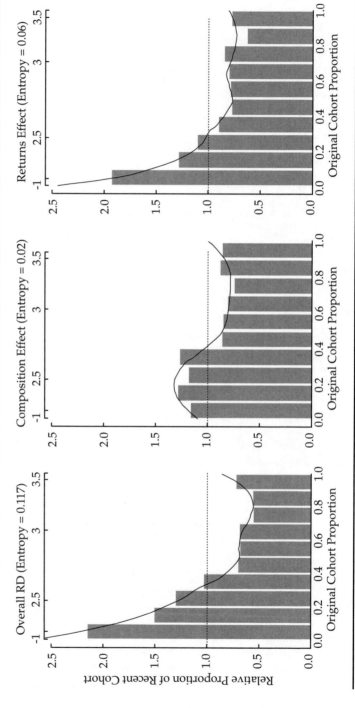

*Source:* Authors' compilation.

tic cannot be exactly additively decomposed, the relative magnitudes across the different panels are informative (Handcock and Morris 1998). The composition effects are around one-third the size of the returns effects. So we can say that roughly 75 percent of the difference in the final wage distributions between the cohorts is coming from the changes in returns, and 25 percent from the changes in composition.

Because the returns effects are the more important, it is worthwhile to pursue them a bit further. In figure 6.10, the returns effects are broken down into those associated with education (the experience and instability effects) and the "residual" differences associated with the intercept, age, and experience terms. This is not an exact decomposition, because it is not sequential. Rather, it shows what each set of effects would have done on its own.

The results are, again, striking. The two education-mediated effects behave in a similar fashion—either alone would have generated a large growth in the bottom decile of the wage distribution as well as smaller increases in the next lower deciles. This is not simply a story of shifts toward the bottom, however; if it were, we would have seen much stronger declines in the top deciles. The fact that we do not is indicative of an additional polarizing of the distribution, which should not be surprising, given the results reported in the previous section. Those with a college degree have managed to hold on to traditional levels of wage growth and are thus pulling further away from the middle. The entropy statistics suggest that if the two returns effects were acting independently, the lower returns to experience would account for about 60 percent of the changes, and the higher penalties for job instability would account for most of the remaining 40 percent.

Finally, the right panel shows the differences in residual returns between the cohorts, as represented by the intercept, age, and experience terms. Given the parameters we selected for the model, these effects represent the residual cohort differences for college graduates. Overall, the entropy statistic shows that these residual differences are quite small, clearly a lower order of magnitude than the other returns effects or all of the compositional effects combined.

## Who Won and Who Lost?

These figures raise interesting questions about who managed to hang on at the top of the wage distribution and who fell into the bottom. The next chapter focuses on low-wage workers, so here we concentrate more on the top end of the distribution. Specifically, in table 6.6

**Figure 6.10   Education-Mediated and Residual Returns Effects on the Relative Final Wage Distribution**

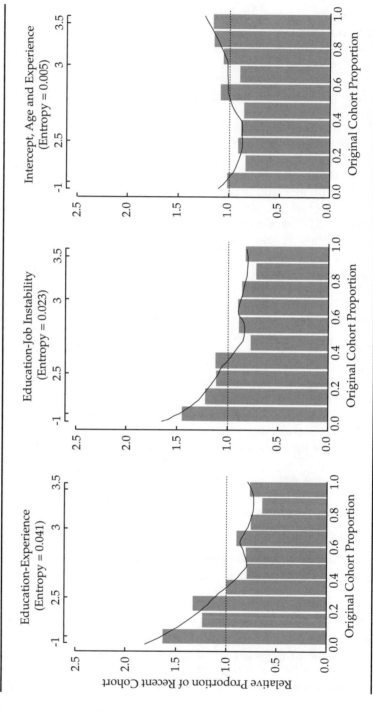

*Source:* Authors' compilation.

Table 6.6    Composition of the Top Final Wage Decile, by Cohort
(Percentage)

| Category | Original Cohort | Recent Cohort | Change[a] |
|---|---|---|---|
| Education | | | |
| High school dropout | .8 | .5 | −.3 |
| High school graduate | 12.6 | 8.7 | −3.8 |
| Some college experience | 21.3 | 13.3 | −8.0 |
| Bachelor's degree or higher | 65.3 | 77.4 | 12.2 |
| Industry | | | |
| Goods producing | 54.9 | 40.2 | −14.6 |
| Low-end services | 21.5 | 17.5 | −4.1 |
| High-end services | 23.6 | 42.3 | 18.7 |
| Occupation | | | |
| Blue-collar | 21.8 | 8.8 | −12.9 |
| Sales, service, and clerical | 12.1 | 11.9 | −.2 |
| Professional, managerial, and technical | 66.1 | 79.3 | 13.2 |

Source: Authors' compilation.
Note: Based on predicted permanent wage at age thirty-six and last reported industry, occupation, and education, for respondents aged thirty to thirty-seven. Decile cutpoints defined by the ninetieth percentile of the original cohort's wage distribution.
[a]Recent minus original cohort.

we take the predicted permanent wage for each respondent at the age of thirty-six from the baseline model and identify whether it fell into the top decile of the original cohort distribution.[19]

The table shows the composition of the top decile by education industry and occupation. For both cohorts, this has always been the preserve of the most educated. The share of top decile going to college graduates, however, has increased by 12.2 percent in the recent cohort, so that more than three-quarters of this exclusive group is now in their hands. Industry membership is less skewed but has also changed over time. In the original cohort, workers in goods-producing industries made up a narrow majority of those in the top decile, with the remainder pretty evenly split between the high and low ends of the service sector. In the recent cohort, however, workers in goods-producing industries constitute only 40 percent of the top decile, largely because of declining employment in these industries. The high end of the service sector, by contrast, gained a whopping 19 percent of the decile. A similar story obtains for occupations. Professionals and managers have traditionally claimed the lion's share of the top decile. In the recent cohort, however, their share has risen by 13 percent, giving them nearly 80 percent of the decile membership, while the big losers have been blue-collar workers, whose share has fallen from 22 percent to 9 percent.

These aggregate trends, however, mask some specific industry shifts. In figure 6.11, we break up the industry categories to show where the real gains and losses in top decile membership have happened. The bars represent the ratio of top decile share to population share, so values greater than 1 indicate that the industry has a larger fraction of the top decile than expected, and values less than 1 indicate the opposite. The most striking pattern is the marked overrepresentation of the finance, insurance, and real estate industries in the top decile of the recent cohort—with only 5 percent of the working population employed in these industries (table 6.7 gives labor force share in each industry), they claim more than 16 percent of the top decile. No other industry shows such a disproportionate presence or has seen such a disproportionate increase in recent years. The next largest ratio, and the only other one in the recent cohort with a value well above 1, is professional services. Workers in this industry are now twice as likely to be in the top decile as expected.

For most other industries, workers in the recent cohort are now less likely to make it into the top decile of the wage distribution. Some of the largest declines are in the low end of the service sector, especially retail trade (which makes up the majority of the trade category) and recreation and entertainment. Moreover, the employment shares of these industries have grown from about 15 percent to 18 percent of the population, so these declines reflect pure wage losses. Further analysis also shows that the retail trade sector is massively overrepresented in the bottom decile, by a factor of nearly six.

When we break these trends down by education group, it turns out that finance, insurance, and real estate, and professional services are also the only industries in which college graduates have made significant gains. In all other industries, college graduates in the recent cohort are now less likely than those in the original cohort to make the top decile. Thus the so-called education effect at the top of the wage distribution is being largely driven by about one-third of the college graduates who work in these two service industries—very specific gains, indeed, for a very small group of workers.

So, is anyone doing better in the recent economy? We can answer this question by comparing the counterfactual and observed wages from figure 6.9 at the individual, rather than the aggregate, level. This tells us which workers in the recent cohort have higher predicted wages in the new economy than they would have had in the old economy. Comparing these predictions, we find that only 10 percent of the recent cohort are doing better in the new economy, and 99

**Figure 6.11    Industry Underrepresentation and Overrepresentation in the Top Earnings Decile**

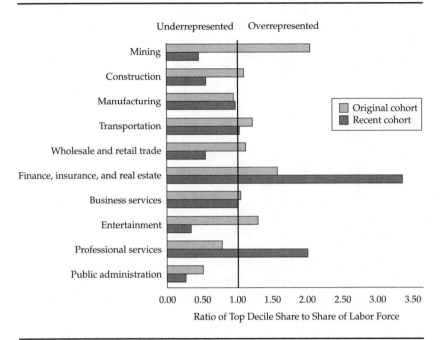

Source: Authors' compilation.

**Table 6.7    Industry Share of Labor Force, by Cohort (Percentage)**

| Industry | Original Cohort | Recent Cohort | Percentage Change |
|---|---|---|---|
| Mining | 2.4 | 1.2 | −50.0 |
| Construction | 9.8 | 13.4 | 36.7 |
| Manufacturing | 28.6 | 23.8 | −16.7 |
| Transportation | 9.6 | 8.7 | −9.4 |
| Wholesale and retail trade | 14.5 | 16.4 | 13.1 |
| Finance, insurance, and real estate | 5.6 | 4.9 | −12.5 |
| Business services | 4.0 | 7.8 | 95.0 |
| Entertainment | 1.0 | 1.6 | 60.0 |
| Professional services | 13.0 | 12.1 | −6.9 |
| Public administration | 9.0 | 6.1 | −32.2 |

Source: Authors' compilation.

percent of them are college graduates. If they do better, it is not by much: an increase of 4 percent at the median and an increase of 7 percent at the upper decile. In addition, though college graduates may be almost the only ones who do better in the new economy, in fact only 35 percent of them actually experience the benefit of their credential. For the 65 percent who do worse, their losses are surprisingly large, 8 percent at the median and 20 percent at the lower decile.

## Summary

The findings in this chapter have taken us a long way toward understanding the prospects for upward mobility in postindustrial America. Much has changed, and some of the well-known effects from previous research can now be recast in light of our longitudinal evidence.

The single most important finding to come out of our analyses is that long-term wage growth—upward mobility—has deteriorated for young men who entered the labor market in the 1980s. We estimate that permanent wage growth for sixteen- to thirty-six-year-old workers has fallen by 21 percent from the original to the recent cohort. Moreover, these are permanent changes, not to be erased by a few years of strong economic growth. In addition, economic mobility has also become more unequal. Permanent wage trajectories are significantly more polarized in the recent cohort, by about 20 percent. The net result of wage stagnation and polarization is a race to the bottom. Fully a quarter of the workers in the recent cohort have permanent wage gains that place them in the bottom decile of the original cohort's distribution. This indicates a massive downshift in earning standards. Polarization also means that the heart of the middle class has been hollowed out, with 40 percent fewer workers now landing in the central part of the wage growth distribution. In addition, though some workers (few in number) have managed to retain their grip at the top, they are typically not doing better than their predecessors.

For many, the favored explanation for these trends is education. Indeed, we find that workers without a college degree, three-quarters of the population, have seen the strongest hits to their long-term wage growth (with declines on the order of 15 to 27 percent). College graduates, though insulated to a large degree, nevertheless also show a mild decline of 3 percent. Relatively speaking, they are better off, but in absolute dollar terms they have barely managed to hold their ground.

This part of the story is not new, of course. What is new is that we have been able to clarify the actual mechanisms that lie behind the lower wage growth of less educated workers in recent years. About 60 percent derives from declining returns to experience, which indicates that the new economy has brought with it a harsh process whereby disadvantage builds on itself and cumulates over time. About 40 percent derives from stronger penalties for job instability, which means we can no longer afford to ignore public anxiety about downsizing, subcontracting, and other forms of contingent work. Overall, these two changes account for the bulk of the wage deterioration experienced by workers in the recent cohort. Moreover, they alone appear to explain the growth in inequality.

Finally, if we focus on workers who are still doing relatively well in the new economy, it should come as no surprise that they are most likely to be college graduates (accounting for 77 percent of the top decile). The great majority of college graduates, however, never make it that far—in fact, 65 percent are doing worse now than if they had entered the labor market in the late 1960s and early 1970s.

All of this puts a very different spin on the story of rising returns to education. Researchers who look at data closely have always pointed out that this story is about losses at the bottom, not gains at the top (Gottschalk 1997; Houseman 1995; Bound and Johnson 1992). We can now say more. Harsher penalties for job instability have played a significant role in generating those losses at the bottom, at the same time that instability itself is on the rise. The few gains at the top are being driven by a minority of college graduates who hold jobs in two small and privileged industries—finance, insurance, and real estate, and professional services. We may idolize the fearless new breed of Wall Street consultants, and they do indeed represent the winners in the new economy. But they are only a small fraction of the population, perched above the majority of workers who can no longer expect stable careers that lead to a solid, family-sustaining wage.

# = Chapter 7 =

# The Growth
# in Low-Wage Careers

T HE ANALYSES in this book have cast a wide net, analyzing labor
market trends across a broad spectrum of workers. Along the
way, we have paid attention to differences by education, work
experience, occupation, and other dimensions that determine who
succeeds and who does not. Yet on the whole our interest has been in
documenting how the morphology of the entire labor market has
changed, from top to bottom.

Events over the past few years, however, suggest that a more specific focus is needed as well. The advent of welfare reform and its
"work first" policies are shifting the attention of researchers and the
public alike to the question of mobility at the bottom of the labor
market. When welfare-to-work initiatives were implemented in 1996,
the overriding concern was simply with moving welfare recipients
into the labor market. Because of the tight labor market and strong
economy, this step has not proved as difficult as first conceived. Between August 1996 (when welfare reform was enacted) and Septem-
ber 1999, an astonishing 4.9 million people had left the welfare rolls, a
reduction of 40 percent (Collins 1999). Job placement has not been the
problem.

Rather, troubling questions have emerged about job quality and the
ability of low-wage workers to move onto a stable path of work and
wage growth. From state after state, the evidence suggests that former welfare recipients are, in the main, working in low-wage, high-
turnover, dead-end jobs whose earnings are frequently still not
enough to lift a family out of poverty (General Accounting Office
1999; Loprest 1999; Handler and White 1999). Particularly worrisome
are reports of severe economic hardship, with some working families
reportedly running out of food between paychecks or unable to pay
rent or utility bills. Policy makers now have to grapple with a broader

set of issues. How does the low-wage labor market operate? Are there any entry-level, low-wage jobs that can lead to solid wage growth over time? If so, what characterizes these jobs, and what steps are necessary to give workers access to them? If not, what steps are necessary to move workers up and out of this sector? These are questions that go far beyond the specific population of welfare recipients and that, again, go to the heart of question of mobility and opportunity in the United States.

Welfare reform has therefore placed the problem of low-wage jobs on the public agenda in a way that the rise in wage inequality never managed to do. In so doing, it has also highlighted the fact that we have surprisingly little detailed information on the nature of these jobs, the workers who hold them, the careers they do (or do not) build, and changes at the bottom of the labor market over time.[1] We do have a pretty good sense of the demographics of low-wage workers: they tend to be disproportionately young, female, and minority, without college education, and concentrated in retail trade and other low-end service occupations. They have a greater incidence of unemployment and nonparticipation in the labor force. In addition, their numbers have increased since the 1970s (Bernstein and Hartmann 1999; Acs and Danziger 1993; Schrammel 1998).

We know much less about the dynamics of low-wage employment. How persistent is it over the life cycle? What are the mechanisms by which low-wage work becomes chronic? Are all low-wage jobs unstable, or are they perhaps too stable, because they lead nowhere? Is lack of skills the entire story, or are there also structural barriers that trap workers in the low-wage job cycle? Perhaps most important, how has all of this changed over time? These types of questions have generally not been asked about low-wage workers, partly because of data limitations. Where they have been asked, the samples have typically been restricted to welfare recipients and focused on program evaluation (see review in Cancian et al. 1999). However, information on the very poor after they have gone through training and education programs is not necessarily generalizable to the working poor as a whole (see review in Plimpton and Nightingale 2000). More important, restricting the studies to specific populations tends to lead to analyses that focus attention on the attributes of individuals rather than the attributes of jobs and the reward structures individuals face. As the previous chapters suggest, this reward structure has changed, and for those at the low end of the market, the new economy offers much less than it once did.

The goal of this chapter is to use our unique data set to begin to understand how workers move through the low-wage sector. We obviously cannot answer all of these questions, but our longitudinal data allow us to give insight into the dynamics of work at the lower end of the labor market. Specifically, we step back from the more technical, model-driven analyses of the previous chapters and, instead, offer concrete descriptions of the experience of low-wage workers, both poor and working poor, on a variety of dimensions. The strength of our data and measures is fourfold. First, we focus on workers who are earning low wages over the long run, not just temporarily passing through that state. This means that we are isolating low-wage careers in which there is no upward mobility. Second, our data capture dynamics not normally available to researchers, such as wage growth and job instability over time and starting and ending occupations and industries. We can therefore identify the circumstances under which a worker actually gets caught in the low-wage trap rather than just describe his characteristics at one point in time. Third, our focus is on white men. This puts us in the traditional core of the labor market, where we can observe the dynamics of low-wage careers not confounded by race and sex discrimination. Fourth, our data are comparative. We can therefore examine whether the low-wage labor market has changed between the two cohorts and whether the disadvantages faced by low-wage workers in the recent cohort signal a structural change that may require a structural solution.

Ideally, this type of inquiry would also focus on women and other race and ethnic groups. It is worth remembering, however, that 63 percent of the working poor in 1997 were white (Bernstein and Hartmann 1999). Our hope is that the following analyses might serve as a template for future research that includes women and people of color as well.

## Defining Low-Wage Workers

Although most of us have an intuitive understanding of low-wage work—high turnover, low-wage, dead-end jobs—it is in fact difficult to define and measure precisely. We might prefer to define it in terms of characteristics of the jobs themselves, but data limitations mean that we must base our measure on the workers who hold those jobs. This raises an issue of temporal dynamics. Poorly paid employment can be transitional, with no impact on long-term well-being (teenagers holding McDonald's jobs for short spells is one example). If we base our measure on a cross-sectional definition of low-wage workers—in a given interview week, for example—we may end up tracking these short-term spells in addition to long-term ones. A tighter definition would track workers who are frequently or even constantly employed in low-wage jobs. Here too, however, there is ambiguity. Individuals often live with families whose other members may bring in additional income, so that the family as a whole would not be considered poor or working poor. Complicating all of the above, we do not have agreement on what constitutes a poverty-level wage. The government's formal definition is notoriously outdated, dating back to the 1960s and using an archaic computation method (Porter 1999).

Given these caveats, a common way of defining a low-wage worker is in relation to some cutoff dollar amount in hourly wages. Although there is no single "correct" cutoff, researchers often use a multipier of the official poverty threshold (for example, 1.25 or 1.5). Such multipliers are simply a reasonable tool for capturing a group of workers who earn what we would intuitively consider low wages.

In this analysis, a respondent is considered a chronically low-wage worker if his permanent hourly wage at the age of thirty-four is less than eleven dollars an hour (in 1999 dollars).[2] This definition has several important features. First, the cutoff point is above the poverty line because we want to capture the working poor as well as those who are working right at or below the poverty line. Second, this is a worker-based measure: we use the individual respondent's wages (not his family's total income), and the measure therefore describes the respondent's economic welfare (not his family's).[3] Third, this is by design an absolute measure, based on a real dollar amount of income below which a person is considered poor or working poor. It therefore differs from relative measures, which can vary according to the movement of other earners' wages. Fourth, this cutoff ensures sufficient sample sizes to support a meaningful analysis.

Finally, and perhaps most important, we use the respondent's permanent wage at the age of thirty-four. This is a critical point. Recall from the previous chapter how we measure permanent wages. We look at an individual's entire trajectory of wages over the full survey and smooth those wages of short-term fluctuations to identify the long-term trend. So if by the age of thirty-four a respondent's permanent wage qualifies as low, then the respondent is truly stuck on a long-term, low-wage career trajectory. Our measure therefore has a strong advantage over cross-sectional definitions, which are contaminated by the presence of workers who are inadvertently caught in the net—for example, teenagers working in retail jobs for the summer. By using longitudinal data and insisting on a long history of employment in low-wage jobs, we are isolating the population that is of concern to policy makers.

In what follows, we compare the experiences of chronic low-wage workers between the original and recent cohorts. Here, however, un-like in previous chapters, cross-cohort comparisons are not our only concern. Even if no changes over time are evident, simply gaining more information on the lack of mobility of low-wage workers in the current economy is illuminating and important.

## The Prevalence of Low-Wage Careers

We begin by presenting a context for our low-wage cutoff definition. As shown in table 7.1, the official 1999 poverty threshold for a family of four translated into hourly wages of $7.97. A full-time, year-round job at this wage would garner only $16,580 in earnings (perhaps giv-ing credence to those who argue that the poverty line should be raised). The second column gives the cutoff line we use to define a low-wage worker, $11.00 an hour. At full-time year-round work, this wage would yield annual earnings of $22,880—a more realistic amount but still not close to what the average American would con-sider a comfortable, basic income, especially since many low-wage jobs are not full-time. It is also important to remember that many of the workers in the low-wage group had hourly earnings that fell well below the cut-off line. In the recent cohort, for example, these workers earned an average of $8.70 an hour, which even at full-time, year-round work only translates into an annual salary of $18, 096—very close to the poverty line. In short, we are clearly capturing workers with jobs that do not pay well. Finally, in the last column we show wages at twice the poverty line, or $15.95 an hour. We use this cutoff to separate mid-wage from higher-wage workers, so that we have three comparison groups in our analyses. Although rough, these defi-nitions do a good job of grouping workers in different parts of the wage ladder.[4]

The first question, of course, is whether the prevalence of low-wage careers has changed. Table 7.2 indicates that it has, indeed,

Table 7.1    Cutoff Points for Wage Groupings (1999 Dollars)

| Category | Official Poverty Line[a] | Low-Wage Cutoff | Mid-Wage Cutoff |
|---|---|---|---|
| Hourly wage (dollars) | 7.97 | 11.00 | 15.95 |
| Yearly earnings (dollars)[b] | 16,580 | 22,880 | 33,170 |
| Multiplier of poverty line | 1.00 | 1.38 | 2.00 |

Source: Authors' compilation.
[a]In 1999, for a family of two adults and two children.
[b]From full-time, year-round job.

Table 7.2    Share of Workers in Each Hourly Wage Group, by Cohort (Percentage)

| Cohort | Low Wage (less than or equal to $11.00) | Mid-wage ($11.00 to 15.94) | Higher Wage ($15.95 or more) |
|---|---|---|---|
| Original | 12.2 | 32.0 | 55.8 |
| Recent | 27.6 | 35.9 | 36.5 |

*Source:* Authors' compilation.
*Note:* All percentages are person based.

more than doubling from 12.2 percent of workers in the original cohort to 27.6 percent in the recent. Our low wage cutoff has thus effectively captured those in the bottom decile of the original cohort's final permanent wage distribution, as shown in figure 6.9. To appreciate the meaning of these shifts, it is important to remember that we are not capturing a greater incidence of, say, students working part-time at Wal-Mart during high school and college. The definition of low-wage work used here focuses only on those workers who are "stuck," over the long run, at the bottom of the labor market, and so this constitutes a truly worrisome trend.

Figure 7.1 presents the permanent wage profiles for the three wage groups.[5] The lines are weighted by the percentage of workers falling into each group, so that thicker lines represent a greater proportion of the sample. In both cohorts, the profile for low-wage workers shows the chronic low pay and stagnation over time that we commonly think of as characterizing the careers of the working poor. These profiles stand in stark contrast to those of mid- and higher-wage earners, who experience real wage growth during their careers, in line with our more common notions of upward mobility. The problem for policy makers is that the number of chronic low-wage workers has grown in recent years (as shown by the greater thickness of the bottom line in the recent cohort) and that the low-wage trajectory has fallen even lower than in the past.

This description, then, forms the basis of the remainder of our chapter. We examine how low-wage workers differ from other workers, hoping to gain some insight into why their numbers have risen during the past several decades.

## Education

The most obvious route into such an analysis is to look at the role that education plays. As the findings in chapter 6 suggest, however, the

**Figure 7.1  Long-Term Wage Growth Patterns, by Cohort**

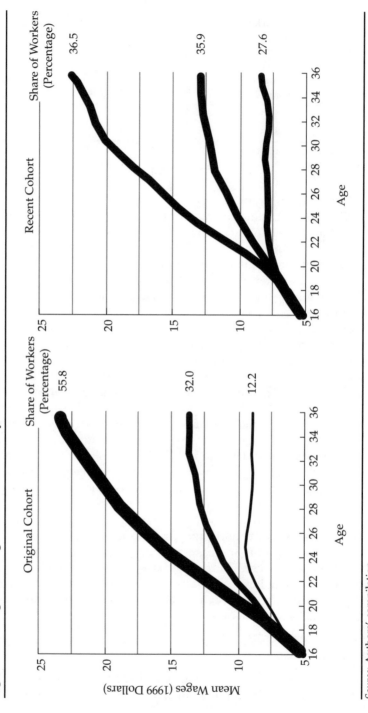

*Source:* Authors' compilation.
*Note:* Workers are assigned to a low, middle, or high growth group based on their permanent wage at age thirty-four (see text for details). Displayed trajectories are mean wages for all of the workers in a group, and as such do not reflect within-group variability.

Table 7.3    Distribution of Wage Groups Within Each Education Category, by Cohort (Percentage)

| | Original Cohort | | | Recent Cohort | | |
|---|---|---|---|---|---|---|
| Final Education Level | Low Wage | Mid- Wage | Higher Wage | Low Wage | Mid- Wage | Higher Wage |
| High school or less | 14.4 | 36.1 | 49.5 | 35.3 | 42.9 | 21.8 |
| Some college experience | 10.5 | 34.4 | 55.1 | 25.4 | 35.0 | 39.6 |
| Bachelor's degree or higher | 10.4 | 23.8 | 65.8 | 14.1 | 22.8 | 63.2 |

Source: Authors' compilation.
Note: All percentages are person based.

results are not as straightforward as one might expect. Table 7.3 presents the percentage of low-, mid-, and higher-wage workers at each level of education.[6] Those with the least amount of schooling, a high school diploma or less, have seen a strong rise in low-wage careers, more than doubling from 14.4 percent of workers in the original cohort to 35.3 percent of those in the recent. Workers with some college experience were hit just as hard in proportionate terms—their percentage of low-wage workers more than doubled. Perhaps most surprising of all, workers with bachelor's degrees also shared in this trend. True, the absolute prevalence of low-wage workers is much lower for this well-educated group. Nevertheless, an increase from 10.4 percent in the original cohort to 14.1 percent in the recent represents a proportionate rise of 36 percent, not a trivial amount.

These findings can be interpreted in two ways. On the one hand, the "shift toward the bottom" was less pronounced for educated workers, indicating that high levels of education have served to insulate them against the recent trends in wages. On the other hand, no group has escaped these trends, regardless of education. This is especially noteworthy because we are focusing on the prevalence of chronic cycling among low-wage jobs. The fact that college-educated workers are showing an increase in such cycling underlines a recurrent theme throughout this book: even some of the most educated workers in our economy have seen an absolute deterioration in life chances. In particular, workers with some college experience have shifted their relative standing, looking less like college graduates (in the original cohort) and more like high school graduates (in the recent cohort). This should raise a red flag to policy makers. Because prescribing attainment of a four-year college degree for the entire population is unrealistic, much of education and training policy has focused on encouraging two-year degrees, occupational certificates, and other forms of postsecondary education. Yet our data (and that of others) show that these initiatives, though well intentioned, are unlikely to solve the problems of downward mobility that a majority of the workforce now faces.

## Industries

As is well known and as we documented earlier, there has been a pronounced shift from manufacturing industries to the service sector over the past several decades. The manufacturing sector has historically had higher unionization rates and has paid better wages than the service sector. One might imagine, then, that the number of poor and working poor has grown simply because there are now more service sector jobs. At this point, however, we have solid evidence that deindustrialization has not been the main force driving the stagnation and growing inequality in wages, though it has played a role (compare chapter 6 and Dinardo, Fortin, and Lemieux 1996). We also know from chapter 6 that industrial shifts have played virtually no part in the doubling of workers in the bottom decile of the old wage distribution. It is not so much compositional shifts that are at work here as changes in the pay structure within industries. This point warrants further illustration, using our data. In the following analyses, we examine the last industry reported by respondents, that is, the industry in which they were working at the age of thirty to thirty-seven. The idea is to isolate those industries that are most likely to generate low-wage careers over the long run (as opposed to jobs that are poorly paid within any one year).

Table 7.4 gives the percentage of chronic low-wage workers by industry for both cohorts.[7] This isolates the changes in the wage structure. If nothing about the wage structure had changed during the past thirty years and only the mix of industries had shifted, then we would expect the figures for the original and recent cohorts to be identical.[8] The percentage of low-wage workers in the labor force would have grown simply because there had been a shift in employment toward low-wage service industries. However, this simple scenario clearly does not hold: all industries show an increase in the incidence of low-wage careers for the recent cohort; and there is considerable variation in the magnitude of that increase. It should come as no surprise that industries at the bottom of the service sector, such as retail trade and business services, have seen a doubling of low-wage workers.[9] For example, weekly earnings for nonsupervisory workers in retail trade dropped from 69 percent of the national aver-

Table 7.4   Low-Wage Share of Each Industry, by Cohort (Percentage)

| Industry | Original Cohort | Recent Cohort | Percentage Change[a] |
|---|---|---|---|
| Construction, mining, agriculture | 15.9 | 30.6 | 92.5 |
| Manufacturing | 10.0 | 23.0 | 130.0 |
| Transportation and communications | 10.1 | 23.4 | 131.7 |
| Wholesale and retail trade | 21.2 | 46.5 | 119.3 |
| Business and repair services, entertainment and recreation, personal services | 21.3 | 40.7 | 91.1 |
| Finance, insurance, and real estate | 8.1 | 9.1 | 12.3 |
| Professional services | 23.0 | 27.8 | 20.9 |
| Public administration | 9.7 | 11.2 | 15.5 |
| All industries | 12.2 | 27.6 | 126.2 |

Source: Authors' compilation.
[a] Original to recent cohort.

age in 1970 to 58 percent of the national average in 1999 (U.S. Department of Labor 1999). By contrast, at the upper end of the service sector (professional services and the finance, insurance, and real estate industries), there has been much less change. The results for manufacturing and transportation and communication industries are also startling: the percentage of poor and working poor has climbed by roughly 130 percent in both. This is clear evidence of the effect of deunionization and structural changes within these historically well-organized industries.

In general, then, much more has happened to change the wage structure than a shift in the industrial mix. The nature of the employer-employee contract has changed within industries, and one result has been a greater incidence of poor and working poor careers.[10]

Finally, though the data presented in table 7.4 is illuminating, it does not directly tell us where low-wage workers are most likely to be employed. Table 7.5 therefore reorients the analysis, showing the industrial mix within wage groups (the middle group has been dropped for the sake of brevity). The basic trends are clear. Although all workers have been subject to the effects of deindustrialization, higher-wage workers still tend to work in higher-wage industries, lower-wage workers in lower-wage industries. The bottom of the service sector—retail trade, personal services, entertainment and recreation, and business and repair services—continues to employ a disproportionate number of the poor and working poor.

What is important here is that these "bottom" industries now em-

Table 7.5   Industry Share of Each Wage Group, by Cohort (Percentage)

| Industry | Original Cohort | | Recent Cohort | |
|---|---|---|---|---|
| | Low Wage | Higher Wage | Low Wage | Higher Wage |
| Construction, mining, agriculture | 14.6 | 14.0 | 17.2 | 12.6 |
| Manufacturing | 19.1 | 29.8 | 18.7 | 26.3 |
| Transportation and communications | 6.9 | 12.3 | 7.1 | 10.7 |
| Wholesale and retail trade | 21.1 | 11.7 | 25.9 | 10.3 |
| Business and repair services, entertainment and recreation, personal services | 8.9 | 5.1 | 15.8 | 8.4 |
| Finance, insurance, and real estate | 2.8 | 6.4 | 1.6 | 9.2 |
| Professional services | 20.3 | 10.4 | 11.4 | 15.1 |
| Public administration | 6.1 | 10.3 | 2.4 | 7.6 |

Source: Authors' compilation.

ploy 42 percent of the recent cohort, up from 30 percent in the original. Low-wage careers, growing in number, are becoming more and more concentrated in a handful of industries. Especially if this trend continues, there is true cause for concern that a new type of segmentation is emerging. The employment trajectories of these industries are typically very flat, with the large majority of workers employed in frontline sales and service occupations, supervised by a few managers. Career or skill ladders have never been common and are even less so now (Bailey and Bernhardt 1997; Macdonald and Sirianni 1996). For a public policy aimed at boosting workers out of the low-wage job cycle, concentration in these industries presents a serious challenge. To wit, in the original cohort, workers stuck in low-wage jobs may still have ended up in professional services, public administration, or manufacturing and may eventually have been able to move up higher with training in industry-specific skills. Today, however, in retail trade industries, for example, such intervention is unlikely to yield much. Instead, a much more difficult strategy will be required, focused on retraining workers in an entirely new set of skills to enable movement across industries. Later in the chapter we pursue the issue of industry mobility and segmentation in greater depth.

## Job Instability and Its Consequences

Any talk of low-wage careers inevitably contains the image of cycling among short-term, dead-end jobs. In previous chapters, we have seen repeated evidence of a strong connection between job instability and

Table 7.6    Attainment of Steady Jobs by Workers Aged Thirty-Four to
Thirty-Seven, by Wage Group and Cohort (Percentage)

| Current Tenure | Workers with Full-Time Jobs | | | Percentage Gap (Low to High) |
| | Low Wage | Mid-Wage | Higher Wage | |
| --- | --- | --- | --- | --- |
| One year or longer | | | | |
| Original cohort | 70.3 | 80.0 | 83.9 | 16.2 |
| Recent cohort | 59.6 | 75.1 | 85.1 | 39.0 |
| Percentage change, original to recent | −15.2 | −6.1 | 1.4 | |
| Three years or longer | | | | |
| Original cohort | 45.5 | 60.0 | 69.4 | 34.4 |
| Recent cohort | 32.2 | 56.2 | 68.1 | 52.7 |
| Percentage change, original to recent | −29.2 | −6.3 | −1.9 | |

*Source:* Authors' compilation.

lack of long-term wage growth. It is worth pinning down that connection in simple descriptive terms.

In table 7.6, we examine the ability of workers to attain steady jobs. We focus on older workers aged thirty-four to thirty-seven who are employed full-time and ask how long they have been with their current employers. If a "steady job" is defined as one in which a worker has been employed for at least one year, steady employment has declined by 15.2 percent for low-wage workers in recent years, and only 59.6 percent of them can now expect to attain this goal. This can perhaps best be understood by comparison with workers on higher-wage career paths, 85.1 percent of whom were able to attain stable jobs by their mid-thirties. This stability gap between low- and higher-wage careers has more than doubled in recent years. In the original cohort, there was only a 16.2 percent difference in the likelihood of stable employment for the two groups. In the recent cohort, the gap has widened to 39 percent. If we restrict the definition of a stable job to tenure of at least three years, the stability gap between low- and higher-wage career paths becomes even more pronounced. The majority of mid- and higher-wage career paths are characterized by this type of long-term, full-time job by the mid-thirties. By contrast, less than one-third of those with low-wage careers in the recent cohort managed to secure such steady jobs. Indeed, virtually all of the increase in the stability gap between low- and high-wage career paths has been driven by the decline in stable employment among those with low-wage careers.

Unstable employment thus appears to have played a much more prominent role in producing chronic low wage growth in recent years. To get a better picture of the link, in figure 7.2 we compare the average change in log wages for job changers and nonchangers in both cohorts.[11] First, notice the simple fact that low-wage workers experience less wage growth than other workers, no matter what they do. This, of course, is one of the reasons they end up being classified as low-wage workers in the first place. Note also that they have less to gain from job changing than do other workers. This puts them at a distinct disadvantage in the labor market, because as we have seen in chapter 5, job changing early in the career is a key mechanism through which workers build a path of upward mobility. For the poor and working poor, that mobility strategy has not worked well historically, and in the recent cohort, it has actually become quite detrimental. This is the most dramatic message from these graphs: in the recent cohort, the returns to job changing are now actually negative for low-wage workers.[12] These workers would be better off staying with the same employer, but as we have just seen, finding a stable job has become more and more difficult for them.

It should be noted that only a portion of separations from employers are voluntary, and even "voluntary" choices are probably quite limited for workers at the bottom of the labor market. A Wal-Mart job may look better than one at McDonald's because of, say, better hours or more convenient store location, but the gain in wages or promotion opportunity is minimal and, in the long run, after accounting for inflation, may even be negative.

Finally, with evidence of rising job instability, a natural question is whether there have also been accompanying increases in wage volatility, especially for those earning close to the minimum wage, for whom even small variations in earnings are likely to have important consequences for day-to-day life. Jumps and dips in wages from one period to the next mean that low-wage workers are faced with a great deal of uncertainty about income and are hampered in making long-term financial plans. Such periodic fluctuations in cash flow and the crises they engender have often been noted in research on the poor and working poor (Handler and White 1999).

One measure of such wage volatility is the transient variance we examined in chapter 6.[13] For example, consider the average low-wage worker from the recent cohort who is in his mid-thirties. He can expect his hourly wages to fluctuate between $6.58 and $10.20 from one year to the next (in 1999 dollars). Assuming a full-time work sched-

**Figure 7.2    The Returns to Changing and Not Changing Jobs, by Wage Group**

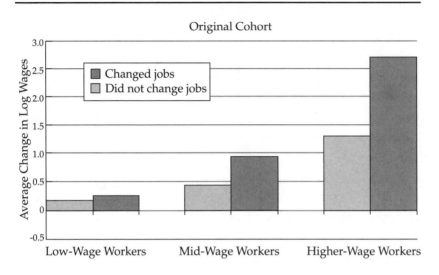

Original Cohort

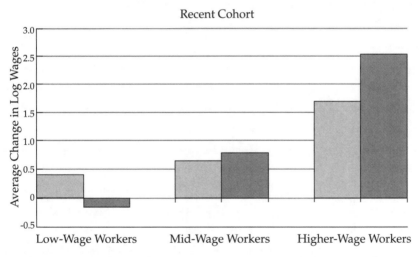

Recent Cohort

*Source:* Authors' compilation.

ule, this means that weekly earnings would swing between $263 and $408. With earnings this close to subsistence, such variation can mean the difference between meeting the rent and getting evicted. On the positive side, an increase of a dollar an hour can have significant benefits. Our calculations show that these low-wage workers face a 30 to

40 percent chance of falling below the poverty line at any point in time. The fact that this threat has gotten stronger for the recent cohort underscores the point that rising job instability has had ripple effects on many other aspects of economic well-being.

## The Growing "Stickiness" of Low-Wage Careers

We have now assembled several different pieces of the low-wage career puzzle, but the dynamics by which such careers unfold over time remain unclear. We therefore shift to a longitudinal analysis to try to pinpoint some of the mechanisms by which a worker gets stuck on a flat wage trajectory. Although we cannot resolve issues of causality here, a good description of some of these mechanisms will make an important contribution to our understanding of what needs to be explained in future research.

We start by returning to the concept of a low-wage sector, as distinct from a low-wage worker. A growing proportion of low-wage earners can be found in a handful of sectors and occupations that traditionally pay poorly and have high turnover. These are jobs that, before the resurgent economy of the late 1990s, were routinely offered as evidence in heated debates about the future of the country: hamburger flippers, cashiers, room cleaners, data entry operators, retail clerks, building maintenance workers, and so forth. These are also jobs that, at least historically, many workers passed through when they were young, serving as entry points into the greater labor market. So are they a trap or a springboard? That is the question to which we now turn.

To understand the role the low-wage service sector plays in career formation, we need a working definition of this sector so that we can measure it. The definition we adopt here combines aspects of both industry and occupation. We start by singling out service industry jobs that paid full-time, full-year median wages below 1.5 times the poverty line for a family of four.[14] For both cohorts, these low-wage service industries were the same: eating and drinking places, retail trade, private household services, business services, repair services, personal services, entertainment and recreation services, and welfare and religious services. We then add the restriction that the occupations held in these industries could not be managerial, professional, or technical. Effectively, this isolates frontline jobs in low-wage service industries. For the sake of brevity, we refer to this simply as the "low-wage sector."

With this definition in hand, we then divide our young workers'

Table 7.7  The "Stickiness" of Employment in Low-Wage Sectors, by
Cohort and Wage Group (Percentage)

| Wage Group | Workers Starting Careers in Low-Wage Sector[a] | Workers Still in Low-Wage Sector Later in Career[b] |
|---|---|---|
| Original | | |
| Low wage | 58.6 | 49.4 |
| Higher wage | 46.7 | 17.9 |
| Recent | | |
| Low wage | 65.7 | 59.8 |
| Higher wage | 57.8 | 20.2 |
| Percentage to increase (original to recent) | | |
| Low wage | 12.2 | 20.8 |
| Higher wage | 23.7 | 12.5 |

*Source:* Authors' compilation.
*Note:* All percentages are person based. See text for definitions.
[a]At ages sixteen to twenty-five.
[b]Of workers who started careers in low-wage sector, those who ended up in low-wage sector at ages twenty-six to thirty-seven.

careers into an early portion (from the age of sixteen to twenty-five) and a later portion (from the age of twenty-six to thirty-seven) and ask whether in each interval, the respondent was seen holding a low-wage sector job at least once.[15] Table 7.7 illustrates how entry into the low-wage sector at the start of the career is related to the eventual wage trajectories that workers achieve. In both cohorts, it is clearly the case that chronic low-wage workers are more likely to have entered the labor market in low-wage service industries and occupations, as compared with workers with higher-wage career paths (we exclude the mid-wage group for the sake of simplicity). Yet the difference is not as large as one might expect, reiterating the point made earlier, that many Americans start their careers in these types of jobs. Moreover, the table shows that entry into the bottom of the labor market has become more common in the recent cohort, across all wage groups. In fact, the greatest increase, proportionately, can be found among higher-wage workers, who are now 23.7 percent more likely to have started their careers in the low-wage sector.

Do early jobs matter? In the last column of table 7.7, we ask the following: of those who started working in the low-wage sector, what percentage were still working in that sector later in the career? Descriptively, what we are capturing here is the "stickiness," or pull, of low-wage industries and occupations (we address causality later).

Table 7.8   The Role of Job Instability in the "Stickiness" of the
            Low-Wage Sector

| Low-Wage Sector Employment | | Job Instability Rate | |
|---|---|---|---|
| Started | Ended | Early (Ages 16 to 25) | Late (Ages 26 to 37) |
| No | No | .66 | .53 |
| Yes | No | .74 | .58 |
| Yes | Yes | .74 | .63 |

*Source:* Authors' compilation.
*Note:* Sample limited to low-wage workers in recent cohort. The row for workers who did not start in the low-wage sector but ended there was omitted because of the small number of observations.

The likelihood of low-wage sector employment in later years has increased for workers on both wage paths, but for workers who experience high wage growth, only about 20 percent remain in this sector. Workers on a stagnant wage trajectory are more likely to have been stuck in the low-wage sector over the long run—in both cohorts one-half or more of those are still in this sector at the end. The concentration of low-wage careers in this sector has increased in the recent cohort, however, by 20.8 percent.

Thus the bad-job trap has become tighter for those at the bottom of the wage distribution. There is more to this story, however: the bad-job trap is also a job instability trap. This can be seen in table 7.8, in which we focus on low-wage workers in the recent cohort only, summarizing their job instability rate by labor market entry point.[16] Most workers are changing jobs a lot during the early stage of the career, but even so, employment in the low-wage sector is associated with higher rates of instability. When we compare job instability by labor market location at ages twenty-six to thirty-seven, instability appears to be more persistent for workers who started and ended in a low-wage service job—their two-year turnover rate is .63 even as they reach their mid-thirties. By contrast, workers who managed to escape the low-wage sector have fared better. Their job instability rate falls by 22 percent, to .58. Thus there is a clear correlation between job instability and working in a low-wage sector.

## Causality and Public Policy

How should these findings be interpreted? At the very least, we have described one of the key mechanisms by which workers end up trapped in low-wage careers. They are more likely than others to have entered the labor market in the low-wage sector—service industries and occupations that pay poorly and that have high turnover. Many workers pass through these types of jobs early in the careers, however. What truly differentiates the working poor is their continued dependence on low-paying unstable service jobs over the long run.

To some, this may simply signify a lack of skills. If so, then the above findings are nothing more than yet another illustration of the consequences of not having enough human capital. We would push the interpretation further, however. There is now enough research on low-wage service industries to tell a more sophisticated—and more accurate—story. The lesson from a variety of industries (ranging from retail trade to financial services) is that service firms' strategic stratification of their customer markets, based on price, quality, and level of customer service, has resulted in a similar stratification of service jobs and the wages associated with each submarket.

The outcome for workers has been not just a polarization in wages but also a splitting of the paths that previously connected jobs and created careers. For example, different department stores now specialize in either high-income, middle-income, or mass markets, resulting in less-varied jobs and less-elaborate career ladders within any one store. In addition, training for incumbent workers has declined and managers are increasingly hired from the outside, leaving fewer opportunities for skill acquisition and upward movement within firms. Exacerbating this trend, service firms are also consolidating entry-level jobs into centers that are geographically or organizationally separate from higher-tier jobs (for example, customer service phone representatives or temporary workers in health care). Even technology has not proved a panacea, because the same technology often increases skill requirements in some parts of the organization while decreasing them in others.[17]

In our view, then, the growing "stickiness" of low-wage, high-turnover jobs in the service industries reflects not just inadequate skills. It also reflects the structure of those industries—bad jobs, lack of training, lack of career ladders—effectively signaling a segmented labor market. Although we cannot offer definitive evidence for this argument, we can show some suggestive evidence, by way of a series of graphs that trace career profiles under different scenarios.

In figure 7.3, we take the recent cohort and focus only on workers who never went beyond a high school diploma, thus roughly controlling for skill level. We also choose only those high school graduates who truly started their work lives at the "bottom" of the labor mar-

**Figure 7.3    Mean Wage Paths of High School Graduates Who Began Their Careers at the Bottom of the Labor Market**

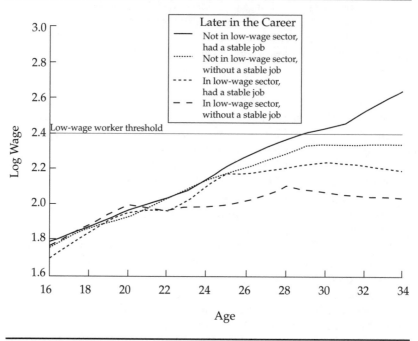

*Source:* Authors' compilation.
*Note:* See text for definitions.

ket: they were employed in the low-wage sector, holding unstable jobs, and paid wages that classified them as low-wage workers.[18] These workers really did have the decks stacked against them. The question is, which of these high school graduates were able to cross above the low-wage threshold by their mid-thirties? The answer is quite clear: those who were able to escape low-wage industries and occupations and at the same time were able to find stable, full-time employment.[19] No other path crosses the low-wage cutoff. Simply moving out of low-wage industries is not enough, and simply finding a full-time, stable job does not suffice, either. Only by doing both can a high school graduate expect a reasonable chance of attaining a livable, family-supporting wage.[20] This graph does seem to signal that "bottom feeder" industries and occupations exert their own pull and depress career mobility. There are few stepping stones for those employed here.

Would these high school graduates have been better served by getting more education? Figure 7.4 indicates that this is not necessarily

**Figure 7.4    Mean Wage Paths of Workers Who Began Their Careers at the Bottom of the Labor Market, Under Different Educational Scenarios**

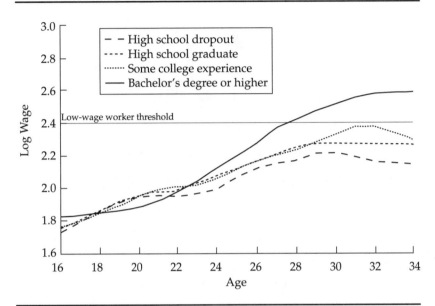

*Source:* Authors' compilation.
*Note:* See text for definitions.

the case. Here we select workers who started their careers in high school, at the bottom of the labor market (as previously defined). We then show the profiles of workers who attained different final levels of education. Only those who eventually earned a four-year college degree managed to reach wages above the low-wage cutoff. This would appear to suggest that more education is the ticket to long-term wage mobility; but things are not that simple. Note that these college-educated workers do only as well as the successful high school graduate from figure 7.3 who managed to find a stable job outside the low-wage sector. Note, as well, that that high school graduate did much better than the average worker here who got some college experience, such as an associate's degree.[21]

A final graph is less academic and more relevant to policy makers. What would happen if we intensified our policy efforts on all fronts? Specifically, what would be the impact if we poured our resources into helping high school graduates attain more education and, through training, find stable full-time work in sectors that provide on-the-job skill acquisition and real career ladders? The likely combined effect is shown in figure 7.5. Again, the sample is workers who

**Figure 7.5    Mean Wage Paths of Workers Who Began Their Careers at the Bottom of the Labor Market but Were Able to Escape It**

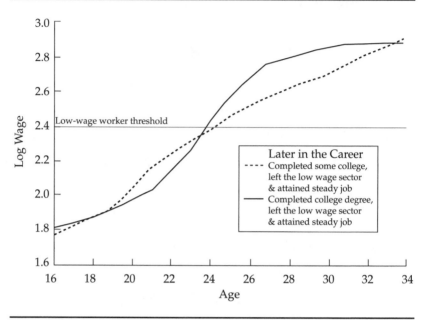

*Source:* Authors' compilation.
*Note:* See text for definitions.

started their careers in the worst labor market position. This time, however, we show the paths of those who were able to continue their education beyond high school, escape the low-wage sector, and find full-time stable jobs. Clearly, that combination is a powerful one, raising permanent wages by the age of thirty-four to about 2.2 times the poverty line—suggestive evidence, at the very least, that an all-out public policy assault on the structural labor market barriers these workers face would pay off.

## Summary

In the context of "work first" welfare reform, it has become more important than ever that we understand low-wage workers and the careers that they do or do not build. We know a good deal about the demographics of these workers and something about their basic labor market characteristics. There is much less information available about how the working poor move through the labor market over time and the dynamics that lead to flat wage trajectories.

This chapter has taken a detailed look at mobility at the bottom of the labor market by focusing on workers who are stuck in low-wage jobs over the long term. Such workers have become more numerous in recent years, rising from 12.2 percent of the original cohort to 27.6 percent of the recent. There has also been disproportionate growth of low-wage careers in service industries and nonmanagerial occupations, a pattern that suggests that deindustrialization has left its mark. The frequency of low-wage careers has risen, however, even in traditional manufacturing industries, so other forces such as deunionization are also at work. Perhaps most important, the increase has not been confined to the least educated. In particular, the prospect of a chronically low-wage career for workers with some college experience now looks much more like that of high school graduates.

We have also provided evidence that supports several common intuitions about low-wage workers. They are less likely to find themselves in steady, full-time jobs even by their mid-thirties. When they change jobs, they see lower wage gains than do other workers. The volatility in their wages is greater, putting them at significant risk of falling below the poverty line from any one year to the next. In addition, they are more likely to be employed in traditionally low-paying jobs in service industries such as retail trade, personal services, entertainment and recreation, and business and repair services.

What is more, all of these markers have become significantly more pronounced in recent years. Thus the low-wage trap has gotten stronger. In particular, service industries and occupations that pay poorly and have high turnover exert a strong pull on the workforce over time, effectively shaping the careers of the working poor. These industries typically have very flat occupational structures, with the large majority of workers employed in frontline sales and service occupations. Career or skill ladders—never common in this sector—are even less common now, and investment in training ranks the lowest among all industries. The stepping stones to long-term wage growth are hard to find here.

We were able to identify several factors that enable workers who start at the bottom of the labor market to get out and attain a living wage by their mid-thirties. The results may be surprising, however, to those familiar with the rhetoric about the need for upgraded skills in the new economy. For high school graduates with the decks stacked against them, finding a full-time, stable job outside the low-wage sector is all it takes. In fact, the payoff to this route equals or even exceeds the payoff to higher education.

Of course, combining the two routes is the best bet of all, and so there are clear and direct policy implications here: we need to invest

# Chapter 8

## Policies to Restore the American Dream

THIS IS a book about what has happened to economic mobility during the past thirty years of economic restructuring. Some parts of this picture have already been drawn by others. On one side are the well-documented changes in labor market structure. The "new economy" has been shaped by a long-term shift from manufacturing to service industries and by more recent changes in employment relations at the firm level. On the other side are the equally well documented changes in worker outcomes. There has been a long secular decline in median wages for men, and wage inequality has increased sharply for all. Making a causal link between the structural changes and rising inequality, however, has proved quite difficult. This is not just because the problem is complex but also because the data are, and always will be, historically incomplete.

Our strategy has been to bring a new source of information to the table: longitudinal studies that track workers' careers from the late 1960s onward. We have fully exploited the potential of these data, drawing a map of the new labor market by tracing the paths of the workers who move through it. Whereas cross-sectional studies provide a bird's-eye view of the new economy—the aggregate distribution of wages employers are likely to pay over time—mobility studies provide a "person's-eye" view—the distribution of lifetime wage growth a worker is likely to face.

This focus on upward mobility allows us to analyze the cumulation of advantage and disadvantage over the career. Understanding how the structure of mobility has changed in recent years thus offers a new and different way to assess economic opportunity in postindustrial America. Mobility paths also reveal the dynamics of how inequality has grown. By tracing the movement of workers through different industries and occupations over time, by identifying where job instability is chronic and where skills are (and are not) rewarded, we can begin to make inferences about changes in the employment relationship. Mobility paths therefore capture important, albeit indirect, information about the effects of firm restructuring.

The National Longitudinal Study cohorts provide a remarkable opportunity to observe the emergence of the new economy and its impact. We have used these data to compare two generations of young white men as they entered the labor market, established their working careers, and tried to move up the economic ladder. The original cohort entered the labor market in the late 1960s, at the tail of the economic boom, and was followed until the end of the 1970s. The recent cohort entered the labor market in the early 1980s, after the onset of economic restructuring, and was followed through the first half of the 1990s. After briefly recapping our central findings here, we discuss what we believe these findings imply about economic restructuring and the policy responses needed to offset some of its more negative effects.[1]

## Key Findings

Our main finding is that economic mobility has deteriorated in the new economy, so that workers now face the prospect of more limited and more unequal wage growth from ages sixteen to thirty-six. Job instability has also risen in recent years, and this rising instability appears to play an important role in explaining the mobility trends. It plays a particularly strong role in the dynamics that are generating a growing number of workers caught in low-wage careers. We review these findings in more detail below.

### Economic Mobility Has Declined and Become More Unequal

Our findings clearly document that long-term wage growth has worsened for most workers. Median wage growth by midcareer has fallen by 21 percent in recent years, and the distribution of the remaining gains has become sharply more unequal. The 90:10 wage decile ratio, for example, is now 20 percent higher for workers in their mid-thirties. The net impact of wage decline and polarization is a race to the bottom. More than one-quarter of the workers in our recent cohort did not even manage to double their wages after more than a decade and a half in the labor force. As a result, the heart of the middle class has been hollowed out: there are now 40 percent fewer workers in the central part of the wage growth distribution than there were three decades ago.

At the very top, we do find a small core of workers who have managed to hold their ground; these are mostly college graduates. This is the kind of finding that makes headlines and that leads to the constant reiteration of the growing importance of skill in the global economy. Frequently overlooked is the fact that not all college graduates are doing this well. Fully three-quarters have failed to reach the top decile of the wage growth distribution by their mid-thirties, and 65 percent have had to settle for lower wage gains in the new economy than they would have enjoyed in the old economy, given their skills. Another neglected dimension of the education story is the trends for workers just behind college graduates: the 20 percent of the recent cohort that acquired some college training but not four-year degrees. In the 1980s and early 1990s, these workers did barely better than high school graduates, sharing in the strong declines in long-term wage growth. It is important to understand that these are workers with associate's degrees, certificates, and occupation-specific training—surely indicators of solid skills—yet the new economy is not rewarding their investments.

Finally, we have documented the actual mechanisms that lie behind the declining mobility of workers without a college degree. One element in this change is the declining returns to experience, an indication that the new economy has brought with it an unforgiving process whereby disadvantage builds on itself and cumulates over time. The other element is stronger penalties for job instability, which means we can no longer afford to ignore public anxiety about downsizing, subcontracting, and other forms of the externalization of work. Overall, these two changes account for the bulk of the wage deterioration that workers in the recent cohort experienced. Moreover, they alone explain the growth in inequality.

## Job Instability Has Increased

Job instability in the recent cohort has risen by about 14 percent, regardless of education level. Although we might have expected the youngest workers to be the chief targets of this rising instability, it is instead the workers in their mid-thirties who have seen the sharpest increases. This finding has important implications, because developing permanent relationships with employers becomes increasingly critical for wage growth during this stage in life.

The rise in job instability is probably not news to those who work for a living; their anxiety about job loss has shown up in poll after poll. Empirical documentation of this simple fact, however, has eluded economists for many years. About a quarter of the increase is associated with the shift in employment to the service sector, especially low-wage, high-turnover industries; but there has also been a decline in job stability within industries. Thus not only are young adults in the recent cohort suffering from greater reliance on the "unstable" service sector, they are also not benefiting as much from jobs in traditionally stable industries such as manufacturing.

Job instability turns out to be one of the key factors in explaining the deterioration of wage growth in the recent economy. It has taken its toll in two ways. The first is through its effects on the tenure distribution: median tenure with the current employer has fallen by about 20 percent for workers in the recent cohort, and lower tenure means lower wages. The second is through changes in the returns to tenure: the penalties for short tenures have risen, primarily for those without a college degree. For young workers, this means that the benefits of job shopping are sharply reduced, and for older workers, it means that those who continue to change employers fall further and further behind. The typical worker in the recent cohort has thus been hit on two fronts: he is changing jobs more often at the same time that penalties for instability have risen.

## The Low-Wage Career Trap Has Expanded Its Grip

The prevalence of low-wage careers has more than doubled, increasing from 12 percent in the original cohort to 28 percent in the recent cohort. These are not teenagers taking afterschool jobs at McDonald's to earn spending money, but rather mature workers chronically cycling through bad jobs over the long run, and we find that they have two things in common. One is that they are increasingly trapped in just a handful of industries, such as retail trade, personal services, entertainment and recreation, and business and repair services. These industries offer few opportunities for wage growth, promotion, and training, making it difficult for workers to escape their grasp. The other is their inability to find stable full-time employment by the time they reach their mid-thirties—indicating a type of job churning that becomes increasingly harmful as workers grow older.

The good news is that we have been able to identify routes of escape from the trap. For high school graduates, finding a stable job outside the low-wage service sector is all it takes to cross over the threshold and attain reasonable long-term wage growth. In fact, the payoff to this route equals or exceeds the payoff to getting more education. The down side, of course, is that both job instability and the low-wage service sector have grown in recent years so that the structural basis for chronically low-wage careers is now firmly entrenched.

# What Are the Implications of These Findings?

Market economies always generate inequality to a lesser or greater degree. Yet strong growth has usually been associated with rising wages and declining inequality, at least since World War II. Judging by the limited wage mobility that workers are now achieving, one might think that the economy is in shambles. Of course it is not, and that is the puzzle.

Readers of the mass media could be forgiven for being surprised to hear that 90 percent of white male workers are doing worse now than they would have done twenty years ago. Our economy is in the midst of the longest postwar expansion on record, and the unlikely combination of strong growth, near-full employment, and low inflation have yielded an optimism that apparently knows no bounds. In 1999, *Newsweek*, in its worker's guide to jobs in the new millennium, focused on those who had reaped high-tech rewards from the expanding economy: "Plenty of fast-growing, high-paying jobs didn't even exist just a few years ago. Who could have predicted the booming demand for Webmasters, desktop publishers, and wireless engineers?" (McGinn and McCormick 1999, 44). The *New York Times Magazine*, while giving a more balanced view, still managed to conclude that "there is no reason why the new freedoms cannot also be a boon to certain kinds of low skilled workers—like cashiers" (Lewis 2000, 48).

This optimism has been bolstered by a modest uptick in median wages that began in 1996. Since our data end in 1994, this raises an important question: Is it possible that the trends we have documented are already a historical curiosity? Or, when placed in the context of other research, do our findings suggest that the unorthodox combination of economic growth, stagnant wages, and growing inequality may be a permanent feature of the new economy?

## *Are the Changes in the Wage Structure Temporary?*

In recent years, wages have begun to rise throughout the wage distribution. This uptick can be seen in the cross-sectional CPS data presented in the first chapter, in figure 1.2. Between 1996 and 1999, men posted gains of 9.2 percent in the bottom decile, 6.5 percent at the median, and 8.7 percent in the top decile. With the greatest gains being made at the bottom of the distribution, inequality started to fall slightly during these four years. We also see evidence of this wage growth for the recent cohort in figure 8.1, in which we supplement our data with two follow-up surveys of the NLSY conducted in 1996 and 1998.[2] It is a bit harder to interpret the NLSY wage increases because they are confounded with the aging of the cohort, and there are no data from the original cohort at these ages to use for comparison.[3] However, the distributional changes observed from 1994 onward are clearly larger than those observed between 1992 and 1994, especially at the bottom of the distribution. Do these findings, evident in both the CPS and NLSY samples, suggest that the long-standing decline in wage growth is soon to be reversed?

One way to gain perspective on these trends is to ask how much of the lost ground has been recovered by the recent uptick in wages. In 1999, the median male wage in the CPS was still 9.1 percent below its 1973 level in real terms, and the 90:10 wage ratio was 22 percent larger, up from 3.6 to 4.4. Similarly, in our data, we can ask whether the additional four years of wage growth that the recent cohort experienced between 1994 and 1998 was enough to bring its workers up to the final wage levels observed for the original cohort. Table 8.1 illustrates the results of this comparison. In 1998, high school graduates in the recent cohort were still more than two dollars (15.1 percent) behind the original cohort, even though they were, on average, four years older. High school dropouts lagged by 15.2 percent, and workers with some college experience by 10.6 percent.[4]

Another way to gain perspective is to consider the cumulative costs of depressed wage growth. At the current rate of wage inflation in the CPS, it will be 2004 before the median male finally earns a wage comparable to that earned in 1973. For the men who will have spent the intervening thirty-one years in the workforce, this translates into a substantial cumulative loss in lifetime earnings. To give a sense of the magnitude of loss for the young men we have studied in the NLSY, table 8.2 presents the cumulative earnings for the recent and the original cohorts during their first twenty years in the labor market.[5] The cohort differences, given in the last column, show a large deficit for every group in the recent cohort. Among those without a college degree, the average deficit of $100,517 is nearly equivalent to the cost of a house ($133,500) or four years of tuition at an elite private college.[6] Even for those with a college degree, the deficit is a substantial $40,000—the equivalent of an SUV for mom and dad and

**Figure 8.1   NLSY Hourly Wage Distributions from 1992 Through 1998**

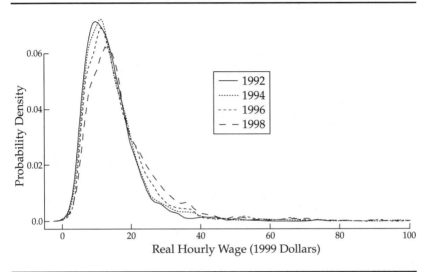

*Source:* Authors' compilation.

a starter car for junior. These losses took two decades to accumulate, and they will not be reversed by a brief period of wage growth. It would take an equally long period of strong growth, on the order of that seen during the 1960s, to erase them.

Finally, it is instructive to examine the greater political and economic context of the recent increase in wages. For those at the bottom of the distribution, the disproportionately large wage gains since 1996 (as illustrated in figure 1.2) reflect the impact of two increases in the minimum wage (in 1996 and 1997) and the decline in unemployment that started in 1993 and that has accelerated in the past few years.[7] It is not surprising that these factors combined to boost wages at the bottom—it would be hard to imagine a better recipe for improving the living standards of low-wage workers. Jared Bernstein and John Schmitt (1998) report that households in the bottom 20 percent of the income distribution received 35 percent of the benefits of the minimum wage increases, even though these households account for only 5 percent of total family income. The impact of the tight labor market is more difficult to quantify, though it has clearly drawn more disadvantaged workers into the workforce and mildly improved wages at the bottom of the distribution. The upshot is that although overall inequality for men started to decline in 1995, this trend was driven entirely by the gains made at the bottom—the top continued to pull

**Table 8.1    The Impact of Four Additional Years of Wage Growth on the Recent Cohort's Wages**

| Final Education Level | Median Wage (Dollars per Hour) | | | Wage Difference[c] |
| | Original Cohort in 1981[a] | Recent Cohort in 1994[a] | Recent Cohort in 1998[b] | |
|---|---|---|---|---|
| High school dropout | 12.58 | 10.00 | 10.92 | −1.66 |
| High school graduate | 16.27 | 12.31 | 14.14 | −2.13 |
| Some college experience | 17.98 | 15.03 | 16.26 | −1.72 |
| Bachelor's degree or higher | 20.15 | 19.38 | 24.38 | 4.23 |

Source: Authors' compilation.
Note: Hourly wages in real 1999 dollars. All figures are person based.
[a]Workers aged thirty to thirty-seven.
[b]Workers aged thirty-four to forty-one.
[c]Recent (1998) − original (1981).

away from everyone else.[8] Given this pattern, it would be premature to declare victory and leave the rest to fix itself. With every minimum wage increase hotly contested on Capitol Hill, and the inevitability of the business cycle, any gains made at the bottom are always at the mercy of politics and market dynamics. It behooves us, therefore, to keep our focus fixed on longer-term trends.

**Table 8.2    Estimated Total Cumulative Earnings from Sixteen to Thirty-Six Years of Age, by Cohort**

| Final Education Level | Total Cumulative Earnings[a] | | Cohort Difference[b] | |
| | Original Cohort[c] | Recent Cohort[c] | Amount[c] | Percentage Change |
|---|---|---|---|---|
| High school dropout | 504,170 | 420,868 | 83,304 | −16.5 |
| High school graduate | 614,373 | 498,593 | 115,780 | −18.8 |
| Some college experience | 640,318 | 537,850 | 102,467 | −16.0 |
| Bachelor's degree or higher | 677,837 | 637,800 | 40,038 | −5.9 |

Source: Authors' compilation.
Note: All estimates are person based.
[a]Based on the sum of annualized, age-adjusted median wages assuming full-time, full-year employment.
[b]Recent − original cohort.
[c]In real 1999 dollars.

The deterioration in upward mobility and job stability that we have documented in this book does not represent a temporary shift, reversible by a few years of strong economic growth. We have measured wage growth for these workers during the period when nearly 70 percent of lifetime wage gains are made. Thus we have observed most of the mobility that they will experience during their careers. The lower level of wage attainment among the recent cohort has already generated a large cumulative deficit in earnings. Absent a truly dramatic shift in the American economy, that deficit will persist, whether in the form of higher levels of indebtedness or lower levels of lifetime savings, over their life course.

The question, of course, is whether new cohorts of workers who are just now entering the labor market will also see a stagnation and polarization in economic mobility. Ultimately, this is a question about causes: whether the trends are easily reversed by more education and training or, instead, reflect more enduring changes in the employment relationship.

## Are the Trends in Economic Mobility the Result of Greater Demands for Skill?

Much of the discussion about rising inequality has settled into the comfortable consensus that changes in the wage structure have been driven by a growing demand for skilled workers. In light of this argument, it remains puzzling that the central feature of the wage trends is not that college graduates have seen their earnings increase but that those without a college degree have seen their wages deteriorate markedly. Moreover, these losses have not been concentrated in "marginal" labor force groups such as part-time workers, women, minorities, or youth. Instead, it is white men working full-time—traditionally the most privileged and protected sector of the labor force—who have been hit the hardest. The fact that they have lost so much ground suggests a more fundamental set of changes, ones that reach deep into the heart of the earnings determination process.

The nature of work has changed considerably over the past half century as production jobs in manufacturing have given way to jobs in a wide array of service sector industries. At the same time, the use of computers has spread into many workplaces (McConnel 1996). This combination—the shift toward nonmanual jobs and the ascent of new technologies—has lead many analysts to diagnose the country's wage problem as one of insufficient skills to meet the growing demand. Skill is a notoriously difficult concept to define and measure, however, and one might legitimately question whether these new jobs require more skill or simply different skills. In addition, while technological change may be somewhat easier to measure, it is not measured often. There is therefore little systematic survey evidence, especially outside the manufacturing sector, that can be used to evaluate directly the hypothesis of skill-biased technological change.

The debate about the impact of technology on skill requirements is hardly new, however, and the history of this debate offers some basic lessons for thinking about current trends. New technology can automate repetitive tasks, thereby raising the skill requirements for the worker who now needs to run a complicated machine. Yet technology can also standardize and compartmentalize tasks, leading to a de-skilling of jobs. Technology is therefore not inherently skill biased, and its effects can be assessed only by examining the context in which it is deployed.

An emerging literature uses firm and industry case studies to ask how technology has affected what actually happens in the workplace—especially in service industries.[9] Perhaps not surprisingly, this research reaffirms what the old debates about technology concluded: depending on the setting, the same technology can either upskill or downskill jobs or eliminate them altogether. In the current economy, one important factor that mediates and sometimes even drives the effect of technology is managerial strategy about how production and the workplace will be reorganized, which workers get access to which technologies, and how technology use will be rewarded.

A good example comes from the banking industry, perhaps the poster child for technological innovation. Larry Hunter and colleagues (2001) compare two major American banks as they restructured their retail banking branches. Both banks significantly upgraded their management information systems, greatly expanded the financial products they offered, and of course upped the ATM transaction flow. Both banks also faced similar skills sets in their tellers, largely high school graduates with long tenures. One bank decided to give tellers access to its new management information system and make them part of the sales force, with a substantial increase in training, while the other did not—and the differences in tellers' wages and mobility opportunities reflected this difference. Simply put, the technological change was the same, but the managerial strategies differed (and importantly, neither proved superior). Where the strategies did converge was in the de-skilling and relocation of back-office work. Improvements in technology made possible the centralization of customer service operations in large off-site call centers; these centers are notorious for their low wages, fast-paced and closely monitored work, and the absence of career ladders.

The upshot is that restructuring and technology can interact to produce different outcomes for workers with the same skill levels, even within a single industry and a single firm. Technology is therefore best seen as enabling rather than determining. We suspect that this is especially true in the wide range of workplaces in which highly specialized knowledge is not required and workers have a basic level of skill that can either be trained either up or not—the decision for managers is to "make or buy" skilled workers. This managerial discretion is a good candidate for explaining the growing inequality within education groups, a finding of virtually every study conducted.

Another way to evaluate the skill argument is to look at just how much better skilled workers are doing in the new economy. Using the most common proxy measure for skill—education—our evidence shows increasing uncertainty in the long-term payoff to higher education. Slightly more college graduates now achieve the kind of wage growth that would have put them in the top decile in the old economy, but at the same time, nearly two-thirds are less upwardly mobile now than they would have been in the past. In fact, the probability of literally flat wage trajectories has increased for college graduates (as for everyone else). Similarly, workers with associate's degrees and the like have clearly invested in additional training to boost their skills, and yet their wage growth is substantially lower now than that of their counterparts two decades ago. These findings make it clear that education does not necessarily protect workers against wage deterioration.

What accounts for this variability? One common argument is that college degrees are too crude a measure—that the skills that are being rewarded in the new economy are more specific, having to do with technology and scientific knowledge. Again, the evidence has not supported this argument. Stephen Rose and Anthony Carnevale (1997) examine wage changes for detailed occupations in the CPS from 1979 to 1995. They find that earnings for professionals in technical and scientific fields stagnated during this period, even in occupations closely tied to technological innovation. For example, among computer systems analysts with bachelor's degrees, earnings rose by only 3 percent over the sixteen years. Engineers, the largest occupation among science-related professionals, actually experienced earnings declines of about 1.5 percent. Yet during this same period, earnings increased by 34 percent for all occupations in the category of "office work"—an increase that was driven by the business professionals and managers outside of scientific or technical fields.[10] Our own findings in chapter 6, based on a less detailed analysis, are consistent with this pattern: the college graduates who made the largest gains during the 1980s and early 1990s were those who worked in the financial sector. It would be a far stretch to call managers, real estate agents, and brokers the leading edge of high technology.

With neither education nor technology able to explain fully the trends in wages and economic mobility, we have to look deeper into the workplace, where the employment relationship is continually contested and reconfigured. A broad indicator of the change in this relationship is given in figure 8.2. The basic assumption of the skill hypothesis is that skilled workers are more productive, and that is why their wages are higher. However, the decoupling of productivity growth from wage compensation growth in recent years strongly suggests that the wage-effort bargain has been changed, especially for men.

Beyond skills and technology lie a number of structural changes that help to explain the trends documented in this book. These changes come under many headings and have been studied in depth in a variety of disciplines: the globalization of trade, the decline of internal labor markets, deunionization, downsizing, the rise of complex interfirm relationships and networks, and the growing use of contingent labor. Our goal here is not to give a complete inventory of these trends and their potential impacts but rather to link our mobility and job instability findings to evidence of changes taking place at the organizational level.

### The Shift Toward Low-Wage Service Industries

The core feature of postindustrialism is, of course, the dominance of service industries. The trend of growing employment in the service sector and shrinking employment in the goods-producing sector is a remarkably long and stable one. By 1999, the share of employment in manufacturing industries had declined to 15 percent, making it smaller than the retail trade industry, while the size of the service sector had risen to 80 percent of the labor force, with service industries alone accounting for 29 percent.[11]

The gap in annual earnings between expanding industries (primarily in the service sector) and contracting industries (primarily in the goods-producing sector) reached ten thousand dollars in the 1980s, a postwar high (Costrell 1988). This is because jobs in the service sector typically pay less, offer fewer benefits, and are more likely to be part-time. The correlation between earnings and employment growth at the industry level from 1973 to 1999 can be seen in figure 8.3. The

Figure 8.2    Index of Productivity and Hourly Compensation Growth, 1973
to 1998

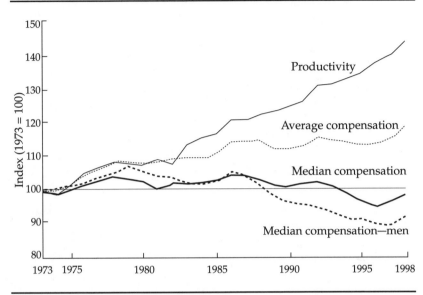

*Source:* Mishel, Bernstein, and Schmitt 2001.

inverse relation is striking: higher-wage industries have generated far
fewer jobs during the past two and half decades than have lower-
wage industries. In fact, retail trade and service industries accounted
for 55 percent of net job growth over this period. However, though
retail industries are fairly homogeneous—low wage and high turnover—service industries are quite stratified. For example, long-term
and home health care is a fast-growing segment of the health services
industry, with wages in stark contrast to those garnered by doctors
and nurses. Similarly, building cleaning and maintenance constitutes
an important, but very low-wage, part of business services.

The upshot is that a rising share of employment in the service sector is consistent with the stagnation in wages and growing inequality
that so many researchers have documented. The exact contribution of
deindustrialization to changes in the wage structure differs from
study to study, but it is clearly a key factor. Our own findings in
chapter 6 show that the wage penalty for low-end service jobs is one
of the largest penalties observed: wages are about 15 percent lower
compared with wages in goods-producing industries. Although the
size of this penalty has not grown over time, the number of workers
experiencing it has. This is the single largest compositional shift in

**Figure 8.3    The Relationship Between Industry Employment Growth from 1973 to 1999 and Average Wages of Non-Supervisory Workers in 1999**

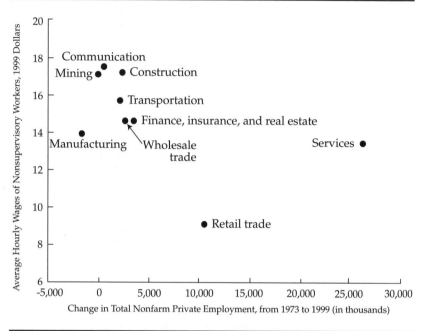

Source: U.S. Bureau of the Census 2000.
Note: Transportation and communication both include various public utilities.

our data, and it explains up to a quarter of the deterioration in long-term wage growth.

Perhaps an even more important question, however, is what the growth in services has meant for upward mobility and employment stability. In chapter 7 we have seen initial evidence that jobs at the bottom of the service sector are "sticky" and over the long term effectively trap workers in low-wage careers. Case study evidence provides some insight into the mechanisms at work here. One of the best places to look is the retail trade industry: it employs almost a fifth of the workforce, with wages that rank at the bottom of the economy. These low-wage jobs are not coming from dinosaur firms that somehow have not yet caught on to the new high-tech credo—just the opposite, in fact. At the forefront of this industry, employing an ever larger number of workers, is the Wal-Mart business model—very productive and technologically sophisticated, but nevertheless requiring a low level of skill of its workforce. On the one hand, the model features a superefficient production process in which each retail operation is linked to the next in a continuous "just-in-time" chain. On the other hand, sales staff basically ring up sales, stock and tidy shelves, and handle layaways. Part-time work is the norm, schedules shift constantly, wages are low and turnover high, and health insurance is too costly for many workers to afford. With sales of $165 billion last year, the Wal-Mart model has put enormous pressure on the industry to follow suit and has even spilled into related industries such as grocery stores.[12]

Is this really cause for concern? One common argument is that the retail sector and other low-wage service industries like it simply serve as a temporary way station for workers—mothers wanting to get out of the house, retirees looking for something to occupy their time, and especially teenagers earning spending money. This is a misleading or at the very least outdated picture. In 1996, only 16 percent of workers in this industry were aged sixteen to nineteen. Fully 44 percent were aged thirty-five or older. With Wal-Mart's strategy driving other competitors to either imitate or perish, more and more retail workers will have little alternative but to depend on this type of job for their long-term livelihood. And in this dependence lies the heart of the problem. Moving up to better jobs is difficult, because this type of service industry has extremely flat job hierarchies. Sales and service occupations make up more than two-thirds of retail jobs, and the average ratio of managerial to frontline workers is one to fifteen. Moving out is equally difficult: retail workers get seven hours of training on average (last among fourteen business sectors), giving them few skills with which to reach for better jobs.

Variations on this story appear in other industries, such as insurance, health care, fast foods, data processing, even the finance sector (for example, see Macdonald and Sirianni 1996). They suggest a clear link to the flat mobility paths, short tenures, and unproductive job searching documented in this book, and especially the growing strength of the low-wage career trap documented in chapter 7.

## The Restructuring of Work

What has happened at the bottom of the service sector is only one piece of a larger puzzle: the economy-wide reorganization of work and production. We do not yet have a full grasp on this complex and still evolving process. There are many signs that mass production and internal labor markets are giving way to new forms of work.[13] There are also a variety of causes, including the globalization of production, governmental deregulation, and deunionization. The question is, how have upward mobility and job stability been affected?

If there is one logo stamped on the new economy, in the minds of both the public and researchers, it is temp work and other forms of contingent labor—and understandably, given the industry's phenomenal fourfold growth since 1982 (Hudson 1999). The stereotype of temp jobs—short lived, with low pay, and leading nowhere—is a powerful symbol of the externalization of labor markets and the anxiety about job loss that seems endemic in survey after survey. Despite the recent emergence of high-skill contingent workers such as lawyers, programmers, and even doctors among the temp workforce, the stereotype still largely holds true. Most temp work is in low-skill occupations such as data entry, industrial assembly, nursing assistance, child care, house cleaning, trucking, and janitorial service, and wages and benefits are almost uniformly lower than those paid for full-time equivalent jobs (Kalleberg et al. 1997).

The problem is that the number of contingent workers is nowhere near large enough to produce the trends that we have documented in this book, even given the strong growth rates. In the CPS survey week of 1997, for example, only 1 percent of workers held a temporary job, 1.5 percent worked as on-call and day laborers, 1.3 percent held contract-company jobs, and 1.3 percent were independent contractors paid wages or salaries (Hudson 1999). Researchers sometimes also count part-time workers (13.6 percent) and the self-employed (4.8 percent) into the contingent category, but the prevalence of such jobs has not changed appreciably since the late 1970s—and our interest here is in changes over time. So although contingent work may well become much more significant in the future, it is unlikely that it has played a major role in generating the rise in job instability and the polarization in mobility paths over the past thirty years.[14]

Temporary work, then, is best considered the tip of the iceberg, just one symptom of a wide variety of restructured work and production arrangements. Hard data on such arrangements are hard to come by, indeed almost nonexistent.[15] This is especially true for subcontracting and outsourcing, one of the least explored forms of restructuring and yet possibly the most important. We are not just talking about Nike's production of its shoes overseas. Subcontracting is redefining the very infrastructure of the domestic economy, with the emergence of complex supplier networks and the shedding of service functions previously performed in-house, such as custodial jobs, payroll and benefits management, data processing, and even entire units such as jobs in restaurants within the hotel industry. We have little data on the prevalence of such outsourcing, except within the manufacturing sector, and this is clearly a critical area for future research. One manufacturing survey has found that from 1986 to 1987, 23.9 percent of firms contracted out at least some of their janitorial services (Abraham and

Taylor 1996). Another analysis of this survey, using a follow-up questionnaire, finds that 57.4 percent of metalworking and machinery plants "usually" outsource some part of their machining operations (Harrison and Kelley 1993). A more recent clue for all industries can be had from the 1999 Staffing and Structure Survey conducted by the American Management Association, which finds that 49.6 percent of firms reported job cuts in 1999, virtually unchanged from the 50 percent in 1995. Of the companies cutting jobs during this five-year period, fully 44.6 percent reported that "the work was transferred to other entities" (for example, outsourcing and subcontracting) (American Management Association 1999).[16]

A related trend is the restructuring of operations within firms. Here, functions that were previously integrated are split off, formed into separate business units, and often relocated geographically. Call centers are perhaps the best illustration: especially in banking and insurance, customer service is now routinely centralized at one location that may be halfway across the country from the firm's headquarters. Whether performed internally or contracted out, this unbundling of operations stems partly from the push by firms to focus on their "core competencies" (a term that has become a mantra for the business sector) and partly to lower their labor costs, especially in unionized firms. As Moss and colleagues (2000) point out in their study of several insurance firms, deintegration does not bode well for frontline workers. The insurance industry has traditionally provided mobility for the less skilled, at least in jobs such as sales and customer service, through on-the-job training and performance-based promotion. When these lower occupational rungs are shifted internally to separate business centers, the ladder is broken; and when the rungs are contracted out altogether, it is frequently to lower-wage (and non-union) firms focused on supplying only a single product or service, offering little by way of job ladders to its employees.

Another form of restructuring that is only now being documented is the growing use of market segmentation. Particularly in the service sector, firms are strategically stratifying their customer markets based on price and quality, resulting in a similar stratification of the work and the wages associated with each submarket. So, for example, in the telecommunications industry, long-distance products are stratified into four tiers. For low-revenue customers, workers provide a small number of services at high volume (nine hundred calls a day), whereas for high-revenue customers, workers are cross-trained and spend much more time with each client (taking as few as thirty calls a day). Rosemary Batt (2001) finds that this segmentation is clearly reflected in wages, and not wholly because of the greater skills required in the upper segments. This trend has been found in industries as diverse as insurance, retail trade, restaurants, information technology, financial services, airlines, and healthcare.[17] The outcome for workers has been not just a polarization in wages but also a splitting of some of the paths that previously connected jobs and created careers. For example, different department stores now specialize in either high-income, middle-income, or mass markets, resulting in less-varied jobs and less-elaborate career ladders within any one store. In addition, managers are increasingly hired from the outside. Such restructuring means fewer opportunities for frontline sales workers to move up to management, merchandise buying, or high-ticket commissioned sales (Bailey and Bernhardt 1997).

Finally, we should consider the introduction of high-performance work systems, which have garnered much interest as a potential balance to some of the negative forms of work reorganization and which are starting to spread beyond manufacturing. Under this model, team-based production and greater employee involvement and decision-making power are leveraged to increase firm productivity; in fact, those productivity effects are now well documented (Ichniowski et al. 1996). The big question, however, is to what extent workers benefit. The picture is mixed in terms of wages: some researchers find positive effects (Appelbaum et al. 2000; Cappelli 1996), whereas others do not (Osterman 2000; Handel and Gittleman 1999). However, no one has as yet studied the long-term impact on worker mobility, and here we can only speculate. A key feature of high-performance systems is the collapsing of many tasks into a few broad jobs that require multiple skills and discretion. This job broadening may present an opportunity for some workers, but it may also create bigger barriers to others. The entry requirements are likely to be greater, and movement up into the next big job classification is likely to mean a greater jump, for which outside education is needed (Moss, Salzman, and Tilly 2000).

The broad picture, then, shows a permanent fading of the traditional career route. As yet, nothing has emerged to take its place.[18] What happens to promotions, raises, and climbing up the ladder of success when employers hire externally for skilled jobs and invest less in entry-level training, especially for new technology? How does a worker with only a high school diploma gain access to firms in which job titles have been collapsed and decision making has been pushed down to multiskilled, autonomous employees working in teams? What happens when low-skill jobs are removed from the organization altogether, through subcontracting and outsourcing, to specialized "niche" firms that frequently pay less for the same work? The traditional routes to upward mobility break down, labor markets become segmented, and greater lifetime inequality results. We therefore see our findings as strong evidence that there has indeed been a shift in the American employment relationship, that the rules of work and career mobility have changed. Until this shift is recognized, a coherent policy discussion focused on both supply-side and demand-side responses cannot occur.

## Policy Options

The changes in the labor market over the past three decades confront us with a difficult question: What kinds of public, private, and community-based policies are required to reverse the long-standing growth in inequality? More concretely, what kinds of institutions, programs, and regulations are needed to improve worker welfare while at the same time maintaining the flexibility that employers are demanding?

That postindustrial America presents us with a new set of policy challenges has not gone unnoticed. The calls for lifelong learning, the expansion of community colleges, the attempt to centralize the government's training and placement services through a one-stop system, all signal a growing awareness of the changing nature of work. In fact, a number of comprehensive inventories of policy options already exist, and it is not our purpose to reiterate them; interested readers should consult Paul Osterman's *Securing Prosperity* (1999).

Instead, we focus here on strategies for influencing long-term wage growth over the course of the career.[19] This focus highlights why the traditional policy approach of education and training, though clearly integral, does not suffice to address the myriad problems currently in evidence in the labor market. The supply-side approach must be balanced with policies that ensure workers access to quality jobs, economic security, and employment stability. There are a number of compelling reasons for this expanded approach.

First and foremost, education and training policies can improve upward mobility only if there are enough career paths for the trained workers to fill. Especially at the bottom of the labor market, however, firms are succeeding with bottom-line strategies that emphasize cost cutting and low wages and that in the process generate jobs that lead nowhere. Higher up, the growing practice of siphoning off jobs that are not part of a firm's "core competency" has resulted in broken career ladders, with components of that ladder spread across subcontractors, temp agencies, and even different geographic regions. It is hard to argue that such strategies exist merely because of an inadequate supply of skilled workers. They are proving efficient and competitive against "higher road" models and will continue to prevail unless explicitly addressed.

A second motivation for targeting the demand side of the economy is that skills alone do not protect workers against wage and job instability. Our current employment laws are modeled on the permanent lifetime job, assuming only infrequent and temporary layoffs. These laws are inadequate to the task of protecting workers who are not covered by union contracts, who have only tenuous relationships with employers, and who are frequently unemployed between jobs.

A third point is that a more volatile and fluid labor market puts severe pressure on current job-matching systems. As job instability rises, the problem for firms is to find, screen, hire, and train an increasing number of workers in a short time. For workers, job search becomes more complex and more consequential as time spent with one employer grows shorter and as the responsibility for ensuring long-term wage growth increasingly resides with the individual. Education cannot solve this coordination and information problem.

Finally, as a society we need to ensure that there are many paths to upward wage mobility. We have neither the dollars nor the infrastructure to educate everyone to be a programmer or managerial consultant—and why should we want to? The country's job structure is a pyramid, and many critical tasks are performed at its base. From a societal standpoint, these workers provide essential services and they should have access to a living wage that can support a household over the long run.

In short, a policy of education and training alone is unlikely to solve the problem of limited mobility in the postindustrial economy. We also need policies that touch the employment relationship directly, that address the problems of career development and long-term wage growth documented in this book. How to do this? In our minds, four strategies are needed: the creation of career ladders outside of firms, the strengthening of career ladders within firms, improvement of low-wage jobs, and improvement of labor market coordination.

## Constructing External Career Ladders

Probably the main concern in policy discourse has been with the rise in job instability and the consequent need for new career structures. From the worker's standpoint, frequent job changes might be tenable if they are accompanied by advancement into higher positions and if benefits are portable across employers. This indicates the need for labor market institutions that support multiemployer careers. Workers could shift among firms according to demand but gain portable and recognized skills in the process, so that upward mobility would occur incrementally across different organizations and churning between low-wage jobs could be avoided. An important requirement is that workers receive long-term and generalized training, not just short-term training for immediate firm needs.

## Constructing or Strengthening Internal Career Ladders

Because they are tied to the old employment system, internal labor markets are often seen as antiquated and impractical in a highly competitive environment. Yet it is premature to abandon an emphasis on internal promotion. In many industries and niches, the nature of work and certification lends itself to a graded system of upward mobility as skills are progressively gained at each level (for example, health care, telecommunications, banking, education). Indeed, especially in the current tight labor market, we are beginning to hear concern in the business community that the downsizing and dismantling of internal labor markets during the 1980s may have been too extreme. Employee motivation and productivity are hard to sustain in an unstable work setting that offers few chances for upward movement and in which little is invested in on-the-job training. Thus in theory at least, internal labor markets make sense for a number of occupations and industries.

## Improving Low-Wage Jobs

Ultimately, however, policies focused only on mobility ladders (whether external or internal) are not enough. Low-wage and dead-end jobs will continue to serve as the mainstay of employment for significant numbers of workers. In the early 1990s, it was hoped that firm reorganization and a greater emphasis on customer service, teamwork, and modern technology might upgrade the quality of these jobs—that firms would choose a high-performance strategy. As we have just seen, however, especially in service industries there is evidence to suggest that workplace innovations rarely trickle down to affect entry-level, low-skill jobs. We may simply have to recognize that tasks such as preparing hamburgers, cleaning hotel rooms, and ringing up sales will not be significantly transformed. If this is the case, then an important policy goal continues to be the guarantee of a livable income for low-skill work. This is what the unionized manufacturing sector was able to do in the past for a core group of frontline, semiskilled workers: provide decent wages with benefits and with regular wage increases over the career span.

## *Improving Labor Market Coordination*

Finally, the increased movement of workers between employers raises a host of new coordination issues. In the past, employers and prospective workers typically found one another by relying on a mix of informal networks, headhunters, private job-matching firms, and public agencies. Such an ad hoc system does not respond well to rapid changes in skill requirements. Nor does it easily handle a faster cycle of job openings, screening, and hiring. Informal networks are especially worrisome in the context of a more volatile labor market–job-finding networks run the risk of reproducing inequality because they tend to be segregated by skill level, income, race, and gender (Newman and Lennon 1995). In short, the job-matching process needs to be given a formal structure, through better information and coordination, in which intermediary institutions serve as a clearinghouse where employers can list their jobs and job seekers can learn about job openings and requirements.

## Policy Implementation

What is needed to implement these four strategies? Part of the answer lies in legislation. Almost any attempt to mediate the new employment relationship needs to be supported by laws and regulations in several areas.[20] One of the most important is reform of the unemployment insurance system. Currently, access to its benefits is based on the outdated model of long-term employment and stable earnings with one company, perhaps interrupted by temporary layoffs. The result is that only about a third of those who are unemployed receive unemployment insurance benefits (McMurrer and Chasanov 1995). In particular, temporary, part-time, seasonal, and low-wage workers, as well as independent contractors, are usually not eligible because of the nature of their work and careers. Reform is also clearly needed in the provision of benefits. The current structure of health care and pension benefits is employer based and militates against portability, yet portability is precisely what the externalization of work requires. Simply asking workers to buy their own benefits is not tenable, as evidenced by the large number who are currently uninsured and who do not have their own retirement accounts. Last, several steps are needed to ensure that the wage floor is not just a bottomless well: indexing the minimum wage to inflation, expanding the earned income tax credit (EITC), and the continued adoption of living-wage ordinances are all effective strategies for preventing wage deterioration at the bottom of the distribution.

These and other steps, however, will be effective only if they are combined with actual changes in the employment relationship itself. Otherwise, these legislative strategies will simply support the practices that are responsible for growing inequality in the first place. For example, however important the EITC has been to low-income families, it has the effect of allowing low-wage employers to continue business as usual. Ultimately, policy makers will have to confront the fact that the negative trends in workers' long-term economic welfare will be reversed only by changes in the way firms behave.

On the ground at least, there is evidence that this point has hit home. Around the country, a diverse set of organizations and programs are trying in some way to move beyond the traditional approach of workforce development. Included are union-run initiatives, multiemployer alliances, community-based organizations, worker-owned companies, occupation-based associations, and collaborations between public and private partners. The initiatives use a wide array of approaches, which vary in the extent to which they touch the core of the employment relationship. For example, some simply try to improve the quality of the job match through labor market coordination; others try to pool resources on the worker side, acting as "proxy" employers; and an increasingly common strategy is to provide training that is directly linked to employers, with guaranteed jobs at the end. These and other approaches have been comprehensively reviewed by Osterman (1999), Laura Dresser and Joel Rogers (1997), and Françoise Carré and Pamela Joshi (1998).

Here we briefly outline the most developed and most promising of these models: sectoral partnerships that marshal as many resources as possible to push participating companies toward a high-performance, "mutual gains" model, one in which both firms' profits and workers' wages and careers are sustained. These partnerships usually include a critical mass of employers and unions in a given industry or sector, as well as any number of public partners, such as community colleges, Private Industry Councils, and community-based organizations. The logic is simple, at least in theory: provide collective solutions to problems that single firms cannot afford or are unable to devise on their own, with the price tag of solid wages, job security, and career ladders for workers.

One of the most developed examples is the Wisconsin Regional Training Partnership (WRTP), a consortium of manufacturers, unions, and public sector partners in the Milwaukee metropolitan area, founded in 1992. The goal of the WRTP is to support the creation of high-performance workplaces and quality jobs in the region and to ensure an adequate supply of skilled workers to fill those jobs. More than sixty employers from metalworking, electronics, plastics, and related industries are members—a significant share of the regional market. They employ roughly sixty thousand workers, who are represented by industrial and craft unions. At the core of the partnership is a series of channels for communication, planning, and implementation between employers and unions to solve common problems. Joint management-labor working groups focus on three issues: plant modernization (a key need in this sector), training of incumbent workers (to enable modernization and internal promotion), and training of new workers (through a program to link inner-city residents to good jobs). The cornerstone of the partnership is the set of Workplace Education Centers, which are on-site at most of the member firms and are linked to technical colleges in the area. These centers provide skills upgrading and training to meet changes in production and technology as well as basic education and preparation for the general educational development (GED) test. These centers were initially subsidized by public funds, but the employers now spend twenty million dollars to sustain them. New initiatives by the partnership include a program to convert temporary jobs back to permanent jobs in member firms and the creation of a "supplier network" of organizations in city neighborhoods to link disadvantaged workers to training and job openings.

Another example illustrates the feasibility of this approach in the service sector. The San Francisco Hotels Partnership Project was created in 1994 as part of a multiemployer contract between eleven first-class hotels and the largest union in the industry. The immediate goals of this project are to provide job security for workers and to increase the competitiveness of the member hotels. The ultimate goal is to increase the upward mobility of the largely immigrant workforce. At the core of the partnership lies a series of problem-solving teams that address long-standing workplace issues, staffed by workers, managers, and neutral facilitators and translators. To date, the focus has been on intensive team-building training (to overcome a history of hostile labor-management relations) and skills training for workers. Classes in English as a second language, in particular, have been especially important, because the language barrier has created a virtual divide between the "back house" jobs in housekeeping, kitchen work, and maintenance and the better "front house" jobs requiring interaction with customers. Several recent pilot projects have addressed the broader issue of workplace reorganization. In one hotel

the entire kitchen area was restructured: twenty-seven kitchen qualifications were collapsed into three, and two job titles were eliminated
altogether. (This was one of the main concerns of the employers, that
rigid job titles hinder flexibility in how workers are deployed.) The
union and its workers were involved in every part of the reorganization, and wages and seniority rules were renegotiated. On the agenda
for the next five years are pilot projects to improve hotel restaurant
operations, housekeeping operations, health and safety, and career
ladder opportunities.

The promise of sectoral partnerships is that they can begin to reverse the breakdown of career ladders and rebuild upward mobility
for workers without college degrees—at their best, they actually
change the nature of the jobs being created.[21] How is this possible?
Again, the incentive for employers lies in the collective goods and
services that can be provided by a collaborative structure. For example, it is difficult for single firms, especially the smaller ones that pop-
ulate the service sector, to know exactly how to modernize and implement new technologies, never mind to find the resources for
retraining workers. Shared resources on the first front, and joint training pools on the second, can make the difference between choosing
the high road or sticking with the low road. Similarly, the ubiquitous
concern over poaching can be solved with multiemployer collaboration. When firms "share" a group of workers in an effectively closed
labor market, they also share the costs of screening and training—the
loss of one worker is offset by the ability to hire another who is similarly trained. Collaboration across employers can also improve sectoral competitiveness. Under this scenario, competition between single firms gives way to the larger goal of improving the global
performance of a domestic industry. Firms thus "lay down arms" and
jointly pursue the high road—in fact, this was the initial motivation
behind the WRTP, the need to remain competitive in the global economy.[22]

Finally, it is also important to recognize that a low-wage business
strategy brings its own set of costs, shirking, absenteeism, and lack of
commitment on the part of the workforce. These are incentive problems that the traditional internal labor market was good at solving
and that the new joint initiatives can also address. For example,
worker-management teams charged with modernizing the workplace
yield many of the benefits of employee involvement (Blinder 1990;
Levine and Tyson 1990).

What is compelling about this list of incentives is that they address
many of the complaints commonly heard from the business community: high turnover, lack of skills, low productivity, lack of worker

commitment. The hope, then, is that employers might voluntarily commit to improving worker welfare at the same time that they pursue flexibility and profits. The question, however, is whether the above incentives are sufficient in the absence of unions. Several experiments in nonunion settings are currently under way, and in the end, the answer will most likely depend on the specific industry and labor market being targeted.

This is the most common critique of sectoral partnerships, that they rely heavily on the presence of unions. This is true; but the picture is a bit more complicated. First, though union density is quite low overall, it actually remains significant in major metropolitan areas and in big firms across a host of industries (not just manufacturing and hospitality but also grocery stores, health care, telecommunications, and construction, to name just a few). In fact, this is precisely the goal of the partnership model: to become firmly established in core regions and with key employers and then to use that leverage to reform the rest of the sector. Second, the role of unions is not simply (or even mainly) to "force" the partnerships onto employers. Perhaps even more important is that they are the best source of worker voice: joint initiatives of the type just described can only succeed with sustained input from the worker side. This is not a platitude. Over and over again, employers trying to change their production and service delivery systems have quickly learned that knowledge from the floor—about what should be improved, whether the new technologies and machines are working, safety issues, what training should actually look like—is critical to the process. So at least in theory, alternative forms of worker representation could be used to build sectoral partnerships.

That said, there is no question that in very low-wage service industries, the "high-road" carrot is unlikely to work. High-skill strategies are a hard sell at the bottom of the service sector, and in the likely absence of governmental regulation, the only thing that will make an appreciable dent in the quality of poor jobs here is an all-out unionization assault. To their credit, unions are beginning to realize this need, though the obstacles to organizing a high-turnover service workforce are enormous. A new type of unionism will be needed, one that is multiemployer and occupationally based. Pursuing such a strategy will take significant reform on many fronts—not only in labor's willingness to adopt a new constituency and new organizing tactics but, more important, in labor law itself (Greenhouse 1997). As with our laws that govern employment, labor law has become outdated, based as it is on a single-site unionism that allows little room for the new structures of work and nonstandard workers (Commission on the Future of Worker-Management Relations 1994).[23] Reform here is critical: a 1994 survey finds that 32 percent of nonunion workers would like to have a union (42 percent if management were not opposed), and an even larger percentage would like to see some type of workplace representation (Freeman and Rogers 1999).

## Conclusion

Images of Silicon Valley exert a strong pull on how our nation perceives postindustrial America. The reality is both different and more interesting. The new economy does indeed hold the promise of a prosperity that could be widely shared. That promise will not be realized, however, by pursuing a naive policy goal of transforming every worker into a computer programmer or managerial consultant. The story of the past three decades is not about the rise of technocracy, in which knowledge workers have finally come to rule. Rather, it is a story about economic restructuring, in which the employment relationship has been deliberately reconfigured within and between firms. It is a story about power and the extent to which we as a nation have been unwilling to mediate the imbalance of power that is inherent in a capitalist system. That we have largely dropped the ball should be obvious at this point: declining economic opportunity for a large majority of Americans signals a failure of public responsibility.

Our choice is simple: either we continue to stand by as the market makes it more profitable for firms to defect from the employment relationship, or we try, with a combination of carrots and sticks, to engage them in the process of rebuilding that relationship. History has repeatedly shown that unregulated markets do not produce optimal outcomes for both workers and firms. In some cases it is simply too attractive for firms to shift their costs to workers and the public purse, as with health care and retirement benefits. Even if the costs of an unregulated system begin to exceed the benefits for firms, however, the invisible hand may still not suffice. Educating and training workers, for example, is a classic public goods problem. Any single firm is individually better off by letting other firms invest in training and then poaching the workers; but if all firms do this, none benefit, and all are worse off.

Any number of innovative external programs can be devised that do not ask firms to change their calculus—providing job-matching services, alleviating substandard wages through tax credits, and anticipating future training needs through community college programs—but these ad hoc mechanisms can never replace a coherent system of industrial relations. Markets work best when their weaknesses are systematically redressed through policy; the question for the future is who will be at the table when these decisions are made.

# = Appendix A =

## Variable Definition
## and Construction

THIS APPENDIX provides a reference for the variables that are
used throughout the book. We discuss only variables that require elaboration. For straightforward variables such as marital
status or region of residence, the interested reader is referred to the
*NLS Users' Guide* (Center for Human Resource Research 1995).

As described in chapter 2, we make use of data from two cohorts
from the National Longitudinal Surveys. The first is the National Longitudinal Survey of Young Men (NLSYM): a nationally representative
sample of young men was first interviewed in 1966 and reinterviewed
yearly until 1981, except for four skipped years. The second is the
male sample of the National Longitudinal Survey of Youth (NLSY): a
nationally representative sample of young men was interviewed
yearly from 1979; for this sample, we use data up to 1994.

In preparing the variables used in our analyses, we were guided by
one key principle: any measures used to compare the two cohorts had
to be identically constructed. To a large extent, we could rely on the
comparability in the basic structure of the data sets. Each cohort was
followed for sixteen years, from the ages of fourteen to twenty-one
until the ages of thirty to thirty-seven. We therefore observe the members of each cohort at exactly the same ages, with similar information
on education, work history, and job characteristics. Occasionally, however, there are some differences between the survey instruments and
procedures used in the two cohorts, and in such cases we have made
extensive efforts to ensure that the measures we construct retain full
comparability. Often this means sacrificing a finer level of detail,
which may be present in only one of the cohorts, to gain full comparability between them.[1]

Four primary differences between the cohorts affect our variable
construction: the four missing years in the original cohort; the fact

that for the original cohort, information is collected only on the CPS job; the inability to identify a return to a previous employer in the recent cohort if the intervening spell is longer than two years; and the shifting interview window in the recent cohort. The first two differences are most important.

First, the four missing years will affect any measure that depends on the cumulation of values across years, because the original cohort has several two-year gaps and the recent cohort does not. Examples of measures that would be affected are the rate of job changing, age at first full-time job, and total number of unemployment spells.

Second, whereas data on the recent cohort were collected on up to five employers since the last interview, in the original cohort data were consistently collected only on the respondent's main CPS job. In this book, therefore, we focus exclusively on the CPS employer, and all job-related information pertains to this employer.[2] In practice, the information loss is not great, because the holding of more than one job at any one point in time is not common and because incorporating two jobs in our wage models, for example, would have been a truly daunting task. Moreover, the focus on the CPS employer allows congruence with other research in the labor economics field. The only place there is a strong impact is on our measure counting the total number of employers reported by a respondent by the last year of the study; we discuss this variable in more detail later in this appendix.

The CPS employer is identified in the same way across both cohorts in all survey years: a respondent who held more than one job at the time of the survey was asked to focus on the one at which he worked the most hours. Our definition of the CPS job also required at least ten hours of work a week and at least nine weeks of cumulated tenure (Center for Human Resource Research 1995). See chapter 2 for more detail on the CPS definition.

In the discussion that follows, we begin with the basic variables, such as education and work experience, and then move to the derived measures, such as labor force transition sequences, employer changes, and cumulative number of employers. The derived measures are presented in the order of the chapters in which they appear.

## Basic Variables

The NLS collects information on a number of work and education-related measures that are typically quite straightforward when used in a cross-sectional analysis. These measures require more care in this setting, where longitudinal and cross-cohort consistency must be maintained.

## Education

Educational attainment is measured for every year in which the surveys were administered, with similar questions for both cohorts. When respondents missed a survey year, retrospective information was collected to establish enrollment and attainment. To construct our measure of educational attainment, we use information on both years of education completed and degrees received to date: respondents coded as high school graduates or college graduates must actually hold those degrees. Thus someone reporting twelve years of education but not reporting a high school diploma is coded as a high school nongraduate. Similarly, someone reporting sixteen years of education but not reporting having a college degree is coded as having "some college experience." Our analyses typically focus on four education categories: high school nongraduates; high school graduates, including GED holders; respondents with some college experience but no four-year degree; and respondents with a four-year college degree.

## School Enrollment

In most analyses, we use the NLS measure of school enrollment provided for each cohort, which indicates whether the respondent was enrolled during the survey week. This measure is defined in the same way for both cohorts. For analyses that focus on the effects of enrollment on other variables measured in the survey week, this is the appropriate measure to use. Analyses that compare rates of enrollment between the cohorts over time, however, are complicated by shifting interview windows (see figure 2.2): whereas the original cohort was interviewed in the autumn of each year (consistently capturing the academic term), the interview period for the recent cohort shifted from the winter to the summer months in the second half of the sixteen-year panel (increasingly missing the academic term). For analyses in which we compare the prevalence of enrollment by age between the cohorts, we therefore constructed another variable. This alternative measure asks whether the respondent was enrolled during the past twelve months, and it is strictly comparable across the two cohorts. Where necessary, we adjust the respondent's age to reflect the timing of that enrollment. This variable is used in chapter 3 in the labor force transition analysis.

## Work Experience

People often work part-year because of spells of unemployment, schooling, or other activities. To obtain a measure of work experience, cross-sectional surveys would have to collect retrospective information on weeks worked since the respondent first entered the labor market, and this is unlikely to be reliably reported unless the person is a recent entrant. As a result, researchers must often use the proxy of "potential experience" instead, defined as age minus years of education minus six. This does not measure how long a respondent has actually worked but only how long he could have worked if he never worked during school and worked continuously after completing his schooling. "Potential experience" overstates the true number of years worked by about 15 percent for men (Light and Ureta 1995).

Few surveys collect information on the actual number of years worked to date because it is difficult to measure accurately. Because they are longitudinal, the NLS and NLSY surveys have the advantage of being able to collect accurate information on weeks worked in each year. As a result, we do not have to settle for the potential experience measure: we have data on actual cumulative weeks worked. This measure is not affected by missed interviews in either cohort, because respondents were asked to provide retrospective information for the years in which they were not interviewed.

The raw variable is, however, affected by the respondent's age at entry into the survey. For both cohorts, the recording of weeks worked begins in the twelve months preceding the first survey. This variable is therefore truncated for respondents whose work histories extend further back. To create a standardized untruncated measure, we constructed a variable that represents the number of months worked since the respondent turned sixteen years of age. For respondents who were fourteen to sixteen years old in the first year of the survey, we have exact information on this variable. For respondents who entered the survey after the age of sixteen, we imputed the missing months of experience. We did so by forming a matrix of age (seventeen to twenty-two) by enrollment (currently enrolled in high school, currently enrolled in college, or currently not enrolled) for those who entered the survey before the age of seventeen, and calculating the mean observed experience. These means were then imputed to the truncated cases, from the appropriate age-enrollment cell. The accuracy of this imputation method was first checked on the untruncated sample. Specifically, we performed the imputation for half of the respondents observed before the age of seventeen (using the other half for estimating the means) and then compared the predicted values to the actual observed values. The predictions were remarkably accurate; age and current enrollment are clearly strong predictors of weeks worked in this early stage of the career.

## Tenure

Both cohorts have comparable information on weeks of continuous tenure with the respondent's current employer. We stress continuous, because in the recent cohort it is not possible to identify returns to a previous employer if the intervening spell was longer than two years. For the original cohort, all tenures were calculated using the job start date.

For the recent cohort, the tenure data is taken from the work history array for the appropriate CPS job. This tenure variable is truncated, however, if the job started before January 1, 1978 (one year before the survey began). We therefore use the job start date to identify jobs that began before 1978 and add the difference back to the truncated tenure for those jobs. We also checked the accuracy of all other array-reported tenures using the job start date and cleaned them where necessary.

## Industry and Occupation

In each cohort, we measure the industry and occupation of the respondent's CPS job. Both dimensions are classified using codes from the 1970 census, as these were the only codes consistently available for both cohorts. For the recent cohort, 1980 codings were available, as well. Industry codes have not changed much over the past three decades, and so here, we could have converted the original cohort's 1970 codes to 1980 codes. Occupational codes have changed significantly, however, and imputing 1970 codes to 1980 codes is known to be particularly difficult and inaccurate.[3] This means that our occupational data should be interpreted with care, because the 1970 codes reflect categories used thirty years ago and may not accurately reflect the actual content of jobs held by the recent cohort. To minimize this effect, we use highly aggregated occupational categories (at the one-digit level). Nevertheless, we give more substantive weight to industry trends and effects throughout the book.

## Wages

We focus on hourly wages rather than yearly earnings because the latter are confounded by hours and weeks worked and the number of jobs held during the year. The former allow us to approximate more closely the market distribution of wage offers and, by extension, the opportunities available to different groups in the labor force.

The measure we use is the respondent's hourly wage at his CPS job in the week preceding the interview. This measure is constructed by the NLS, using direct information if the respondent reported his earnings as an hourly wage and from questions on the weeks (or months) and hours worked in the past year if the respondent reported in other units. We exclude respondents from the wage analyses in the years during which they are self-employed or working without pay. Analyses are based on the natural log of real wages in 1999 dollars, using the personal consumption expenditure (PCE) deflator.[4] This deflator tends to be more conservative than the commonly used consumer price index (CPI) deflator.

In both cohorts, roughly 5 percent of the wages required imputation owing to either invalid skips or censoring by the NLS. Our imputation scheme used a contextual stratification of the wage profile (that is, whether the missing wage was at the beginning, middle, or end of a sequence) and a regression model based on nearby wages, age, and current education level (Rubin 1987, 258). The imputed wages retain both the level and the variability of the wages in each context.

The wages have also been cleaned, with extremely low wages (below one-quarter of the minimum wage) and extremely high wages (cross-sectional outliers with longitudinal inconsistency) removed from the analyses. This amounts to the removal of fewer than 1 percent of the wage observations for both cohorts.

Finally, we should note that our data set has the same problem as any data source on wages: we do not observe wages for the long-term unemployed. This is, of course, an unsolvable problem; a respondent's wages cannot be observed if he is not working. In terms of our analysis of mobility paths, this means that we are not be able to observe the "careers" of workers who are unemployed or out of the labor force for all of the years they are in the survey.

## Derived Variables

To summarize specific features of the 16-year work histories of these respondents, we derived several variables from combinations of simple measures. For these derived variables, the need for cross-cohort consistency required careful consideration of the missing data patterns unique to each cohort. We designed each measure carefully, and subjected each derived variable to diagnostic tests to ensure that cohort differences would not be confounded with artifacts of survey administration.

### Labor Force Transition Sequences

In chapter 3, we describe the sequencing of enrollment and labor force participation that makes up an individual's transition from school to work. This is a person-based analysis, in which each person contributes one transition sequence. We first define an individual to be in one of three states in each year: exclusively enrolled in school, working while enrolled, or not enrolled. The sequences themselves are then defined to capture the ordering of those three states over time as the individual enters the labor market. Specifically, we define three sequences: exclusive continuous enrollment, continuous enrollment while working, and noncontinuous enrollment (that is, movement back and forth between schooling and the labor market).

"Enrollment" is defined as any incidence of school enrollment during the previous year. "Working" is defined to be consistent with this definition: we consider an individual to have worked during the previous year if he reports more than twenty-six weeks of work, whether part-time or full-time. By spanning more than half of the year we ensure that there will be some overlap with the regular school year. Respondents are coded "working while enrolled" if, using the definitions stated earlier in this appendix, they are working and enrolled in the same survey year. An individual who has only a summer job and does not work during the school year is coded as "not working" while he is in school. Unfortunately, this approach excludes from "working while in school" individuals who work for only one semester of the academic year Thus our measure may underestimate the true amount of working while enrolled, but it does so consistently across both cohorts.

To construct comparable sequences across the two cohorts, it is necessary to restrict the sample to the twelve matched years shown in table 2.1, because including the additional four years for the recent cohort would raise the probability of observing noncontinuous enrollment relative to the original cohort. We also exclude respondents who were not enrolled in school at least once during the survey, because it is not possible to classify them with respect to continuity of enrollment. This removes individuals who enter the study having already completed their education, but it does so consistently for both surveys.

## Employer Separations

In chapter 4, we examine the question of whether job instability has risen in the recent cohort. For this analysis, we need to identify the time at which a respondent separated from a previous employer. To do this we use the unique employer identification codes provided by the NLS in each cohort.

We focus on the respondent's CPS employer at the time of the survey. In the original cohort, the CPS employer is assigned an employer code that is unique across all interview years. In the recent cohort, unique identification of the CPS employer is possible only between any two consecutive years. By successively linking pairs of years, however, we can trace a unique CPS employer over any time span as long as that employer is present in each survey year. We have restricted our use of the employer codes in the original cohort to match this constraint.

Recall that four noncontiguous years are skipped in the original cohort survey. This means that we cannot construct an unbroken series of year-to-year employer comparisons. We therefore construct a series of two-year employer comparisons. These are strictly matched between the two surveys, so that we are comparing job changes at exactly the same ages and at exactly the same time during the survey period. There are six such comparisons for each cohort, and they are evenly spaced across the survey time span. Table 2.1 shows the years used for the analyses in chapter 4 and defines the six comparisons being made for each cohort. This matching strategy allows us to conduct a rigorous and controlled comparison across cohorts in job instability, but the reader should remember that as a result, we are not counting all recorded jobs and job changes for the respondents. For example, our analysis of the number of cumulative employers in chapter 4 is an underestimate in absolute terms but is an accurate estimate of the relative difference between the two cohorts.

We define a job separation as follows: For each two-year comparison, the risk set in year $t$ is all employed respondents, neither self-employed nor working without pay, who are also observed in year $t + 2$. If the respondent is unemployed or out of the labor force in year $t + 2$, an employer separation occurred. If the respondent is employed in year $t + 2$, then the employer code for the CPS employer in year $t$ is compared with the CPS employer code in year $t + 2$. An employer separation occurred if these codes differ. The empirical two-year separation rate is thus calculated as the number of respondents who have left their year $t$ employer by year $t + 2$ divided by the total number of respondents in the risk set in year $t$.

After the risk set was defined, we dropped person-year observations outside the sixteen-to-thirty-four age range to ensure adequate sample sizes within age groups. Observations in which the respondent was self-employed or working without pay were also excluded. The resulting sample sizes and mean number of observations contributed by respondents are given at the top of table 4.1.

## Cumulative Number of CPS Employers

In chapter 6, we examine the cumulative impact of job instability on wage attainment. One of the measures we use to capture the effects of job instability is the cumulative number of different employers reported by the respondent at his last interview. To ensure comparability between cohorts and across individuals within cohorts, a number of issues must be addressed.

As always, we restrict the focus to CPS jobs. We know consistently for both cohorts whether the CPS employer in the current year is the same as the CPS employer in the previous year. Our measure cumulates the total number of different CPS employers the respondent has worked for across the entire survey span; it is a person-based measure.

The final cumulative number of CPS employers, measured in this way, is dependent on the number of years a person is observed. It is therefore important to establish whether differences in the pattern of missingness across the two cohorts compromise the comparability of this measure. The NLS changed its retention rules between the two cohorts; respondents in the original cohort were dropped from the survey after two missed years, whereas respondents in the recent cohort were pursued for a much longer time and were often drawn back into the survey. One result, as mentioned in chapter 2, is a greater attrition rate in the original cohort. Another result is that there are longer sequences of missing years for the recent cohort (because respondents could reenter the survey after a long absence). In the recent cohort, however, the NLS also improved its retrospective collection of missing data for respondents who returned to the panel. The net result is that the recent cohort has substantially less missing data on CPS employers: 95 percent of the eligible recent cohort is missing no data over the years, compared with 71 percent of the original cohort. The majority of those missing data in the original cohort are missing only one or two years, but this could still potentially bias the cumulative number of employers downward in the original cohort.

A simple test for bias is to see whether the cumulative number of employers is different for the full sample as compared with the sample of respondents who missed no interviews. These data are shown in table A.1. A slight downward bias in the full sample is evident for both cohorts: the fraction reporting only one or two cumulative employers is 2 or 3 percentage points higher than in the restricted sample, and there is a corresponding drop in the fraction reporting six or more employers. We are not so much interested in the absolute level of this variable, however, as in its difference between the two cohorts.[5]

This difference is surprisingly similar in the full and the restricted sample. Regardless of the sample used, the story is quite clear: the recent cohort reports a higher total number of employers. There is

Table A.1   Cumulative Number of CPS Employers, by Cohort
(Percentage)

|  | Original Cohort | Recent Cohort | Difference[a] |
|---|---|---|---|
| All respondents |  |  |  |
| One to two | 21.0 | 12.9 | −8.1 |
| Three to five | 56.9 | 55.3 | −1.6 |
| Six or more | 22.1 | 31.7 | 9.6 |
| Respondents with no missing employment data |  |  |  |
| One to two | 17.7 | 11.3 | −6.4 |
| Three to five | 54.8 | 53.9 | −1.1 |
| Six or more | 27.5 | 34.8 | 7.3 |

*Source:* Authors' compilation.
*Note:* All percentages are person based.
[a]Original cohort minus recent.

little evidence here to justify restricting the sample to cases with no missing data, as this would result in the loss of nearly 30 percent of the original cohort sample. We have run all of the analyses that use this measure on both samples, and there are no substantive differences in the findings. We report, then, the findings for the full sample.

To ensure comparability within cohorts, we standardize all respondents so that the job cumulation count starts at sixteen years old. For respondents who entered the survey after the age of sixteen, we impute the missing number of employers using a model based on those who entered the survey before the age of seventeen. This approach parallels the one used to impute the unobserved weeks of experience described earlier in this appendix. The model predicts the mean number of jobs for respondents with no missing data, based on age and years of experience since the age of sixteen, as $\hat{y}_{ij} = \alpha_i + \gamma_j$, where the $\alpha$ coefficients are dummies for age and the $\gamma$ coefficients are dummies for years of experience. These predicted means are then used at the start of the cumulation for respondents who are seventeen to twenty-two years old at entry into the survey.

# = Appendix B =

## Validation and Attrition Analysis for Job Change Measure

I N THE context of a research field that has not been able to reach consensus on trends in job instability, the significant increases for the recent cohort that we find in chapter 4 require a second look. On the one hand, we might expect the NLS data to yield different findings, because they focus on young adult men only, they extend from the late 1960s to the early 1990s and thus capture a longer time span, and they allow for a direct, clean measure of instability. On the other hand, it may be the case that other characteristics of the NLS data are generating an artificial increase in instability. In particular, the higher attrition rate in the original cohort (25.8 percent, as against 7.8 percent in the recent cohort) raises important questions about the interpretation of our findings. If respondents who are lost to attrition are also more likely to be unstable in their job change behavior, then our cohort effect for job instability may be upwardly biased by the lower rates of attrition in the recent cohort. We use two strategies to examine the potential confounding effect of attrition. First, we benchmark the NLS job change estimates against estimates based on the PSID and the CPS. This exercise is important in its own right, as it contributes to cross-data-set validation in the field. Second, we develop several model-based adjustments to our instability estimates for the impact of attrition.

We begin by comparing job change estimates from the NLS with estimates from the two other main data sets in the field. We use Daniel Polsky's (1999) series for the PSID and Jay Stewart's (1998) series for the CPS; both address some of the well-known problems with changes in measures and question wording over time. If attrition in the original cohort introduces bias, then the job instability estimates from the recent cohort will match up well with those of the other data sets (since attrition in the recent cohort was negligible), whereas those from the original cohort will not.

Two factors complicate a simple comparison. First, because neither the PSID nor the CPS extend far enough back in time, they provide only two time points that we can use to compare the recent with the original cohort. Both of these years, however, fall toward the end of the series, when the greater attrition rate in the original cohort is most likely to make itself felt. Second, members of the two NLS cohorts age throughout the sixteen-year survey period, and the skipped interview years in the original cohort mean that we sometimes have to use two-year instead of one-year job change rates. With these considerations in mind, tables B.1 and B.2 present the best comparisons that can be constructed, showing the specific age ranges and years used in each case. For all three data sets, the samples are white working men who are not self-employed. We also reweighted the NLS and PSID distributions to the CPS distribution within age-education cells, so that the analysis is not confounded by differences in composition; in practice, this reweighting has a minor effect.

Table B.1 gives the NLS-PSID comparison, using either one-year or two-year job change rates. For the NLS, these rates are once again calculated using the unique employer codes; for the PSID, these rates are calculated using information on job tenure (Polsky 1999). For both, the measure is the proportion of respondents working at time $t$ who left their time $t$ employer at either time $t + 1$ or time $t + 2$, depending on which comparison is being made. The two sets of estimates match up remarkably well; none of the differences is statistically significant. Note in particular the close agreement in 1980 for the original cohort, the next to last year of that panel in which the rate of attrition peaks. This is a solid indicator that the greater attrition

Table B.1   Comparison of Separation Rate Estimates from the NLS and the PSID

| Year | Age Range | Measure | Cohort | NLS | PSID | Difference (NLS − PSID) |
|------|-----------|---------|--------|-----|------|--------------------------|
| 1978 | 26 to 32 | 2-year rate | Original | .3668 | .3652 | .0016 |
| 1980 | 28 to 34 | 1-year rate | Original | .2292 | .2104 | .0188 |
| 1989 | 26 to 32 | 2-year rate | Recent | .4078 | .4177 | −.0100 |
| 1991 | 28 to 34 | 1-year rate | Recent | .2420 | .2389 | .0031 |

*Source:* PSID data from Polsky 1999.

rate in the original cohort is not driving our finding of changes in job
stability over time.

Table B.2 shows our comparison of the NLS with the CPS estimates. This comparison is more problematic because the two data sets
have different measures and risk sets. Stewart's (1998) CPS measure is
a 14.5-month job change rate that is inferred using several decision
rules for respondents who had worked at least one week in the previous year and who were not students or recent graduates. By contrast, the NLS measure is a one-year job change rate calculated directly for respondents who were working during the week of the
previous year's survey. The results of comparing across these different measures are not clear. As a rule, the NLS estimates are lower
than the CPS estimates, as one might expect, given the way the measures are defined (one-year change rates for the former, 14.5-month
rates for the latter). The size and significance of the differences varies
considerably, however, both within and between cohorts. Especially
worrisome is the variability in the differences within the recent cohort, which has very little attrition. Our sense is that it would be
difficult to reconcile these two data sets without considerably more
analysis, along the lines pursued by Jaeger and Stevens (1999). It
should be noted, however, that these authors also find a divergence
between the CPS and PSID estimates in the 1970s, though not in the
1980s and 1990s.

Our second attrition analysis is a model-based sensitivity analysis.
We make several adjustments to our estimate of the cohort difference

Table B.2   Comparison of Separation Rate Estimates from the NLS and
the CPS

| Year | Age Range | Cohort | NLS[a] | CPS[b] | Difference (NLS − CPS) |
|---|---|---|---|---|---|
| 1975 | 23 to 31 | Original | .2721 | .3351 | −.0630* |
| 1980 | 28 to 36 | Original | .2108 | .2591 | −.0483* |
| 1988 | 23 to 31 | Recent | .3001 | .3452 | −.0451* |
| 1989 | 24 to 32 | Recent | .2942 | .3198 | −.0256 |
| 1990 | 25 to 33 | Recent | .2653 | .3228 | −.0575* |
| 1991 | 26 to 34 | Recent | .2474 | .2890 | −.0416* |
| 1992 | 27 to 35 | Recent | .2546 | .2705 | −.0159 |
| 1993 | 28 to 36 | Recent | .2713 | .2727 | −.0014 |

Source: CPS data from Stewart 1998.
[a]Measure is one-year rate.
[b]Measure is 14.5-month rate.
*$p \leq .05$.

in job stability from chapter 4, based on potential differences in the behavior of those lost to attrition. First, they may have higher levels of job instability than those who never leave the survey cohort. Second, they may also be less likely to be eligible for the risk set that defines the job change sample. In both cases, respondents lost to attrition do not contribute enough "unstable" observations to the original cohort sample, and as a result the cohort effect is overstated. Our strategy in calculating the adjusted cohort effects, therefore, is, effectively, to "add back in" the missing observations for those lost to attrition. Because we are conducting a hypothetical experiment asking, "What would the cohort effect have been if no one had been lost to attrition?" we cannot estimate the adjusted cohort effect empirically from the data. Instead, we derive an expression for this adjusted effect that allows us to incorporate any greater propensity to change jobs among those lost to attrition and to equalize the number of observations contributed by both attrition groups.

We begin by adding several terms to model 1 in chapter 4:

$$\text{logit}(P[Y_{ijt} = 1 \mid X_{ijt}, J_{ijt}, U_{it}, C_i, \phi_i, A_{ijt}])$$
$$= \theta_o X_{ijt} + \theta_1 J_{ijt} + \theta_2 U_{it} + \theta_3 C_i + \theta_4 A_{ijt} + \theta_5 CA_{ijt} + \phi_i.$$

The model now includes two attrition-related terms: $A_{ijt}$, a dummy variable indicating whether person $i$ in job $j$ in year $t$ is lost to attrition after year $t + 2$, given that he has not left the cohort before, and $CA_{ijt}$, the interaction between attrition and cohort. Thus $\theta_4$ represents the attrition effect for the original cohort, and $\theta_5$ represents the incremental difference in the attrition effect for the recent cohort. (Later, we suppress the references to the characteristics $X_{ijt}, J_{ijt}, U_{it}$, and $\phi_i$). Under this model, the average log-odds of a two-year job change for a randomly chosen person-year with given characteristics from cohort $k$ is

$$\overline{\text{logit}}(P[Y_{ijt} = 1 \mid C_i = k])$$
$$= \text{logit}(P[Y_{ijt} = 1 \mid C_i = k, A_{ijt} = 0]) \, P(A_{ijt} = 0 \mid C_i = k)$$
$$+ \text{logit}(P[Y_{ijt} = 1 \mid C_i = k, A_{ijt} = 1]) \, P(A_{ijt} = 1 \mid C_i = k)$$
$$= \theta_o X_{ijt} + \theta_1 J_{ijt} + \theta_2 U_{it} + \theta_3 k + \phi_i$$
$$+ \theta_4 \, P(A_{ijt} = 1 \mid C_i = k) + \theta_5 k \, P(A_{ijt} = 1 \mid C_i = k).$$

The attrition-adjusted cohort effect is then simply represented as

$$\overline{\text{logit}}(P[Y_{ijt} = 1 \mid C_i = 1]) - \overline{\text{logit}}(P[Y_{ijt} = 1 \mid C_i = 0])$$
$$= \theta_3 + \theta_4 \, [P(A_{ijt} = 1 \mid C_i = 1) - P(A_{ijt} = 1 \mid C_i = 0)]$$
$$+ \theta_5 \, P(A_{ijt} = 1 \mid C_i = 1).$$

The first term ($\theta_3$) represents the cohort effect for a respondent who was not lost to attrition. The second term represents the differential odds that a respondent lost to attrition experiences a job separation before being lost, multiplied by the difference in attrition rates between the two cohorts. If those who are lost to attrition are more unstable, $\theta_4$ will be positive, and as the difference in attrition rates is negative, the adjustment will lower the estimate of the cohort effect. The third term represents the differential in the attrition effect for the recent cohort multiplied by the attrition rate in the recent cohort. If, among respondents lost to attrition, those in the recent cohort are more unstable than those in the original cohort, then $\theta_5$ will be positive, and this adjustment will increase the estimate of the cohort effect.

To calculate an adjusted cohort effect based on this derivation, we need to estimate two sets of quantities: $\theta_3$, $\theta_4$, and $\theta_5$, and the conditional probabilities of attrition. We estimated the former using the modified logistic regression model (equation 1) and obtained $\theta_3$ = 0.3478, $\theta_4$ = 0.2902, and $\theta_5$ = 0.0039. Note that among respondents lost to attrition, those in the recent cohort are in fact relatively more unstable than those in the original cohort. We might expect this, given that the recent cohort was pursued more rigorously for continued participation in the survey; any respondents who still managed to drop out of the survey are thus likely to be particularly unstable individuals.

We next estimated the conditional probabilities of attrition that we use in our derivation. The idea here is to construct these probabilities as though the unobserved years of respondents lost to attrition had been included in the analysis. We accomplish this by defining the fraction of respondents who dropped out at the level of the individual rather than at the level of person-years, so that the number of person-year observations contributed by those lost to attrition and those who remained throughout the survey years is equalized. There are three ways these fractions can be defined:

1. *The fraction of respondents lost to attrition in the risk set.* The fraction of respondents in the job-change risk set who eventually drop out is 0.1603 in the original cohort and 0.0545 in the recent cohort. In using these fractions, we are effectively adding the person-years that would have been contributed by respondents who left the sample, had they not dropped out.

2. *The fraction of respondents lost to attrition in the risk set, equalized for eligibility.* In addition to the adjustment made in the previous defi-

nition, we also need to account for the fact that among respondents lost to attrition, those in the recent cohort were more likely to make it into the job change risk set than those in the original cohort. We do so by equalizing the proportion of those who dropped out who are eligible for the risk set, yielding an adjusted attrition fraction of 0.1996 for the original cohort.

3.  *The fraction of respondents lost to attrition in the full sample.* Finally, the strongest adjustment would use the fraction of respondents who dropped out for each cohort in the full sample (all available survey years). The fraction of persons in the full sample who ever worked and who are lost to attrition is 0.2323 in the original cohort and 0.0658 in the recent cohort.

The adjustments based on each of these three methods are provided in table B.3, along with the unadjusted estimate from model 1 in table 4.2, for comparison. Although in all cases the attrition adjustment reduces the estimated cohort effect, the reductions are modest. Under method 1, the adjusted cohort effect is 0.3172, an 11.3 percent decrease in the unadjusted value. Under method 2, the adjusted cohort effect is 0.3058, a 14.5 percent decrease in the unadjusted value. We consider this the most accurate adjustment, because it removes both types of attrition bias from the job change sample. Finally, under method 3 the adjusted cohort effect is 0.2996, a 16.2 percent decrease. We feel less comfortable with this adjustment, because it uses estimates from the job change sample (that is, $\theta_3$, $\theta_4$, and $\theta_5$) and applies them to a sample that is not included in the instability analysis as conducted for this book. Even with this most conservative adjustment, however, the recent cohort still has 35 percent higher odds of a job change.

The adjustments are modest under all methods for two reasons. First, the cohort difference in attrition ranges only from 11 percent (method 1) to 16 percent (method 3), so the proportional reweighting is not substantial in any of the methods. Under these conditions, the estimated attrition effect ($\theta_4$) would have to be about 5.5 times larger to fully negate the size of the cohort effect.

Second, the recent cohort attrition differential ($\theta_5$) is positive, so that it offsets the negative adjustment made by the main attrition effect. It makes sense that among respondents lost to attrition those in the recent cohort are more "unstable" than those in the original cohort, given the difference in retention rules in the two panels. In the original cohort, any respondents missing two sequential interviews were dropped from the survey, whereas such respondents in the re-

**Table B.3   Attrition Adjustments to the Cohort Instability Effect**

| Category | Unadjusted | Adjustment[a] | | |
|---|---|---|---|---|
| | | Method 1 | Method 2 | Method 3 |
| Fraction of respondents lost to attrition | | | | |
| Original cohort | .16 | .16 | .20 | .23 |
| Recent cohort | .06 | .06 | .06 | .07 |
| Cohort effect | .3577[b] | .3172 | .3058 | .2996 |
| Standard error | .052 | .042 | .042 | .042 |
| Adjustment | | −.0405 | −.0114 | −.0062 |
| Percentage adjustment | | 11.31 | 14.50 | 16.23 |

*Source:* Authors' compilation.
[a]See text for definition of adjustment methods.
[b]Taken from model 1 in table 4.2.

cent cohort remained eligible and were pursued for future interviews with great effort. Respondents of the recent cohort who were nevertheless lost to attrition therefore are likely to represent "hard core" dropouts. We found support for this conjecture by examining respondents in the recent cohort who would have been dropped from the survey under the rules used in the original cohort (about 9 percent of the sample). These "hypothetical" dropouts have attributes and outcomes that fall in between the "hard core" dropouts and the retained sample. This result suggests that the additional respondents lost to attrition in the original cohort are a moderate group.

In sum, both the cross-data-set comparisons and the model-based adjustments suggest that though a slight attrition bias does exist in the original cohort, it does not alter the statistical significance or the substance of our findings in chapter 4.

# = Appendix C =

## Relative Distribution Methods

D ISTRIBUTIONAL methods are becoming increasingly popular among labor economists and other social scientists who study the trends in earnings (Creedy 1985, 1998; Dinardo, Fortin, and Lemieux 1996; Picot, Myles, and Wannel 1990). From informal visual displays like the decile ratios in Lynn Karoly's (1993) review of the recent trends in inequality to more formal techniques like quantile regression, researchers have been grappling with how best to represent and analyze the recent distributional changes in earnings. Means and variances—the basis for traditional statistical approaches to such data—leave much of the information in a distribution untapped. In this book we therefore sometimes turn to relative distribution methods to permit a more detailed analysis of the trends in earnings inequality. In this appendix we give a brief technical description of these methods.[1]

If we want to compare the distribution of earnings for two groups (say, C and R, for comparison and reference groups, respectively), we might think about starting with a density ratio: the ratio of the proportion of members of the two groups at each level of the earnings scale. The value of this ratio will vary along the length of the earnings scale. If it takes the value 1, the two groups have equal probability of earning at that level, and if it rises above (or falls below) 1, the group in the numerator has a higher (or lower) relative probability. The value of the ratio is also directly interpretable. For example, if it takes the value 1.5, members of group C are 50 percent more likely to earn at that level than members of group R. The relative distribution is essentially a rescaled version of this density ratio.

An example is shown in figure 6.6. In the top panel of figure 6.6, the distributions of the permanent wage gains for each cohort are plotted (the PDFs, or probability density functions). The bottom panel presents the plot of their relative distribution (the recent cohort as compared with the original, so the original cohort is the reference group here). The rescaling maps the earnings levels on the horizontal axis to the quantiles of the reference group distribution. Technically, the relative distribution is a transformation of the data from two distributions into a single distribution that contains all of the information necessary for scale-invariant comparison. A simple way to think about the relative distribution is that it assigns the raw values in the comparison distribution the rank they would have in the reference distribution. This distribution of relative ranks (the relative data) can then be plotted and analyzed in a number of ways.

The transformation that defines the relative distribution is sometimes called the "grade transformation" (Cwik and Mielniczuk 1989). It provides the basis for many well-known measures of distributional difference, such as the Kullback-Leibler distance ("relative entropy"), and special cases give rise to the Lorenz curve and Gini index. Recent theoretical and statistical developments now allow relative distributions to provide a general framework for analysis: graphical displays that simplify exploratory data analysis, a statistically valid basis for the development of hypothesis-driven summary measures, and location, shape, and covariate decompositions that identify the sources of distributional changes within and between groups. The relative distribution can provide this general framework for analysis because it represents a theoretically rich and substantively meaningful class of data in a fundamental statistical form: the probability distribution.

## Technical Definition of the Relative Distribution

Denote the cumulative distribution function (CDF) of a measurement for a reference group by $F_o(y)$. In the example from figure 6.15, this is the CDF of permanent wage gains for the original cohort. Denote the CDF for the comparison group by $F(y)$. In figure 6.15, this is the CDF of permanent wage gains for the recent cohort. The objective is to study the differences between the comparison distribution and the reference distribution.

Let $Y_o$ and $Y$ be random samples from $F_o$ and $F$, respectively. We suppose that $F_o$ and $F$ are absolutely continuous with continuous densities and common support. The *grade transformation* of $Y$ to $Y_o$ is defined as the random variable, $R = F_o(Y)$. As $R$ is obtained from $Y$ by transforming it by the function $F_o$, it is continuous with outcome space $[0, 1]$. We can express the CDF of $R$ as

$$G(r) = F(Q(r))\ 0 \leq r \leq 1.$$

where $R$ represents the proportion of values and $Q(r) = \inf_y\{y \mid F_o(y) \geq r\}$ is the quantile function of $F_o$. The PDF of $R$ is

$$g(r) = \frac{f(Q(R))}{f_o(Q(R))}, \ 0 \leq r \leq 1.$$

If the two distributions are identical, then the CDF of the relative distribution is a 45-degree line and the PDF of the relative distribution is the uniform PDF.

The relative distribution is an intuitively appealing approach to comparing distributions because the relative data, PDF, and CDF all have clear, simple interpretations. The relative data can be interpreted as the percentile rank that the comparison value would have in the reference group. The relative PDF, $g(r)$, can be interpreted as a density ratio. This can be seen more easily by expressing the relative PDF explicitly in terms of the original measurement scale, $y$. Let the $r$th quantile of $R$ be denoted by the value $y_r$ on the original measurement scale; so the $y_r$ corresponding to $R$ is $Q(r)$. The relative PDF is then the rescaled density ratio

$$g(r) = \frac{f(y_r)}{f_o(y_r)}, \ y_r \geq 0. \tag{C.1}$$

The relative CDF, $G(r)$, can be interpreted as the proportion of the comparison group whose attribute lies below the $r$th quantile of the reference group. Note that even though the relative CDF is explicitly scaled in terms of quantiles, the implicit unit of comparison is the value of the measurement on the original measurement scale ($y_r$ representing the quantile cutpoint).

The relative density simplifies comparison in several ways. In contrast to the direct PDF overlay in figure 6.15, which requires the viewer to construct the differences between the two curves at each point on the scale, the relative density codes this comparison directly in terms of a ratio. It provides a simple visual (and numerical) signal for information that exists but is not easy to process in the original PDF overlay (Chambers et al. 1983; Cleveland and McGill 1984).

In general, the relative distribution is invariant to the scale of the distributions (up to a monotone transformation). For example, in our application, we would obtain the same relative distribution using raw wage gains as we do from using the logarithm of wage gains.

If the designations of reference and comparison group were reversed, the relative PDF and CDF would be symmetric around the distributional equivalence axis (net of the rescaling), and the substantive findings would be equivalent. As a result, choosing the reference distribution is much like choosing a reference category in dummy variable regression: it changes the direction, but not the meaning, of the estimate. In our comparison of the two cohorts, it is natural to use the original cohort's distribution as the reference, because we are testing whether the wage distribution has changed in the recent cohort.

## Decomposing the Relative Distribution

When more complex modeling is required, these methods can be used to isolate specific effects. For example, what would the distributional comparison look like if only the median had shifted down, or if the education composition of the population had not changed? In general this involves constructing a counterfactual distribution. Through sequential pairwise comparisons among observed and counterfactual distributions, the overall difference can then be decomposed and analyzed.

One of the primary uses of decompositional techniques is to isolate the effects of distributional changes in location and shape. If the comparison distribution is a simple location-shifted version of the reference distribution—that is, if $F(y) = F_o(y - c)$ for some constant $c$—then the difference between the two distributions can be parsimoniously summarized by this shift. In general, we can consider the counterfactual distribution describing the reference group location adjusted to have the same mean as the comparison group. The CDF of this distribution is $F_{oL}(y) = F_o(y - \rho)$, where $\rho$ is the mean of $Y$ minus the mean of $Y_o$. A comparison of $F_{oL}(y)$ with $F_o(y)$ isolates the location shift as both distributions have the shape of the reference distribution, $F_o$. A comparison of $F(y)$ with $F_{oL}(y)$ isolates the shape shift as both distributions have the same mean, that of the comparison distribution, $F$. It is natural to make these comparisons using the corresponding relative distributions. Denote the relative PDF of $F_{oL}(y)$ to $F_o(y)$ and $F(y)$ to $F_{oL}(y)$ by $g_o^{oL}(r)$ and $g_{oL}(r)$, respectively.

Their relationship can be represented in terms of the density ratios from equation (C.1), as

$$\frac{f(y_r)}{f_o(y_r)} = \frac{f_{oL}(y_r)}{f_o(y_r)} \times \frac{f(y_r)}{f_{oL}(y_r)},$$

or, in more heuristic terms,

$$\begin{matrix} \text{Overall relative} \\ \text{density} \end{matrix} = \begin{matrix} \text{density ratio for} \\ \text{the location difference} \end{matrix} \times \begin{matrix} \text{density ratio for} \\ \text{the shape difference} \end{matrix}$$

The graphical display of the relative densities $g(r)$, $g_o^{oL}(r)$, and $g_{oL}(r)$ provides a useful visual summary of the relative size and nature of the three components in the decomposition.

The other primary target of decompositional analysis is to adjust for covariates. In its simplest form, this analysis can be used to standardize two populations in terms of one variable—say, education—to isolate any residual differences. In more complex modeling contexts, this approach can be used to isolate the impacts of multivariate changes in population composition and changes in returns. This approach leads to a fully distributional generalization of the Blinder-Oaxaca regression decomposition (Blinder 1973; Oaxaca 1973).

The idea is applied to the comparison of final wages between the two cohorts in chapter 6. The counterfactual distribution is based on putting the recent cohort through the original cohort economy—that is, predicting their wages using the original cohort model coefficients. Where the Blinder-Oaxaca approach would restrict the focus to the mean effects, however, this approach compares the full distributional impact. To isolate the returns effects, we take the relative distribution of the observed wage distribution for the recent cohort to the counterfactual distribution of wages. To isolate the composition effects, we take the relative distribution of the counterfactual distribution to the observed wage distribution for the original cohort. In appendix D, we describe the construction of this counterfactual distribution based on the mixed-effects model for wages.

# = Appendix D =

## Permanent Wage Estimation

MANY OF the questions studied in this book involve comparisons of individual-specific wage growth trajectories between and within the cohorts. In this appendix we describe the statistical modeling framework used to analyze these trajectories. The longitudinal (or panel) nature of the NLS requires that the dependence of the responses within individuals be explicitly modeled. These models must specify the nature of the dependencies so as to determine the influence of potentially endogenous explanatory covariates on the wage growth trajectories.

The starting point is a simple linear regression model. Additional components are used to smooth an individual's wages of short-term fluctuations. The full model specifies a set of fixed effects to capture the average curve of the wage growth trajectory over age, a set of random effects to isolate the heterogeneity in permanent wage gains among individuals, and a residual term to represent the transitory components of wage change within each individual trajectory. This type of model has been used to examine the role of transitory variability in the growth in wage inequality (Duncan, Boisjoly, and Smeeding 1996; Gottschalk and Moffitt 1994; Haider 1997; Moffitt and Gottschalk 1995; Stevens 1996). The model allows a unique wage trajectory for each person across his work history, smoothing out fluctuations in wages that can result from temporary disturbances such as the business cycle.

The permanent and transitory components of wage trajectory heterogeneity are specified as follows:[1]

$$y_{it} = \mu_{it} + e_{it},$$

where $y_{it}$ is the log of the real wage of individual $i$ in year $t$. The average wage growth trajectory $\mu_{it}$ is specified by

$$\mu_{it} = \beta_0 + \beta_1 l_{it} + \beta_2 q_{it} + \gamma x_{it},$$

where $l_{it}$ and $q_{it}$ are the linear and quadratic age terms, respectively, and $x_{it}$ represents individual- and age-specific covariates. Examples of covariates are education, experience, occupation, industry, and job change characteristics. The coefficients $\beta_0$, $\beta_1$, $\beta_2$, and $\gamma$ are average-level ("fixed-effect") parameters. We have parameterized $l_{it}$ as the age of individual $i$ in year $t$ centered on age sixteen and $q_{it}$ as the quadratic term centered on age sixteen. The random effects component is specified as

$$e_{it} = p_{it} + u_{it},$$

where we define $p_{it}$ as the permanent component and $u_{it}$ as the transitory component. We model $u_{it}$ as mean-zero and allow the variance of $u_{it}$ to vary by calendar year to capture any business cycle effects. The permanent component is specified by

$$p_{it} = b_{0i} + b_{1i} l_{it} + b_{2i} q_{it}.$$

Thus $p_{it}$ is a random quadratic representing the deviation of the individual-specific wage growth trajectory from the average wage growth trajectory. Under this parameterization, $b_{0i}$, $b_{1i}$, and $b_{2i}$ are time-invariant latent values representing the deviations from their fixed-effects counterparts.

The individual-specific wage growth trajectory is the combination of the average wage growth trajectory and the individual-specific deviation, $\mu_{it} + p_{it}$. The parameters in our model are estimated using restricted maximum likelihood (REML). In addition to being asymptotically efficient under the assumption of Gaussianality, this approach produces asymptotic standard errors and covariances for the fixed and random parameter estimates. This approach provides the best linear unbiased predictor (BLUP) for the individual-specific wage growth trajectories.

Clearly, the relative magnitudes of the transitory and permanent components will vary under different model specifications. For the questions we address in this book, however, the systematic heterogeneity in individual wage growth trajectories by age is of primary substantive interest. It represents in the most direct way the idea that long-term wage growth has become more unequal between the two cohorts. For this reason, we choose to define the permanent component of wage growth, with linear and quadratic age effects, at the individual level. Other studies have specified the permanent and transitory effects in different ways, and this can have an impact on the findings. Gottschalk and Moffitt (1994) build less structure into the permanent component, allowing a random effect only for the age intercept. This forces all systematic trajectory heterogeneity into the transitory component and, as a result, tends to overestimate wage instability. Their conclusion that wage instability is the primary cause of the growth in cross-sectional wage inequality is largely driven by this assumption in their model.

Several subsequent papers have introduced alternative structure to the permanent component, in addition to the random linear and quadratic specification we have adopted. The added structure can take forms such as changes over time in the returns to specific covariates (Katz 1994) or period-specific variance components (Haider 1997). It is also possible to consider models that specify the permanent component in an autoregressive-moving average (ARMA) form (Baker 1997). Given the nature of wage growth and the specification of the fixed effects in the model, the interpretation of the ARMA form is less desirable. The addition of an AR(1) component to our random quadratic form does not change our substantive interpretations.

The individual-specific effects (ISE), $b_{0i}$, $b_{1i}$, and $b_{2i}$, can be further modeled in a variety of ways. A purely cross-sectional specification that excludes the permanent component assumes conditional independence of the wages for the same individual. This is not credible and is firmly rejected by the likelihood ratio test. The subsequent specification of a sophisticated model for the ISE conditional on the covariates can follow many routes. Fitting the ISE as fixed effects (as in Topel and Ward 1992) avoids the need to assume that these effects are orthogonal to the other regressors, and it is an attractive approach. In our situation this is infeasible, as we would have an additional two thousand unrestricted nuisance parameters. As we have at most twelve observations for each individual, and often less, direct estimation of the ISE as fixed effects is not generally appropriate.

As an alternative to this approach we specify the ISE through a mixed-effects specification. The simplest form of this assumes that the values, conditional on $x_{it}$, are independent between individuals. We hierarchically model $b_{0i}$, $b_{1i}$, and $b_{2i}$ as samples from a mean-zero trivariate Gaussian distribution with a general unstructured covariance matrix between the parameters. These covariances are then inferred from the data. We refer to this specification as the mixed-effects model.

Another alternative is to use a population-average model that does not specify the ISE but adjusts for the individually specific covariance in the estimation. This is usually achieved by solving generalized estimation equations. The results are similar to those we report in this book, but we have trimmed them to avoid additional complication and to save space.

Following Chamberlain (1984), we might instead exploit the fact that the mean log wage for each individual is a minimally sufficient statistic for their ISE $b_{0i}$. We can therefore use the distribution of log wages conditional on the covariates and the mean log-wages to obtain a conditional likelihood function that does not depend on the $b_{0i}$. This approach leads to the commonly used change regression model. The conditional maximum likelihood estimator is a consistent estimator of the coefficients as the number of individuals goes to infinity and the number of time periods is fixed. The power of the procedure is that it places no constraints on the distribution of the $b_{0i}$ conditional on the covariates. However, the coefficients of within-person time-invariant factors, such as the cohort effect, are completely confounded with the ISE and hence cannot be estimated without further restrictions. Respecifying the period effect as a linear trend is not a solution, as the coefficient on calendar time is too highly correlated with the coefficient on the age variable. In addition, more sophisticated forms are necessary to incorporate the other ISEs, $b_{1i}$ and $b_{2i}$.

In general, the ISEs are probably correlated with the covariates. For example, $b_{1i}$ may represent family support networks, uncaptured in the other covariates. This could be related to the total number of job changes—that is, individuals who change jobs a lot may have weak family support networks. Of course, much care must be taken in specifying these relationships to ensure they represent the causal relationships. For example, we might expect the family support networks to influence job changing, rather than the reverse. In the presence of correlation between $b_{1i}$ and $x_{it}$ the usual mixed-effects models and ordinary least squares (OLS) estimators produce biased and statistically inconsistent estimates of $\beta_0$, $\beta_1$, and $\gamma$. One way to capture this dependence is to model further the ISEs by decomposing them into a component for the mean effect of $x_{it}$, an additional error term unrelated to the covariate. For example, we can specify the constant term $b_{0i}$ by

$$b_{0i} = \phi m_i + v_i, \tag{D.1}$$

where $m_i$ is the average value of $x_{it}$ for individual $i$ and $v_i$ is a transitory component. The latter is assumed to be independent of $m_i$ and the residual disturbance $u_{it}$. The coefficient vector $\phi$ represents the correlation between the latent individual effect and the level of the covariates.

Obviously many other specifications of this relationship are possible (for example, median or standard deviation of the covariate). In chapter 6 we specify $m_i$ to be the total number of job changes observed for an individual from sixteen through thirty-six years of age. This attempts to capture the relationship between an individual's latent effect and his level of job changing. This specification can be generalized for multiple ISEs, such as $b_{0i}$, $b_{1i}$, and $b_{2i}$. The full model for log-wages is then a mixed-effects model with an individual-specific intercept term and an additional fixed effect representing the means of the endogenous covariates. We refer to the additional hierarchical specification of equation (D.1) as the Chamberlain mixed-effects models. Each of the mixed-effects models described here can be fit using the standard programs: Singer (1998) describes the use of PROC MIXED in SAS, and Bates and Pinheiro (1997) describe the use of linear mixed effects models in S-PLUS.

Finally, we consider the construction of counterfactual distributions based on these mixed-effects models for the wage growth trajectories. Counterfactual distributions are discussed in appendix C in the context of relative distribution methods. Their use leads to a fully distributional generalization of the Blinder-Oaxaca regression decomposition. An example of a counterfactual distribution is our simulation of putting the recent cohort through the original cohort economy. The resulting distribution of outcomes is then compared with the actual outcomes experienced by the recent cohort in the recent economy. Consider the mixed model for both cohorts:

$$y_{it}^c = \beta_o^c + \beta_1^c l_{it}^c + \beta_2^c q_{it}^c + \gamma^c x_{it}^c + p_{it}^c + u_{it}^c,$$

where the additional superscript, $c$, represents coefficients or covariates from the original ($c = o$) or the recent ($c = r$) cohorts. There are four components to this model: the covariates, the estimated coefficients (or "returns"), the permanent ISEs, and the transitory ISEs. Denoting these by c, f, p, and t respectively, let $y(c, f, p, t)$ denote the vector of log-wages,

$$\beta_o^f + \beta_1^f l_{it}^c + \beta_2^f q_{it}^c + \gamma^f x_{it}^c + p_{it}^p + u_{it}^t,$$

where ($f = o$ or $r$), ($p = o$ or $r$), and ($t = o$ or $r$) represent the cohort from which the values are taken. Thus $y(o, o, o, o)$ are the log-wages from the original cohort and $y(r, r, r, r)$ are the log-wages from the original cohort. In addition, $y(r, o, r, r)$ are the log-wages from the recent cohort where the fixed-effects coefficients ($\beta_o$, $\beta_1$, $\beta_2$, and $\gamma$) are those from the original cohort, and all other values are from the recent cohort. These log-wages have the fixed-effects returns of the original cohort while retaining the covariate composition and other variance components of the recent cohort. Thus $y(r,o,o,o)$ can be interpreted as the log-wages for individuals in the recent cohort had they been subjected to the economic conditions of the original cohort.

The treatment of the permanent and transient variance components of the counterfactual wages requires additional specification. The permanent ISE for an individual in the recent cohort under the original cohort economy is defined to be the permanent ISE for that individual scaled by the ratio of the standard deviations of the permanent ISEs in the original to the recent cohort. Thus individuals retain the rank and relative position of their ISE, while the absolute magnitude is scaled to be consistent with the population-level scale of the original cohort. The transient ISEs for recent cohort individuals under the original cohort conditions are defined analogously: the residual log-wage rescaled to the population-level variance of the transient ISEs in the original cohort. The counterfactual permanent and transient effects of an individual in the original cohort under the recent cohort economy are defined in a similar manner.

Combinations of these four components can produce a range of counterfactual log-wages that can be compared using the relative distribution methods of appendix C. A compositional effect can be defined as the distributional difference between $y(r,o,o,o)$ and $y(o,o,o,o)$. A returns effect can be defined as the distributional difference between $y(r,r,r,r)$ and $y(r,o,o,o)$. A covariate-only returns effect can be defined as the distributional difference between $y(r,r,r,r)$ and $y(r,o,r,r)$. A specific-covariate returns effect can be arrived at by altering only the coefficients of specific variables and holding the other factors fixed. This last idea is used in chapter 6 to measure the distributional effects of cohort differences in job change returns. Each of these counterfactual log-wages facilitates comparisons that isolate an interpretable aspect of the difference between the two cohorts.

# = Notes =

## Chapter 1

1.  Similarly, although the rate of downsizing (a net reduction in a firm's workforce) has declined noticeably in the current economic boom, we continue to see a persistent pattern of job elimination coupled with job creation (American Management Association 1999).

2.  For detailed reviews of these trends, see Levy and Murnane 1992, Danziger and Gottschalk 1993, and Mishel, Bernstein, and Schmitt 1997b.

3.  For a review of the research on the less-dominant supply-side effects, such as immigration and the increased labor force participation of women, see Topel 1997.

4.  See the symposium in the 1997 summer issue of *Journal of Economic Perspectives*.

5.  For a review of quantitative labor economics research, which addresses these institutional changes, see Fortin and Lemieux 1997.

6.  This description should not obscure the considerable amount of conflict and violence in the history of the Fordist system, especially in the early phases. However, it is also true that the union bargaining model succeeded because it fit with the prevailing mode of industrial organization: it fit the requirement for control, it fit the production process, and it fulfilled the not negligible function of ensuring that consumer demand could keep pace with production.

7.  At its height, union membership stood only at roughly 35 percent (Freeman and Medoff 1984). Especially in the manufacturing sector, however, the threat of unionization often propelled nonunion shops to offer comparable wages and working conditions. As a general rule, then, it is safe to say that the internal labor market represented the work experience of a significant number of American workers.

8.  For more-thorough overviews of changes in the nature of work, see Cappelli et al. 1997, Osterman 1994, Harrison 1994, Smith 1997.

9.  This has sometimes been labeled a shift from a vertical to horizontal division of labor, and there are incipient attempts to describe the struc-

229

ture of the labor market in ways that are closely tied to clusterings of occupations and their ties (or lack of them) to one another (Herzenberg, Alic, and Wial 1998; Carnevale and Rose 1998).

10. More generally, a new body of research is finding that service sector firms are strategically stratifying their customer markets and the services provided to each. This has resulted in a similar stratification of service work and the job quality and wages associated with each submarket and, importantly, a splitting of the paths that previously connected jobs and constituted a career. See chapter 8 for an extended discussion.

11. The restriction to white men was necessitated by limitation in the data. Chapter 2 gives a full treatment of the data sets, sample definitions, and issues concerning representativeness and comparability.

## Chapter 2

1. See tables 1.29.1 and 1.29.2, *NLS Users' Guide* (Center for Human Resource Research 1995).

2. No supplemental samples were drawn for the original cohort (the NLSYM).

3. The interested reader can consult the *NLS Users' Guide* (Center for Human Resource Research 1995) for details.

4. A third question, whether specific measures such as job tenure or wages are comparable across the two cohorts, is addressed on a variable-by-variable basis in the main body of the book.

5. To different degrees, the two surveys oversampled on the basis of race and poverty status; weights were adjusted for oversampling in both surveys

6. Until the March 1976 CPS survey, it was not possible to exclude white Hispanics. We extended the upward limit of the age range from twenty-one to twenty-two because a significant number of twenty-one-year-olds selected for the initial NLS samples had turned twenty-two by the time of the actual first interview.

7. Our adjustment is simple. For everyone in the recent cohort who was interviewed before the end of May, we imputed the years of education that the respondent would have had by the following November (using information on enrollment and years of schooling completed, at the time of both the initial interview and the next year's interview). We also calculated the age that the respondent would have been by the following November, if a birthday occurred in the interim.

8. The model uses a nonparametric specification for age and takes account of the longitudinal cohort dependence in the NLSY.

9. We are not addressing the issue of item nonresponse here. It was generally low, and in those cases in which we did find large differences be-

tween the cohorts (as with union status and the designation of job loss as voluntary or involuntary) we chose not to include the variable in our analyses.

10. For example, if we could recover data on weeks worked during the past year for respondents who were currently working but not for respondents currently unemployed or out of the labor force, we did not recover the data. The number of weeks worked in the past year differs significantly by current working status, and so partial recovery would have introduced bias in the weeks-worked variable. The extent to which bias is introduced in the data cleaning process is a critical issue that has not received nearly enough attention.

11. Starting in 1978, attempts were made to relocate and reinterview respondents who had been previously dropped, but only about a hundred were recovered (Rhoton 1984).

12. We use these weights throughout. To avoid artificially inflated standard errors and significance levels, we rescale the relative population weights back to the actual sample sizes in our data.

13. The measures we consider here are used throughout the book, and details on their construction can be found in subsequent chapters and in appendix A.

14. This marginal effect is calculated by taking the percentage observed for retained respondents and transforming it by the exponentiated log-odds ratio estimate from table 2.5. The transformation is: $100*[\beta\ p \div (100 - p)] \div [1 + \beta\ p \div (100 - p)]$, where $\beta$ is the exponentiated log-odds ratio from table 2.5 and $p$ is the percentage observed for retained respondents.

15. Specifically, non-Hispanic white men aged thirty to thirty-six. We have also adjusted the age distribution of the NLS samples to match the age distribution of the CPS samples (a minor adjustment).

16. Thus, a respondent reporting sixteen years of education was coded as a college graduate only if he actually reported having earned a four-year college degree. This is the preferred measure that we use throughout the book (see chapter 3). However, the CPS version of this measure differs from ours in how workers with "some college experience" are treated, and in this table we adjusted our measure to match that used by the CPS.

# Chapter 3

1. The definition of "final education" and other measures used in this chapter are given in appendix A. Because some respondents are lost to attrition, these figures slightly underestimate the final educational attainment in each cohort.

2. Because of the higher attrition rate in the original cohort, the downward shift evident in table 3.1 is understated. Based on CPS data, we would expect 32.6 percent of the original cohort to have complete a college degree, compared with 27.8 percent of the recent cohort. See table 2.6 for details.

3. The trends for women show a relatively constant increase over this period, which lends some support to this explanation.

4. For arguments to this effect, see Freeman 1976 and Berg 1970.

5. Labor force participation is defined as either working or looking for work.

6. On average, work during these ages tends to be about twenty hours a week and about half of the weeks during the academic year (Ruhm 1997; Stern and Nakata 1989).

7. A small residual state, in which respondents are neither in school nor in the labor market, accounts for less than 5 percent of workers at any given age.

8. We remove Vietnam veterans from this analysis because their schooling was artificially postponed. Including them reduces, but does not eliminate, the strength of the differences that we end up observing. Thus, though college enrollment might have been used to defer service for the nonveterans in the original cohort, their enrollment period was still significantly shorter than that of the recent cohort.

9. We should note that, in general, findings on the impact of work during high school are mixed. Some studies suggest that grades and school completion rates may suffer and that this "premature" transition to adult roles reduces the early investments in human capital that are so important to later economic success. Other researchers find that a well-balanced combination of school and work helps students to learn how to budget time, interact with adults, identify what kinds of jobs they prefer, and make more appropriate decisions regarding additional schooling. A good review of this literature can be found in Stone and Mortimer 1998.

10. Although college graduates are now also entering the labor force at earlier ages, we find no difference in unemployment between the cohorts.

11. For example, among voluntary job quitters in the NLS, 40 percent have a spell of unemployment between jobs (Antel 1991).

12. See the more detailed discussion of labor market transition sequences in appendix A.

13. Respondents who never record any school enrollment while in the survey are not included in this analysis. The sample sizes for this analysis are 2,176 for the original cohort and 2,063 for the recent.

14. Almost everyone in this group combined work with school for some of the years in which they were enrolled.

15. Again, respondents who never record any school enrollment while in the survey are not included in this analysis. The sample sizes for this analysis are 2,177 for the original cohort and 2,061 for the recent.

16. Because the recent cohort remains in school longer, there are more opportunities for them to work while enrolled in school. A measure that controls for this difference is the percentage of time both enrolled and working. We computed this measure and found it larger in the recent cohort for all education groups. Therefore the trend toward increased working while enrolled is true in an absolute and relative sense.

17. This has been found in other studies as well. For example, more than one-quarter of NLS respondents (Marcus 1986) and more than one-third of NLSY respondents (Light 1993) leave school and return at some later point.

18. In figure 3.5 we exclude the Vietnam veterans from the original cohort, because the veterans lost several years of labor market experience during their military service. See chapter 2 for more details.

19. We exclude those who are self-employed or working without pay. These distributions have been adjusted for differences in the age composition of the two cohorts (a very minor adjustment).

20. Retail trade accounts for almost all of the increase in the trade category.

21. Private communication, David Howell, 2000, New School for Social Research, New York.

22. See McCall 1995 and Carnevale and Rose 1998 for evidence along these lines. Stephen Rose also provided a series of CPS tables that substantiate the NLS findings. In addition to the broad CPS analysis described, we also confirmed our NLS estimates in table 2.3 with strict CPS comparisons (that is, using the same years, sample definitions, and age ranges).

# Chapter 4

1. See Schmidt and Svorny 1998 and Bernhardt and Marcotte 2000 for in-depth reviews.

2. James Brown and Audrey Light (1992) find that these employer codes are the best source of employer identification, not only for the NLS data but also compared with the other longitudinal data sets.

3. Table 2.1 shows the years that we use for the analyses below and defines the six comparisons being made for each cohort.

4. For more detail on our job change measure, see appendix A.

5. These are described in detail in appendix B, so we only summarize our findings here.

6. In these graphs, about two-thirds of the cohort differences within subgroups are statistically significant. Because the sample sizes are small in

a number of these subgroups, the power of some of these tests is low, and the propensity for observed significance effectively ends up being a function of sample size.

7. When tenure is measured in months or weeks rather than years, it turns out that the risk of leaving a job actually increases within the first three to six months and declines thereafter (Farber 1994).

8. If we use current education in this graph, the results are similar, except that young workers with some college show high levels of job instability: many of these respondents are still enrolled in college and in the process of finishing their degrees and thus tend to hold short-term jobs.

9. For the original cohort, end dates for jobs are impossible to recover consistently for all years. This induces a form of censoring—that is, interval censoring with variable interval widths—that complicates the usual duration models, so we do not consider them here.

10. We model the $\phi_i$ as conditionally independent given the other regressors and following a mean zero Gaussian distribution. This is a generalized linear mixed-effects model, which we fit by maximum likelihood (McCulloch 1997).

11. Many alternative specifications can be used to examine robustness. The fixed ISE specification (Topel and Ward 1992) is infeasible, as we have a maximum of six observations for each individual, and the conditional maximum likelihood estimator (Chamberlain 1984) does not identify the coefficients of time-invariant factors. We relaxed the assumption of independence by specifying a correlation between the ISE, tenure, and education. We also fit a population-average logistic model using generalized estimating equations instead of the ISE model (Hu et al. 1998). In neither case was the cohort effect appreciably changed.

12. It is likely that during recessions, this relationship reverses, and the rate of job separations actually increases (Marcotte 1996), but we were unable to pull out this effect in the model. Other functional specifications (such as a quadratic) also did not have an effect. We also confirmed our simple specification through a variety of additional diagnostics.

13. We also investigated whether the greater attrition rate in the original cohort may cause us to overstate the cohort difference in stability (because more stable workers are more likely to remain in the sample). Using various adjustment methods, we estimate the cohort differences in the odds of a job change to be between 30.0 and 35.8 percent (see appendix B). Thus though there is indeed evidence of an attrition effect, it does not appreciably reduce the significance of the recent cohort's rise in instability. Moreover, there is very likely another effect—stemming from the role tenure plays in our model—that causes us to underestimate the true difference between the two cohorts. As the recent cohort begins to change employers more frequently than the original cohort, its tenures will become progressively shorter. So toward the end of the time period studied, part of the cohort difference will actually be absorbed by the

effect of tenure. To wit, if we estimate model 1 without tenure, the odds of a job change is even higher for members of the recent cohort. There is unfortunately no simple solution to this problem. Excluding tenure altogether results in a seriously misspecified model (Mincer and Jovanovic 1981), and we have therefore taken the conservative route of including it.

14. Note that current enrollment also helps to explain why youth with some college education had such high separation rates. That is, the coefficient for "some college" in model 1 is cut almost in half in model 2, when we introduce current enrollment and thereby control for the higher instability of jobs typically held while in school.

15. The NLS do not have consistent data on union membership.

16. The same finding obtains if we similarly reestimate models 2, 3, and 4.

17. This missingness is biased toward respondents who become unemployed or leave the labor force—and these groups most likely have different reasons for separation than those moving to new employers.

18. It is important to understand that this table does not measure, for example, a worker's risk of becoming unemployed immediately following an employer separation. Rather, we are asking where workers ended up after a two-year time span, given that they were employed at the outset.

19. We select only workers who have been observed for four or more of the potential six time points in this analysis. In order to control for compositional differences between the two cohorts, we use predicted job change probabilities from model 1. Neither of these decisions significantly affects the results.

20. We confirmed this result by testing for an interaction between cohort and number of previous jobs in model 1 of table 4.2, which was not significant.

21. See appendix A for the definition of this variable.

22. The cohort differences shown here are robust to controls for age, experience, number of missed interviews, and attrition.

23. Recall that we count only CPS employers here in order to define a measure that is strictly consistent across the two cohort. This results in a mild undercount in absolute terms. For example, Hall (1982) finds that in 1978, workers aged thirty to thirty-four averaged 6.7 cumulative employers. Topel and Ward (1992) find that within the first ten years of labor market experience, the typical worker will work for an average of seven different employers. Our measure effectively gives a lower bound estimate of the differences in accumulated employers between the two cohorts.

24. The results are not affected by this choice and are quite similar for the full data set.

25. In this graph we use the full data set that includes all years, to maximize the age of the workers. Because we are not counting jobs and recording

tenure only at the end of the survey, it is not necessary to use the strictly matched data set.

## Chapter 5

1. A similar dynamic obtains within firms. Promotions are a key source of wage growth on the job (as high as 18 percent over the life span), but again, the incidence of promotions declines with experience (McCue 1996).

2. These are identified after controlling for individual- and job-specific effects.

3. We use hourly wages in 1999 dollars, deflated with the personal consumption expenditure (PCE) deflator. See chapter 2 for details on the hourly wage measure and chapter 4 for details on the job change measure and the strictly matched data set used both there and in this chapter.

4. Because the outcome variable is differenced across two time points, we are zeroing out individual-specific effects that are time invariant.

5. Statistical significance in these graphs effectively ends up being a function of sample size. Within each graph, sample sizes differ across the experience groupings because the prevalence of job changing declines dramatically with experience. So, for example, sample sizes are small among job changers with nine or more years of experience and among nonchangers with less than six years of experience.

6. The predicted change in log wages is first estimated at variable means for all control covariates. We then exponentiate and subtract 1, yielding the percentage change in real wages.

7. We use a residualized version of years of experience (and its square), with tenure and prior number of jobs regressed out. The reason is substantive. Controlling for the raw version of work experience either reduces or eliminates the effects of tenure and number of prior job changes. This simply indicates collinearity and the fact that the experience variable is more powerful in capturing the time-based trends for which all three variables are vying. Our interest, however, is in understanding the substantive mechanisms that lead to greater or lesser wage gains, hence we separate the effects by residualizing.

8. See appendix A for details on this variable.

9. The reader may notice that the effect of previous number of jobs differs for the two cohorts. In model 3, however, controlling for the previous wage level erases the cohort difference in the effect of past instability. Thus both cohorts now share the same detrimental effect, controlling for the fact that the recent cohort has on average a lower wage.

10. The effect of previous wages is negative. To understand this, recall that our measure of wage change is relative. If we had used an absolute

measure, then the sign of this variable would be positive. In relative terms, however, low-wage workers actually receive a higher percentage increase in wages than high-wage workers, on average. This is a consistent finding in the literature (Moore, Viscusi, and Zeckhauser 1999).

11.   Specifically, these "smoothed" wages are predicted hourly wages for each respondent at each age, from a mixed-effects wage model that includes random effects for the intercept, age, and age squared term. The model effectively allows a unique wage profile for each person across his full work history, smoothing out fluctuations in wages that can result from temporary disturbances such as the business cycle.

12.   The direct effect of current job change is sufficient—we tested for interaction effects and found none. This accords with the findings of Ann Bartel and George Borjas (1981).

13.   This model was estimated using pairwise deletion, because only 57 percent of the cases had a valid value for both their prior job and their next job. All but 193 of the cases, however, had a valid value for at least one of these jobs, and we did not want to lose their information. Using pairwise deletion means that all of the coefficients for the "prior period" variables were estimated only against cases that had a valid value in the prior period. Similarly, all of the coefficients for the "next period" variables were estimated only against cases that had a valid value in the next period. (Estimating the model for the 57 percent subsample does not affect the substance of our results, though magnitudes differ because the subsample is older and more stable.)

14.   As in our previous models, we have included the $R^2$ estimated with smoothed wages, to underscore the point that we are, in fact, explaining a significant amount of the permanent variation in wage changes.

15.   Because we are collapsing across experience groups, for this analysis we use the difference in (ln) wages that has experience and experience-squared regressed out.

## Chapter 6

1.   See chapter 2 for a discussion of the twelve-year matched files. Our findings do not differ significantly when all sixteen years are used for the recent cohort (except in the case of the variable for cumulative number of employers, which, of course, is sensitive to the number of years counted).

2.   For details on the variables used in this chapter, see appendix A.

3.   The transportation and communication industries are not technically part of the goods-producing sector, but we have included them in this group because they are traditionally unionized and share many of the wage-setting rules of manufacturing industries.

4.   The interval during which the two wage lines converge occurs when college enrollment in the original cohort is about twice as high as in the

recent. The difference in enrollment is likely to be a function of three factors: the shifting interview window for the recent cohort, which places their interview in the middle of the summer months (see figure 2.2), the later enrollment of returning Vietnam War veterans in the original cohort, and effects of the 1974 recession on the original cohort.

5. This is not to ignore the significant effect that year-to-year wage variability can have on economic security.

6. More complicated nonparametric specifications did not provide a better description of the curvature. Also note that we orthogonalize the *age-squared* term with respect to the *age* term.

7. This ANOVA table decomposes the total variation in wages into the sum of the unique contributions of the fixed, permanent, and transient components. We use a forward sequential decomposition to further decompose the permanent component into the contributions of the intercept, age, and age squared.

8. As an aside, note that the total variance in wages over all persons and all years at the bottom of the table is higher for the original than for the recent cohort. This might seem counterintuitive, as we have repeatedly noted the greater wage variance in the recent cohort. What we are seeing here is the influence of the dramatic downshift in the recent cohort mean. When we take all the person-year observations and treat them as a single cross-sectional sample, the mean downshift effectively masks the greater age- or experience-specific variance in the recent cohort's wages.

9. There are also estimated covariances between these random components, which we do not list here. A complete interpretation of the impact of the intercept, linear, and quadratic random components would require that we take into account the covariance between them.

10. The predicted permanent wage for each individual at each time point is a function of the common fixed effects, the random effects, and the covariance of the random effects. The permanent variance at each age can be estimated directly from the covariance matrix of the individual specific parameters.

11. Specifically, we use the best linear unbiased predictors (BLUPs) of the permanent wages at age sixteen and age thirty-six and take the difference. The predicted permanent wage for each individual at each age is a function of the common fixed effects and the individual-specific random effects.

12. See appendix C for details on relative distribution methods.

13. We take the last observed wage for workers lost to attrition, provided they are at least thirty years old.

14. This is about the midpoint of the tenure distribution, though the recent cohort has more observations than the original in the lower category.

15. Given our random-effects specification, coefficients should be interpreted as "within-person" effects. The insignificant direct effect for education therefore means that the acquisition of a high school diploma or college degree makes itself felt as work experience accumulates. For example, one can gauge the instantaneous impact of completing a high school diploma only by comparing the interaction term at nearby levels of experience. So a recent cohort worker with three years of experience gains .021 upon graduating from high school. The penalty of − .032 drops to − .025, so for three years experience, the bump in wages is .021 ([.025 × 3] − [− .032 × 3]). Some college experience combined with five years of work experience results in a predicted gain of .085, and this is in comparison with a high school graduate. One can see that the economic value of a college degree (our reference group) manifests itself over time, through the returns to experience—at this point in our modeling, age is not a strong determinant of wages.

16. This is because we estimated the above models separately for the two cohorts, which obscures the impact of compositional effects.

17. As in table 6.3, we take the last observed wage for workers lost to attrition, provided they are at least thirty years old.

18. There are several ways of constructing the counterfactual distribution and defining the two effects. We have chosen this one because it isolates all attrition effects in the composition term, leaving a clean estimate of the returns effects. This choice also minimizes the impact of attrition in the composition component, as most of the attrition impact is channeled through the education variable. Because the educational coefficient used in the counterfactual distribution is taken from the original cohort, the differences in educational composition are multiplied by a smaller factor than would be the case if the recent cohort coefficients had been used. We have run the decomposition in several other ways, however, and the results do not differ in substance from those presented here. See appendix D for more details.

19. These predicted permanent wages contain all of the heterogeneity we are interested in and exclude only the transient residuals. The deciles are defined by the ninetieth percentile of the original cohort's wage distribution, so the dollar values for the decile cutoffs are the same for both cohorts.

# Chapter 7

1. In labor economics, generic and stylized models of the labor market still tend to dominate. As Jared Bernstein and Heidi Hartmann (1999) note, the neoclassical paradigm does not lend itself to an analysis of the low-wage labor market as a separate entity, distinct in its operation from other parts of the labor market. Alternative theoretical frameworks on segmented and dual labor markets have gone further conceptually but

have typically not provided detailed empirical analysis of the dynamics of those markets—in terms of mobility paths, job changing, and so forth.

2. For us, the key challenge is to set the cutoff line low enough to represent true economic hardship while still ensuring sufficient sample sizes within the low-wage worker group.

3. We do not have consistent data from both cohorts that would allow us to reconstruct the family composition for each respondent and the total family income flowing into the household.

4. For example, the cutoff we use to define low-wage workers is just a bit higher than the wage level that defines the bottom decile of the original cohort's permanent final wage distribution in chapter 6. All of the analyses in this chapter therefore focus on the group bearing the brunt of the largest and most deleterious shifts in the earnings distribution in the new economy.

5. We show smoothed average wage profiles for each wage group. These capture the core of where most curves lie, but it should always be remembered that individual variation about these idealized profiles exists.

6. Education is measured as the final level of education reached by the respondent.

7. We collapsed the 1970 census one-digit industry classification codes into nine categories to ensure sufficient observations in each group.

8. For example, 21.2 percent of workers in wholesale and retail trade in the original cohort were classified as low-wage workers. If only the industrial mix had changed, then we would similarly expect about 21 percent of the recent cohort to be low-wage workers in these industries.

9. The large majority of the retail and wholesale trade category is taken up by retail trade.

10. We should note that this result is remarkably consistent across education levels. Of course, the proportion of low-wage workers within any given industry is less for well-educated workers. The relative increase in low-wage trajectories for the recent cohort, however, is quite consistent, regardless of education level.

11. This is the same measure used in chapter 4: for any two-year span in which we measure whether someone has changed a job, we compute the corresponding change in (ln) wages.

12. Recall that these are deflated wages, so that the returns are negative after taking inflation into account.

13. We can use wage volatility to predict the fluctuation in wages from year to year. In the concrete example that follows, we begin with mean wages for low-wage workers aged thirty-four to thirty-six; taking plus or minus one standard deviation of their volatility forms a predicted range of outcomes. Wages can fall anywhere in this range from one year to the next.

14. The industries were measured, at the two-digit level, in 1981 (for the original cohort) and 1994 (for the recent).

15. Note that this is a "soft" and conservative criterion; we could have required three or more years spent in that sector, for example, which would render the results even stronger.

16. This measure is the same as that used in chapter 4: the proportion of workers changing jobs across a two-year interval.

17. For a broad overview of this field, see Batt 1998. Recent papers in this literature include Batt and Keefe 1998; Bernhardt and Slater 1998; Colclough and Tolbert 1992; Garson 1988; Hunter 1999; and Keltner and Finegold 1999.

18. Specifically, (1) their wages at the age of twenty-four established them as low-wage workers according to our formal definition of "low wage"; (2) they did not have a stable job from sixteen to twenty-five years of age (a stable job is defined as full-time, with tenure of at least three years); and (3) in that age range they had worked in the low-wage sector at least once.

19. Specifically, these measures are whether from the age of twenty-six to thirty-seven, the worker was never observed working in the low-wage sector and was observed at least once in a full-time job with three or more years of tenure.

20. The career profile for any group of workers is a smoothed version of the observed wages. Because variation naturally occurs within groups, we provide in the graph the percentage of workers in each group who permanently make it out of the low-wage group by the age of thirty-four.

21. We do not address selection bias here, so our findings provide an upper bound on the effects of education.

## Chapter 8

1. We strongly encourage the reader to consult the detailed summaries at the end of each chapter, which contain a wealth of important information that we cannot cover here.

2. To maintain comparability to our other analyses, for the 1996 and 1998 wage data we selected the same sample of recent cohort respondents that was used in the rest of the book, selected only the wages of their CPS jobs, and used the NLSY weights.

3. Recall that the original cohort's surveys stopped in 1981, after sixteen years, whereas the recent cohort continues to be surveyed every two years.

4. Only college graduates had managed to make up the lost ground. Note, however, that if we had another four years' worth of wage data for the

original cohort, a college wage gap would reemerge if the original cohort continued to advance at the same rate observed in their final years.

5. To obtain the figures in this table, we assume the age-specific median wage for each cohort is earned by a full-time, full-year worker. The annual earnings are then estimated by multiplying the wage by forty (hours a week) and then times fifty (weeks a year). These annual earnings estimates are summed from age sixteen to age thirty-six to obtain the cumulative totals.

6. The price of the national median existing single family house sold in the first quarter of 1999, as reported by the U.S. Department of Housing and Urban Development (www.huduser.org/periodicals/ushmc.html). The figure is based on sales reported to the National Association of Realtors, a total of 4.8 million homes.

7. This particular confluence of events is quite surprising in itself and seems to bear out the unorthodox arguments made by David Card and Alan Krueger (1995) in their controversial book on the minimum wage, *Myth and Measurement*.

8. The 90:10 wage decile ratio peaked in 1994 at 4.6. Since then it has fallen by 4.2 percent. All of this decline was driven by gains at the bottom of distribution: a 4.8 percent decline in the 50:10 ratio. The 90:50 ratio, by contrast, increased during this period by 0.6 percent (authors' calculations using data from Mishel, Bernstein, and Schmitt 2001).

9. For reviews, see Cappelli 1996 and Moss 2000.

10. Office workers are defined as managers, supervisors, fire sector employees, business professionals, employees of public administration and nonprofits, and support staff.

11. This does not imply that the United States now produces fewer goods, because a concomitant trend has been a steep rise in productivity in the manufacturing sector (Kozicki 1997). However, though manufacturing output may be stable, the mix of jobs has clearly changed, with important effects on wages.

12. This material is drawn from Bernhardt 2000.

13. See the review in chapter 1.

14. That said, an important task for future research is to focus on low-wage workers and the extent to which contingent jobs figure in their entire career span, not just at one point in time. Recent field work conducted by one of the authors in inner-city neighborhoods suggests that temp work, especially in light industry, figures prominently in the working lives of recent immigrants. Jamie Peck and Nik Theodore (forthcoming) find that temp agencies themselves have clearly recognized the best source of short-term labor, inundating Hispanic Chicago neighborhoods with a plethora of hiring branches.

15. See Smith 1997 for an excellent overview of the data, largely based on case studies.

16. American Management Association 1999. Note that this is not a representative survey, and large firms are oversampled. Note also that many of the firms reporting job cuts also reported job creation; only 21.4 percent of the firms actually had a net reduction in jobs, or downsizing, properly defined.

17. Recent papers in this literature include Bailey and Bernhardt 1997; Batt and Keefe 1999; Bernhardt and Slater 1998; Colclough and Tolbert 1992; Garson 1988; Hunter 1999; Keltner and Finegold 1999; MacDonald and Sirianni 1996.

18. It is frequently reported in the business press that employers are starting to rethink their externalization of work, bringing job and workers back inside. Whether this is a long-term trend remains to be seen. Philip Moss, Harold Salzman, and Chris Tilly (2000) have studied the evolution of restructuring in a number of firms. Although they also find this type of rethinking, it resulted in a variety of actions, not all of which reestablished firms' internal labor markets. More than anything, what appears to be happening is a fine-tuning of exactly which jobs should remain core and which should be externalized.

19. Some of the following material draws on Bernhardt and Bailey 1998.

20. What follows is a basic review of complex legal issues. In-depth treatment of these issues can be found in Herzenberg, Alic, and Wial 1998; Wial 1993; duRivage 1992; Kochan and Osterman 1994; and Friedman et al. 1994.

21. Hence, the U.S. Department of Labor has recently put its resources into a review of the partnership model (see Working for America Institute 2000) and has funded several partnerships across the country, including the expansion of the WRTP into several new sectors.

22. See Dresser and Rogers 1997 and Parker and Rogers 1999 for a full discussion of the incentive structure.

23. This is a complex area; see articles in "Labor Law Reform" 1995.

# Appendix A

1. In cases where we found it impossible to construct comparable measures, we dropped the variable from our analyses. This resulted in a number of unfortunate but necessary choices. Among the variables we had to exclude were collective-bargaining coverage and reason for leaving the previous employer.

2. For the NLSY, work-related variables are available in a week-by-week array, known as the Work History File. We used this file to extract almost

all of the CPS job-related information for the recent cohort. It was particularly useful for obtaining the job data for respondents who had missed an interview, as the array has been backfilled with retrospectively collected information from the next interview. It was therefore only necessary to select a week the respondent would have been interviewed and pull the information from the work history array for that week. We selected this week by taking the relative position of the respondent's interview in year 1 of the survey and moving it forward to the missing year. This relative position approach made it possible to accommodate the shifting interview in the recent cohort (see chapter 2 for more information on the interview window).

3.  See Social Science Research Council 1983; Rytina and Bianchi 1984; Bregger 1982. The problem is that many 1970 categories were not simply renamed or divided but, rather, were split up and recombined to form new categories.

4.  The deflator series employed was revised in the third quarter of 1999. Rather than attempting to modify our entire analysis to reflect the adjusted deflator series, we imputed an aggregate factor for the whole year in 1999, based on the information available in the first two quarters and the relationship between quarters in the previous year. This simpler adjustment was found to be robust to several different formulations and was done in consultation with the Bureau of Labor Statistics.

5.  We should point out that even under the best-case scenario (no missing data), the absolute number of CPS employers is a relatively arbitrary measure. One could imagine any number of other indicators of cumulative job instability: for example, a count of all jobs ever held, no matter how short lived and insignificant; alternatively, a count that includes only jobs since the respondent left school, with the aim of identifying job changes that "matter." Our measure ensures strict comparability across the two cohorts and therefore allows us to accurately identify differences in cumulative job changing between them.

# Appendix C

1.  Readers interested in learning more about these methods are referred to Handcock and Morris 1999, which describes the details of the methods outlined here, addresses inferential issues, and develops advanced graphical methods. Additional information is available from the home page (www.stat.washington.edu/~handcock/RelDist).

# Appendix D

1.  We do not consider random walk models here. A comparison of random walk and mixed-effects regression models is given in Baker 1997 and Haider 1997.

# = References =

Abraham, Katherine, and Susan K. Taylor. 1996. "Firms' Use of Outside Contractors: Theory and Evidence." *Journal of Labor Economics* 14(3): 394–424.

Acs, Gregory, and Sheldon Danziger. 1993. "Educational Attainment, Industrial Structure, and Male Earnings Through the 1980s." *Journal of Human Resources* 28(3): 618–48.

Altonji, Joseph G., and Paul J. Devereux. 1999. "The Extent and Consequences of Downward Nominal Wage Rigidity." Working paper 7236. Cambridge, Mass.: National Bureau of Economic Research.

American Management Association. 1999. "AMA Staffing and Structure Survey: Summary of Key Findings." New York: AMA. Downloaded in October 2000 from the World Wide Web at *www.amanet.org/research/pdfs/SHfstrc.pdf*.

Antel, John J. 1991. "The Wage Effects of Voluntary Labor Mobility With and Without Intervening Unemployment." *Industrial and Labor Relations Review* 44(2): 299–306.

Appelbaum, Eileen, Thomas Bailey, Peter Berg, and Arne Kalleberg. 2000. *Manufacturing Advantage: Why High-Performance Work Systems Pay Off.* Ithaca, N.Y.: Cornell University Press.

Appelbaum, Eileen, and Rose Batt. 1994. *The New American Workplace: Transforming Work Systems in the United States.* Ithaca, N.Y.: ILR Press.

Auletta, Ken. 1982. *The Underclass.* New York: Random House.

Autor, David H., Lawrence F. Katz, and Alan B. Krueger. 1998. "Computing Inequality: Have Computers Changed the Labor Market?" *Quarterly Journal of Economics* 113(4): 1169–1204.

Bailey, Thomas, and Annette Bernhardt. 1997. "In Search of the High Road in a Low-Wage Industry." *Politics and Society* 25(2): 179–201.

Baker, George, Michael Gibbs, and Bengt Holmstrom. 1994. "The Internal Economics of a Firm: Evidence from Personnel Data." *Quarterly Journal of Economics* 109(4): 881–919.

Baker, Michael. 1997. "Growth Rate Heterogeneity and the Covariance Structure of Life-Cycle Earnings." *Journal of Labor Economics* 15(2): 338–75.

Bartel, Ann P., and George J. Borjas. 1981. "Wage Growth and Job Turnover." In *Studies in Labor Markets*, edited by Sherwin Rosen. Chicago: University of Chicago Press.

Bates, Douglas M., and Jose C. Pinheiro. 1997. "Software Design for Longitudinal Data Analysis." In *Modeling Longitudinal and Spatially Correlated Data: Methods, Applications, and Future Directions*, edited by Timothy G. Gregoire, David R. Brillinger, Peter J. Diggle, Estelle Russek-Cohen, William G. Warren, and Russell D. Wolfinger. New York: Springer-Verlag.

Batt, Rosemary. 1998. "The Changing Nature of Work in Services." New York State School of Industrial Relations, Cornell University. Manuscript prepared for the National Research Council, Committee for the Enhancement of Human Performance.

———. 2001. "Explaining Wage Inequality in Telecommunications Services: Customer Segmentation, Human Resource Practices, and Union Decline. The Role of Business Strategy and Human Resource Practices." *Industrial and Labor Relations Review* 54 (2,A): 425–49.

Batt, Rosemary, and Jeffrey Keefe. 1999. "Human Resource and Employment Practices in Telecommunications Services." In *Employment Practices and Business Strategy*, edited by Peter Cappelli. Oxford: Oxford University Press.

Bell, Daniel. 1973. *The Coming of Post-Industrial Society*. New York: Basic Books.

Berg, Ivar E. 1970. *Education and Jobs: The Great Training Robbery*. New York: Praeger.

Berg, Peter, and Eileen Appelbaum. 1996. "Financial Market Constraints and Business Strategy in the U.S.A." In *Creating Industrial Capacity: Towards Full Employment*, edited by Jonathan Michi and John Grieve Smith. New York: Oxford University Press.

Berger, Mark C., and Barry T. Hirsch. 1983. "The Civilian Earnings Experience of Vietnam-Era Veterans." *Journal of Human Resources* 18(4): 455–79.

Berman, Eli, John Bound, and Zvi Griliches. 1994. "Changes in the Demand for Skilled Labor Within U.S. Manufacturing: Evidence from the Annual Survey of Manufacturers." *Quarterly Journal of Economics* 109(2): 367–97.

Bernhardt, Annette. 2000. "Performance Without the High: Firms and Technology in Low-End Services." Working paper. Madison: University of Wisconsin, Center on Wisconsin Strategy.

Bernhardt, Annette, and Thomas R. Bailey. 1998. *Making Careers Out of Jobs: Policies to Address the New Employment Relationship*. Published report. New York: Columbia University, Teachers College, Institute on Education and the Economy.

Bernhardt, Annette, and Dave Marcotte. 2000. "Is 'Standard Employment' Still What It Used to Be?" In *Nonstandard Work: The Nature and Challenges of Changing Employment Arrangements*, edited by Françoise Carré, Marianne A. Ferber, Lonnie Golden, and Steve Herzenberg. Champaign, Ill.: Industrial Relations Research Association.

Bernhardt, Annette, and Douglas Slater. 1998. "What Technology Can and Cannot Do: A Case Study in Banking." *Industrial Relations Research Association Series: Proceedings of the Fiftieth Annual Meeting* 1: 118–25.

Bernstein, Jared, and Heidi Hartmann. 1999. "Defining and Characterizing the Low-Wage Labor Market." In *The Low-Wage Labor Market: Challenges and Opportunities for Economic Self-sufficiency*. Published report. Washington, D.C.: Urban Institute.

Bernstein, Jared, and John Schmitt. 1998. *Making Work Pay: The Impact of the 1996–1997 Minimum Wage Increase*. Published report. Washington, D.C.: Economic Policy Institute.

Blau, Francine D., and Lawrence M. Kahn. 1999. "Institutions and Laws in the Labor Market." In *Handbook of Labor Economics*, edited by Orley Ashenfelter and David Card. New York: Elsevier Science.

Blinder, Alan S. 1973. "Wage Discrimination: Reduced Form and Structural Estimates." *Journal of Human Resources* 8(4): 436–55.

————, ed. 1990. *Paying for Productivity: A Look at the Evidence*. Washington, D.C.: Brooking Institution.

Boisjoly, Johanne, Greg J. Duncan, and Timothy Smeeding. 1998. "The Shifting Incidence of Involuntary Job Losses from 1968 to 1992." *Industrial Relations* 37(2): 207–31.

Borus, Michael, Frank Mott, and Gilbert Nestel, eds. 1978. *Counting Youth: A Comparison of Youth Labor Force Statistics in the Current Population Survey and the National Longitudinal Surveys*. Washington, D.C.: U.S. Department of Labor.

Bound, John, and George Johnson. 1992. "Changes in the Structure of Wages in the 1980s: An Evaluation of Alternative Explanations." *American Economic Review* 82(3): 371–92.

Bowers, Norman. 1981. "Youth Labor Force Activity: Alternative Surveys Compared." *Monthly Labor Review* 104(3): 3–17.

Bregger, John. 1982. "Labor Force Data from the CPS to Undergo Revision in January 1983." *Monthly Labor Review* 105(11): 3–6.

Brown, James N., and Audrey Light. 1992. "Interpreting Panel Data on Job Tenure." *Journal of Labor Economics* 10(3): 219–57.

Burdett, Kenneth. 1978. "A Theory of Employer Job Search and Quit Rates." *American Economic Review* 68(1): 212–20.

Cancian, Maria, Robert Haveman, Thomas Kaplan, Daniel Meyer, and Barbara Wolfe. 1999. "Work, Earnings, and Well-being After Welfare: What Do We Know?" In *Economic Conditions and Welfare Reform*, edited by Sheldon Danziger. Kalamazoo, Mich.: W. E. Upjohn Institute.

Cappelli, Peter. 1996. "Technology and Skill Requirements: Implications for Establishment Wage Structures." *New England Economic Review* (May–June): 139–54.

Cappelli, Peter, Laurie Bassi, Harry Katz, David Knoke, Paul Osterman, and Michael Useem. 1997. *Change at Work*. New York: Oxford University Press.

Card, David, and Alan B. Krueger. 1995. *Myth and Measurement: The New Economics of the Minimum Wage*. Princeton: Princeton University Press.

Carnevale, Anthony, and Stephen Rose. 1998. "Education for What? The New Office Economy." Technical Report. Princeton, N.J.: Educational Testing Service.

Carré, Françoise, and Pamela Joshi. 1998. "Building Stability for Transient Workforces: Exploring the Possibilities of Intermediary Institutions Helping Workers Cope with Labor Market Instability." *Radcliffe Quarterly* 84(2): 30.

Center for Human Resource Research. 1995. *NLS Users' Guide 1995*. Columbus: Ohio State University.

Chamberlain, Gary. 1984. "Panel Data." In *Handbook of Econometrics*, edited by Zvi Griliches and M. D. Intriligator. Amsterdam: Elsevier Science.

Chambers, John M., William S. Cleveland, Beat Kleiner, and Paul A. Tukey. 1983. *Graphical Methods for Data Analysis*. Belmont, Calif.: Wadsworth.

Christopherson, Susan. 2001. "Why Do National Labor Market Practices Continue to Diverge in the Global Economy?" *Economic Geography* (Forthcoming).

Cleveland, William S., and Robert McGill. 1984. "Graphical Perception: Theory, Experimentation, and Application to the Development of Graphical Methods." *Journal of the American Statistical Association* 79(387): 531–54.

Cohen, Stephen, and John Zysman. 1987. *Manufacturing Matters: The Myth of the Post-Industrial Economy*. New York: Basic Books.

Colclough, Glenna, and Charles M. Tolbert. 1992. *Work in the Fast Lane: Flexibility, Divisions of Labor, and Inequality in High-Tech Industries*. Albany: State University of New York Press.

Collins, Alvin C. 1999. "Testimony Before the Subcommittee on Postsecondary Education, Training, and Life-Long Learning." Washington, D.C.: U.S. House of Representatives, Committee on Education and the Workforce. Transcript.

Commission on the Future of Worker-Management Relations. 1994. *Fact Finding Report*. Chicago: Commerce Clearing House.

Commission on the Skills of the American Workforce. 1990. *America's Choice: High Skills or Low Wages!* Rochester, N.Y.: National Center on Education and the Economy.

Costrell, Robert M. 1988. *The Effects of Industry Employment Shifts on Wage Growth, 1947–1987*. Testimony Before the Joint Economic Committee. 100 Cong., 2nd session, August 1988.

Creedy, John. 1985. *Dynamics of Income Distribution*. New York: Blackwell.

———. 1998. *The Dynamics of Inequality and Poverty: Comparing Income Distributions*. Northampton, Mass.: Elgar.

Cwik, Jan, and Jan Mielniczuk. 1989. "Estimating Density Ratio with Application to Discriminant Analysis." *Communications in Statistics* 18(8): 3057–69.

D'Amico, Ronald. 1984. "Does Employment During High School Impair Academic Progress?" *Sociology of Education* 57(3): 152–64.

Daniel, Kermit Erik. 1995. "The Marriage Premium." In *The New Economics of Human Behavior*, edited by Mariano Tommasi and Kathryn Ierulli. Cambridge: Cambridge University Press.

Danziger, Sheldon, and Peter Gottschalk, eds. 1993. *Uneven Tides: Rising Inequality in America*. New York: Russell Sage Foundation.

Dertouzos, Michael, Richard Lester, and Robert Solow. 1989. *Made in America: Regaining the Productive Edge*. Cambridge, Mass.: MIT Press.

Diebold, Francis X., David Neumark, and Daniel Polsky. 1997. "Job Stability in the United States." *Journal of Labor Economics* 15(2): 206–33.

Dinardo, John, Nicole Fortin, and Thomas Lemieux. 1996. "Labor Market Institutions and the Distribution of Wages, 1973–1992: A Semiparametric Approach." *Econometrica* 64(5): 1001–44.

Doeringer, Peter B., and Michael J. Piore. 1971. *Internal Labor Markets and Manpower Analysis*. Lexington, Mass.: Heath.

Dresser, Laura, and Joel Rogers. 1997. "Rebuilding Job Access and Career Advancement Systems in the New Economy." Unpublished manuscript. Madison: University of Wisconsin.

Duncan, Greg J., Johanne Boisjoly, and Timothy Smeeding. 1996. "Economic Mobility of Young Workers in the 1970s and 1980s." *Demography* 33(4): 497–509.

Dunlop, John. 1957. "The Task of Contemporary Wage Theory." In *New Concepts in Wage Determination*, edited by George W. Taylor and Frank C. Pierson. New York: McGraw-Hill.

duRivage, Virginia, ed. 1992. *New Policies for the Part-time and Contingent Workforce*. Armonk, N.Y.: M. E. Sharpe.

Edwards, Richard C. 1979. *Contested Terrain: The Transformation of the Workplace in the Twentieth Century*. New York: Basic Books.

Falaris, Evangelos M., and Elizabeth H. Peters. 1998. "Survey Attrition and Schooling Choices." *Journal of Human Resources* 33(2): 531–54.

Farber, Henry. 1994. "The Analysis of Interfirm Working Mobility." *Journal of Labor Economics* 12(4): 554–93.

———. 1997. "The Changing Face of Job Loss in the United States, 1981–1995." *Brookings Papers on Economic Activity: Microeconomics Supplement*: 55–128.

———. 1998. "Are Lifetime Jobs Disappearing? Job Duration in the United States, 1973–1993." In *Labor Statistics Measurement Issues*, edited by John Haltiwanger, Marilyn Manser, and Robert Topel. Chicago: University of Chicago Press.

Fortin, Nicole, and Thomas Lemieux. 1997. "Institutional Changes and Rising Wage Inequality: Is There a Linkage?" *Journal of Economic Perspectives* 11(2): 75–96.

Frank, Robert H., and Phillip J. Cook. 1995. *The Winner-Take-All Society: Why the Few at the Top Get So Much More than the Rest of Us*. New York: Penguin Books.

Freeman, Richard B. 1976. *The Overeducated American*. New York: Academic Press.

———. 1995. "How Much Has De-Unionization Contributed to the Rise in Male Earnings Inequality?" In *Uneven Tides: Rising Inequality in America*, edited by Sheldon Danzinger and Peter Gottschalk. New York: Russell Sage Foundation.

———. 1996. "Labor Market Institutions and Earnings Inequality." *New England Economic Review* (May–June): 157–68.

———. 1997. "Solving the New Inequality." *Boston Review* 21(6): 3–10.

Freeman, Richard B., and James Medoff. 1984. *What Do Unions Do?* New York: Basic Books.

———, eds. 1982. *Why Does the Rate of Youth Labor Force Activity Differ Across Surveys?* Chicago: University of Chicago Press.

Freeman, Richard B., and Joel Rogers. 1999. *What Workers Want*. Ithaca, N.Y.: ILR Press.

Friedman, Sheldon, Richard Hurd, Rudolph Oswald, and Ronald Seeber, eds. 1994. *Restoring the Promise of American Labor Law*. Ithaca, N.Y.: ILR Press.

Gardecki, Rosella, and David Neumark. 1998. "Order from Chaos? The Effects of Early Labor Market Experiences on Adult Labor Market Outcomes." *Industrial and Labor Relations Review* 51(2): 299–322.

Garson, Barbara. 1988. *The Electronic Sweatshop: How Computers Are Transforming the Office of the Future into the Factory of the Past.* New York: Penguin Books.

General Accounting Office. 1999. "Welfare Reform: Information on Former Recipients' Status." HEHS-99-48. Washington: U.S. Government Printing Office.

Ghez, Gilbert R. 1981. "Comment on Bartel and Borjas's 'Wage Growth and Job Turnover.'" In *Studies in Labor Markets,* edited by Sherwin Rosen. Chicago: University of Chicago Press.

Gittleman, Maury, and Mary Joyce. 1996. "Earnings Mobility and Long-Run Inequality: An Analysis Using Matched CPS Data." *Industrial Relations* 35(2): 180–96.

Gottschalk, Peter. 1997. "Inequality, Income Growth, and Mobility: The Basic Facts." *Journal of Economic Perspectives* 11(2): 21–40.

Gottschalk, Peter, and Robert Moffitt. 1992. *Earnings and Wage Distributions in the NLS, CPS, and PSID.* Final Report to the U.S. Department of Labor. Providence, R.I.: Brown University.

———. 1994. "The Growth of Earnings Instability in the U.S. Labor Market." *Brookings Papers on Economic Activity* 2: 217–54.

Granovetter, Mark. 1981. "Toward a Sociological Theory of Income Differences." In *Sociological Perspectives on Labor Markets,* edited by Ivar Berg. New York: Academic Press.

Greenhouse, Steven. 1997. "Deeper Shade of Blue: Unions Concentrating on Lower Rungs of Economic Ladder." *The New York Times,* p. A26, August 10, 1997.

Hacker, Andrew. 1997. *Money: Who Has How Much and Why.* New York: Scribner.

Haider, Steven. 1997. "Earnings Instability and Earnings Inequality of Males in the United States, 1967–1991." Manuscript. Ann Arbor: University of Michigan, Department of Economics.

Hall, Robert E. 1982. "The Importance of Lifetime Jobs in the U.S. Economy." *American Economic Review* 72(4): 716–24.

Handcock, Mark S., and Martina Morris. 1998. "Relative Distribution Methods." *Sociological Methodology* 28: 53–97.

———. 1999. *Relative Distribution Methods in the Social Sciences.* New York: Springer-Verlag.

Handcock, Mark S., Martina Morris, and Annette Bernhardt. 2000. "Comparing Earnings Inequality Trends Using Two Major Surveys." *Monthly Labor Review* 123(3): 48–61.

Handel, Michael, and Maury Gittleman. 1999. "Is There a Wage Payoff to Innovative Work Practices?" Working Paper 288. Annandale-on-Hudson, N.Y.: Jerome Levy Economics Institute.

Handler, Joel F., and Lucie White, eds. 1999. *Hard Labor: Women and Work in the Post-Welfare Era.* Armonk, N.Y.: M. E. Sharpe.

Harrison, Bennett. 1994. *Lean and Mean: The Changing Landscape of Corporate Power in the Age of Flexibility*. New York: Basic Books.

Harrison, Bennett, and Maryellen R. Kelley. 1993. "Outsourcing and the Search for 'Flexibility.'" *Work, Employment, and Society* 7(2): 213–35.

Hayes, Robert H., and William J. Abernathy. 1980. "Managing Our Way to Economic Decline." *Harvard Business Review* 58(4): 67–77.

Heckman, James, and Burton Singer. 1984. "A Method for Minimizing the Impact of Distributional Assumptions in Econometric Models for Duration Data." *Econometrica* 52(2): 271–320.

Herzenberg, Steven, John Alic, and Howard Wial. 1998. *New Rules for a New Economy: Employment and Opportunity in Postindustrial America*. Ithaca, N.Y.: ILR Press.

Hight, Joseph E. 1998. "Young Worker Participation in Post-School Education and Training." *Monthly Labor Review* 121(6): 14–21.

Houseman, Susan N. 1995. "Job Growth and the Quality of Jobs in the U.S. Economy." *Labour* (Special Issue): S93–124.

———. 1997. "Temporary, Part-Time, and Contract Employment in the United States: A Report on the W. E. Upjohn Institute's Employer Survey on Flexible Staffing Practices." Kalamazoo, Mich.: W. E. Upjohn Institute for Employment Research.

Howell, David, and Edward Wolff. 1991. "Trends in the Growth and Distribution of Skills in the U.S. Workplace, 1960–1985." *Industrial and Labor Relations Review* 44(3): 486–502.

Hu, F. B., J. Goldberg, D. Hedeker, B. R. Flay, and M. A. Pentz. 1998. "Comparison of Population-Averaged and Subject-Specific Approaches for Analyzing Repeated Binary Outcomes." *American Journal of Epidemiology* 147(7): 694–703.

Hudson, Ken. 1999. "No Shortage of 'Nonstandard' Jobs." Report. Washington, D.C.: Economic Policy Institute.

Hunter, Larry W. 1999. "Transforming Retail Banking: Inclusion and Segmentation in Service Work." In *Employment Practices and Business Strategy*, edited by Peter Cappelli. New York: Oxford University Press.

Hunter, Larry W., Annette Bernhardt, Katherine L. Hughes, and Eva Skuratowicz. 2001. "It's Not Just the ATMs: Technology, Firm Strategies, Jobs, and Earnings in Retail Banking." *Industrial and Labor Relations Review* 54 (2,A): 402–24.

Hyman, Richard. 1988. "Flexible Specialization: Miracle or Myth?" In *New Technology and Industrial Relations*, edited by Richard Hyman and Wolfgang Streeck. Oxford: Blackwell.

Ichniowski, Casey, Thomas A. Kochan, David Levine, Craig Olson, and George Strauss. 1996. "What Works at Work: Overview and Assessment." *Industrial Relations* 35(3): 299–333.

Ilg, Randy. 1996. "The Nature of Employment Growth, 1989–1995." *Monthly Labor Review* 119(6): 29–36.

Jacoby, Sanford M. 1985. *Employing Bureaucracy: Managers, Unions, and the Transformation of Work in American Industry, 1900–1945*. New York: Columbia University Press.

Jaeger, David A., and Ann Huff Stevens. 1999. "Is Job Stability in the United States Falling? Reconciling Trends in the Current Population Survey and Panel Study of Income Dynamics." *Journal of Labor Economics* 17(4): S1–28.

"Jobs in an Age of Insecurity." 1993. *Time*, November 22, 32–40.

Jovanovic, Boyan. 1979. "Job Matching and the Theory of Turnover." *Journal of Political Economy* 87(5): 972–90.

Kalleberg, Arne L., Edith Rasell, Ken Hudson, David Webster, Barbara F. Reskin, Naomi Cassirer, and Eileen Appelbaum. 1997. *Nonstandard Work, Substandard Jobs: Flexible Work Arrangements in the United States*. Washington, D.C.: Economic Policy Institute.

Karoly, Lynn A. 1993. "The Trend in Inequality Among Families, Individuals, and Workers in the United States: A Twenty-five-Year Perspective." In *Uneven Tides: Rising Inequality in America*, edited by Sheldon Danziger and Peter Gottschalk. New York: Russell Sage Foundation.

Katz, Lawrence. 1994. "Comment on Gottschalk and Moffitt." *Brookings Papers on Economic Activity* 2: 255–69.

Katz, Lawrence F., and Kevin M. Murphy. 1992. "Changes in Relative Wages, 1963–1987: Supply and Demand Factors." *Quarterly Journal of Economics* 107(1): 35–78.

Keith, Kristen, and Abagail McWilliams. 1995. "The Wage Effects of Cumulative Job Mobility." *Industrial and Labor Relations Review* 49(1): 121–37.

Keltner, Brent, and David Finegold. 1999. "Market Challenges and Changing Employment Relations in U.S. Banks." In *Changing Employment Relations in the Banking Industry*, edited by Marino Regini, Jim Ketay, and Martin Baethge. Cambridge, Mass.: MIT Press.

Klerman, Jacob, and Lynn A. Karoly. 1994. "Young Men and the Transition to Stable Employment." *Monthly Labor Review* 117(8): 31–48.

Kochan, Thomas A., Harry Katz, and Robert McKersie. 1986. *The Transformation of American Industrial Relations*. New York: Basic Books.

Kochan, Thomas A., and Paul Osterman. 1994. *The Mutual Gains Enterprise*. Boston: Harvard Business School Press.

Korenman, Sanders, and David Neumark. 1991. "Does Marriage Really Make Me More Productive?" *Journal of Human Resources* 26(2): 282–307.

Kozicki, Sharon. 1997. "The Productivity Growth Slowdown: Diverging Trends in the Manufacturing and Service Sectors." *Economic Review* (Federal Reserve Bank of Kansas City) 82(1): 31–46.

Krueger, Alan B. 1993. "How Computers Have Changed the Wage Structure: Evidence from Microdata, 1984–1989." *Quarterly Journal of Economics* 108(1): 33–60.

Kuttner, Robert. 1983. "The Declining Middle." *Atlantic Monthly*, July.

"Labor Law Reform." 1995. *Industrial Relations* (special issue) 34(3).

Lawler, Edward E. 1986. *High-Involvement Management*. San Francisco: Jossey-Bass.

Levine, David, and Laura D'Andrea Tyson. 1990. "Participation, Productivity, and the Firm's Environment." In *Paying for Productivity: A Look at the Evidence*, edited by Alan S. Blinder. Washington, D.C.: Brookings Institution.

Levy, Frank, and Robert Murnane. 1992. "U.S. Earnings Levels and Earnings

Inequality: A Review of Recent Trends and Proposed Explanations." *Journal of Economic Literature* 30(3): 1333–81.

Lewis, Michael. 2000. "The Artist in the Gray Flannel Pajamas." *New York Times Magazine*, March 6, 45–48.

Light, Audrey. 1993. "The Effects of Interrupted Schooling on Wages." *Journal of Human Resources* 30(3): 472–502.

———. 1994. "Transitions from School to Work: A Survey of Research Using the National Longitudinal Surveys." NLS Discussion Paper 94-18. Washington: U.S. Department of Labor, Bureau of Labor Statistics.

Light, Audrey, and Kathleen McGarry. 1998. "Job Change Patterns and the Wages of Young Men." *Review of Economics and Statistics* 80(2): 276–86.

Light, Audrey, and Manuelita Ureta. 1995. "Early-Career Work Experience and Gender Wage Differentials." *Journal of Labor Economics* 13(1): 121–54.

Loprest, Pamela J. 1992. "Gender Differences in Wage Growth and Job Mobility." *American Economic Review* 82(2): 526–32.

———. 1999. "Families Who Left Welfare: Who Are They and How Are They Doing?" Discussion Paper 99-02. Washington, D.C.: Urban Institute.

Macdonald, Cameron L., and Carmen Sirianni, eds. 1996. *Working in the Service Society*. Philadelphia: Temple University Press.

Magaziner, Ira C., and Robert B. Reich. 1983. *Minding America's Business: The Decline and Rise of the American Economy*. New York: Vintage Books.

Marcotte, Dave E. 1996. "Has Job Stability Declined? Evidence from the Panel Study of Income Dynamics." *American Journal of Economics and Sociology* 58(2): 197–217.

Marcus, Richard D. 1986. "Earnings and the Decision to Return to School." *Economics of Education Review* 5(3): 309–17.

Marini, Margaret Mooney. 1984. "The Order of Events in the Transition to Adulthood." *Sociology of Education* 57(2): 63–84.

McCall, Leslie. 1995. "The Changing Substance and Significance of Occupational Segregation in the United States, 1970–1990." Ph.D. diss., University of Wisconsin, Madison.

McConnel, Sheila. 1996. "The Role of Computers in Reshaping the Work Force." *Monthly Labor Review* 119(8): 3–5.

McCue, Kristin. 1996. "Promotions and Wage Growth." *Journal of Labor Economics* 14(2): 175–209.

McCulloch, Charles E. 1997. "Maximum Likelihood Algorithms for Generalized Linear Mixed Models." *Journal of the American Statistical Association* 92(437): 162–70.

McGinn, Daniel, and John McCormick. 1999. "Your Next Job." *Newsweek*, February 1, 1999, 42–51.

McMurrer, Daniel, and Amy Chasanov. 1995. "Trends in Unemployment Insurance Benefits." *Monthly Labor Review* 118(9): 30–39.

Meisenheimer, Joseph. 1998. "The Services Industry in the 'Good' versus 'Bad' Jobs Debate." *Monthly Labor Review* 121(2): 22–47.

Mincer, Jacob, and Boyan Jovanovic. 1981. "Labor Mobility and Wages." In *Studies in Labor Markets*, edited by Sherwin Rosen. Chicago: University of Chicago Press.

Mishel, Lawrence, Jared Bernstein, and John Schmitt. 1997a. "Did Technology Have Any Effect on the Growth of Wage Inequality in the 1980s and 1990s?" Published report. Washington, D.C.: Economic Policy Institute.

———. 1997b. *The State of Working America, 1996–1997.* Armonk, N.Y.: M. E. Sharpe.

———. 2001. *The State of Working America, 2000–2001.* Ithaca, N.Y.: Cornell University Press.

Moffitt, Robert, and Peter Gottschalk. 1995. "Trends in the Autocovariance Structure of Earnings in the United States, 1969–1987." Manuscript. Baltimore: Johns Hopkins University, Department of Economics.

Monks, James, and Steven Pizer. 1998. "Trends in Voluntary and Involuntary Job Turnover." *Industrial Relations* 37(4): 440–59.

Moore, Michael J., W. Kip Viscusi, and Richard J. Zeckhauser. 1999. "The Anatomy of Jumps and Falls in Wages." In *Research in Labor Economics,* edited by Solomon Polachek. Greenwich, Conn.: JAI Press.

Moss, Philip. 2000. "Earnings Inequality and the Quality of Jobs." In *Corporate Governance and Sustainable Prosperity,* edited by William Lazonick and Mary O'Sullivan. New York: Macmillan.

Moss, Philip, Harold Salzman, and Chris Tilly. 1998. "Corporate Restructuring, Job Structure, and Inequality: Implications for Human Resource Strategies, Skill Development, and Training." Manuscript. Lowell: University of Massachusetts, Department of Regional and Economic Development.

———. 2000. "Limits to Market-Mediated Employment: From Deconstruction to Reconstruction of Internal Labor Markets." In *Nonstandard Work: The Nature and Challenges of Changing Employment Arrangements,* edited by Françoise Carré, Marianne A. Ferber, Lonnie Golden, and Steve Herzenberg. Champaign, Ill.: Industrial Relations Research Association.

Mowery, David C. 1999. "America's Industrial Resurgence: How Strong, How Durable?" *Issues in Science and Technology* 15(3): 41–48.

Murphy, Kevin, and Finis Welch. 1990. "Empirical Age-Earnings Profiles." *Journal of Labor Economics* 8(2): 202–29.

National Center on the Educational Quality of the Workforce. 1995. "First Findings from the EQW National Employer Survey." Report 1. Philadelphia: University of Pennsylvania, National Center on the Educational Quality of the Workforce.

Neumark, David, Daniel Polsky, and Daniel Hansen. 1997. "Has Job Stability Declined Yet? New Evidence for the 1990s." *Journal of Labor Economics* 17(4): S29–64.

Newman, Katherine, and Chauncy Lennon. 1995. "The Job Ghetto." *American Prospect* 6(22): 66–67.

Oaxaca, Ronald L. 1973. "Male-Female Wage Differentials in Urban Labor Markets." *International Economic Review* 14(3): 693–709.

O'Neill, June. 1982. "Review of the National Longitudinal Surveys." NLS Discussion paper. Washington: U.S. Department of Labor.

Osterman, Paul. 1994. "Internal Labor Markets: Theory and Change." In *Labor Economics and Industrial Relations,* edited by Clark Kerr and Paul Staudohar. Cambridge, Mass.: Harvard University Press.

———. 1999. *Securing Prosperity: The American Labor Market—How It Has Changed and What to Do About It*. Princeton: Princeton University Press.

———. 2000. "Work Organization in an Era of Restructuring: Trends in Diffusion and Impacts on Employee Welfare." *Industrial and Labor Relations Review* 53(2): 179–96.

Parker, Eric, and Joel Rogers. 1999. "Sectoral Training Initiatives in the United States: Building Blocks of a New Workforce Preparation System?" In *The German Skills Machine: Sustaining Comparative Advantage in a Global Economy*, edited by Pepper Culpepper and David Finegold. New York: Berghahn Books.

Parsons, Donald O. 1987. "Summary Tables: The National Longitudinal Surveys of Young Males, 1966–1981." Report. Columbus, Ohio: Center for Human Resource Research.

Peck, Jamie, and Nik Theodore. Forthcoming. "Contingent Chicago: Restructuring the Spaces of Temporary Labor." *International Journal of Urban and Regional Research*.

Pfeffer, Jeffrey, and James Baron. 1988. "Taking the Workers Back Out: Recent Trends in the Structuring of Employment." *Research in Organizational Behavior* 10: 257–303.

Picot, Garnett, John Myles, and Ted Wannel. 1990. "Good Jobs/Bad Jobs and the Declining Middle, 1967–1986." Research paper 28. Ottawa: Statistics Canada Business and Labor Market Analysis Group.

Piore, Michael J., and Charles F. Sabel. 1984. *The Second Industrial Divide: Possibilities for Prosperity*. New York: Basic Books.

Plimpton, Lisa, and Demetra Smith Nightingale. 2000. "Welfare Employment Programs: Impacts and Cost-Effectiveness of Employment and Training Activities." In *Improving the Odds: Increasing the Effectiveness of Publicly Funded Training*, edited by Burt S. Barnow and Christopher T. King. Washington, D.C.: Urban Institute Press.

Plunkert, Lois M. 1990. "The 1980s: A Decade of Job Growth and Industry Shifts." *Monthly Labor Review* 113(9): 3–16.

Polsky, Daniel. 1999. "Changing Consequences of Job Separations in the United States." *Industrial and Labor Relations Review* 52(4): 565–81.

Porter, Kathryn. 1999. "Proposed Changes in the Official Measure of Poverty." Report. Washington, D.C.: Center on Budget and Policy Priorities.

Rhoton, Patricia. 1984. "Attrition and the National Longitudinal Surveys of Labor Market Experience: Avoidance, Control and Correction." Ohio State University: Center for Human Resource Research.

Rindfuss, Ronald R., C. Gray Swicegood, and Rachel A. Rosenfeld. 1987. "Disorder in the Life Course: How Common and Does It Matter?" *American Sociological Review* 52(6): 785–801.

Rose, Stephen. 1995. "The Decline of Employment Stability in the 1980s." Report. Washington, D.C.: National Commission on Employment Policy.

Rose, Stephen, and Anthony Carnevale. 1997. *The New Office Economy*. Report. Princeton, N.J.: Educational Testing Service.

Rosenberg, Sam. 1989. "From Segmentation to Flexibility." *Labour and Society* 14(4): 363–407.

Rosenthal, Neal H. 1995. "The Nature of Occupational Employment Growth: 1983–1993." *Monthly Labor Review* 118(6): 45–54.

Rubin, Donald B. 1987. *Multiple Imputation for Nonresponse in Surveys*. New York: Wiley.

Ruhm, Christopher. 1997. "Is High School Employment Consumption or Investment?" *Journal of Labor Economics* 15(4): 735–76.

Rytina, Nancy F., and Suzanne M. Bianchi. 1984. "Occupational Reclassification and Changes in Distribution by Gender." *Monthly Labor Review* 107(3): 11–17.

Schmidt, Stefanie, and Shirley Svorny. 1998. "Recent Trends in Job Security and Stability." *Journal of Labor Research* 19(4): 647–68.

Schrammel, Kurt. 1998. "Comparing the Labor Market Success of Young Adults from Two Generations." *Monthly Labor Review* 121(2): 3–9.

Singer, Judith D. 1998. "Using SAS PROC MIXED to Fit Multilevel Models, Hierarchical Models, and Individual Growth Models." *Journal of Educational and Behavioral Statistics* 23(4): 323–55.

Smith, Vicki. 1997. "New Forms of Work Organization." *Annual Review of Sociology* 23: 315–39.

Social Science Research Council. 1983. "Alternative Methods for Effecting the Comparability of Occupation Measurement over Time." Report of the Subcommittee on Comparability of Occupation Measurement to the Social Science Research Council Advisory and Planning Committee on Social Indicators and the Bureau of the Census. New York, April.

Spilerman, Seymour. 1977. "Careers, Labor Market Structure, and Socioeconomic Achievement." *American Journal of Sociology* 83(3): 551–93.

Stern, David, and Yoshi-Fumi Nakata. 1989. "Characteristics of High School Students' Paid Jobs and Employment Experience After Graduation." In *Adolescence and Work: Influences of Social Structure, Labor Markets, and Culture*, edited by David Stern and Dorothy Eichorn. Hillsdale, N.J.: Lawrence Erlbaum Associates.

Stevens, Ann Huff. 1996. "Changes in Earnings Instability and Job Loss." Manuscript. New Haven: Yale University, Department of Economics.

Stewart, Jay. 1998. "Has Job Mobility Increased? Evidence from the Current Population Survey, 1975–1995." Manuscript. Washington, D.C.: Office of Employment Research and Program Development, Bureau of Labor Statistics.

Stone, James R., III, and Jeylan T. Mortimer. 1998. "The Effect of Adolescent Employment on Vocational Development: Public and Educational Policy Implications." *Journal of Vocational Behavior* 53(2): 184–214.

Swinnerton, Kenneth A., and Howard Wial. 1996. "Is Job Stability Declining in the U.S. Economy?" *Industrial and Labor Relations Review* 49(2): 352–55.

Topel, Robert H. 1997. "Factor Proportions and Relative Wages: The Supply-Side Determinants of Wage Inequality." *Journal of Economic Perspectives* 11(2): 55–74.

Topel, Robert H., and Michael P. Ward. 1992. "Job Mobility and the Careers of Young Men." *Quarterly Journal of Economics* 107(2): 439–79.

U.S. Bureau of the Census. 1999. "Historical Income Tables: People." Table

P-38, "Full-Time, Year-Round Workers (All Races) by Median Earnings and Sex: 1960 to 1998." Washington: U.S. Department of Commerce. Available on the World Wide Web at *www.census.gov/hhes/income/histinc/p38.html*.

———. 2000. "Table A-1. Years of School Completed by People Twenty-five Years Old and Over, by Age and Sex: Selected Years, 1940 to 1999." Washington: U.S. Department of Commerce. Available on the World Wide Web at *www.census.gov/population/socdemo/education/tableA-1.txt*.

U.S. Department of Labor. 1998. *The 1998–1999 Occupational Outlook Handbook.* Washington: U.S. Government Printing Office.

———. 2000. "Nonfarm Payroll Statistics from the Current Employment Statistics: National Employment, Hours, and Earnings." Downloaded in October 2000 from the World Wide Web at *stats.bls.gov/ceshome.htm*.

U.S. Department of Labor. U.S. National Commission on Excellence in Education. 1983. *A Nation at Risk: The Imperative for Educational Reform.* Washington: U.S. Government Printing Office.

Vogel, Stephen. 1996. *Freer Markets, More Rules: Regulatory Reform in Advanced Industrial Countries.* Ithaca, N.Y.: Cornell University Press.

Walton, Richard. 1985. "From Control to Commitment in the Workplace." *Harvard Business Review* 63(2): 77–84.

Wial, Howard. 1993. "The Emerging Organizational Structure of Unionism in Low-Wage Services." *Rutgers Law Review* 45(3): 671–738.

Wilson, William Julius. 1987. *The Truly Disadvantaged.* Chicago: University of Chicago Press.

Wolpin, Kenneth. 1987. "Estimating a Structural Search Model: The Transition from School to Work." *Econometrica* 55(4): 801–17.

Womack, James P., Daniel Jones, and Daniel Roos. 1990. *The Machine That Changed the World: The Story of Lean Production.* New York: Harper Perennial.

Wood, Stephen J., ed. 1992. *The Transformation of Work?: Skill, Flexibility and the Labour Process.* New York: Routledge.

Working for America Institute. 2000. "High Road Partnerships Report: Innovations in Building Good Jobs and Strong Communities." Report. Washington, D.C.: Working for America Institute.

# = Index =

Numbers in **boldface** refer to tables and figures.

dustrial America, 111, 191–94, 199; restoring American Dream, 173–75, 193–94; welfare reform, 12–13, 109, 150–51, 170

political context of wage structure, 179–81

Polsky, D., 66, 210

portability of benefits, 194. *See also* benefits, employee

postindustrialism: and cohort study groups, 22; education level of workforce, 43–44, 62; goods-producing sector, 184; and governmental policies, 111, 191–94, 199; new labor market, 3; and service industries, 184–87; and upward mobility, 16, 19, 111, 148

poverty, 2, 5, 150, 153–55, 159–60, 167

prior vs. current job changes, **82**

production, social organization of, 8

productivity index, **185**

professional occupations, 114, 146

promotion process, 9, 65, 236*n*1

proxy employers, 195

PSID (Study of Income Dynamics), 66, 210–12

public sector, 78

racial convergence, 5

real wages, 93–96, 108, **127**, 132

reengineering, 22

research issues, 65–66

restructuring: and American dream, 173–75, 199; cohort study groups, 22; externalization of labor, 189; globalization of trade, 187; governmental policies, 174, 193; internal labor markets, 9–10, 184, 187–91, 229*n*9, 243*n*18; and job instability, 64, 184; and long-term economic mobility, 126, 141; and low-wage careers, 151, 158–59, 171, 185; and new labor market, 7–10, 17; promotion process, 9; and technology, 182–83; transition

into labor market, 48–50, 53–57, 62; and unions, 8, 55; and upward mobility, 11–19; wage structure, 185; worker-owned companies, 195

Rogers, J., 195

Rose, S., 183

sales occupations, 114

Salzman, H., 243*n*18

San Francisco Hotels Partnership Project, 196

Schmitt, J., 179

school enrollment, 50–52, 63, 77, 86, 202, 206. *See also* education

School-to-Work Opportunities Act of 1994, 2

scientific management, 10

sectoral partnerships, 195–98, 197

*Securing Prosperity* (Osterman), 191

separation, job: and age, **70**, 72; and education, **71**, 72; logistic regressions, **74–76**; and low-wage careers, 162; methodology, 206–7; nonparticipation, 80, 81; rate estimate comparisons, 72, **211–12**. *See also* job changing

service industries: demographics of low-wage workers, 151; and economic mobility, 114, 145, 181–87; high-end vs. low-end, 114; and job instability, 77–78, **79**, 86; low-wage careers, 158–60, 171, 176–77; and market segmentation, 189; occupational shifts, 55–57; and postindustrialism, 184–87; sectoral partnerships, 196–97; stratification of jobs and wages, 167, 185, 230*n*10; transition into labor market, 63; and workplace, 181–87

skill development: and economic mobility, 133, 181–85; in global economy, 175; and job instability, 130, 192; low-skill workers, 87, 190, 193–94, 195; opportunities, 13–14; and restructuring, 9; and